DATE DUE

DEMCO, INC. 38-2931

FREE CULTURE

THE PENGUIN PRESS
NEW YORK
2004

FREE CULTURE

HOW BIG MEDIA USES TECHNOLOGY AND THE LAW TO LOCK DOWN CULTURE AND CONTROL CREATIVITY

LAWRENCE LESSIG

THE PENGUIN PRESS
a member of
Penguin Group (USA) Inc.
375 Hudson Street
New York, New York 10014

Excerpt from an editorial titled "The Coming of Copyright Perpetuity,"
The New York Times, January 16, 2003. Copyright © 2003 by The New York Times Co.
Reprinted with permission.
Cartoon by Paul Conrad on page 159. Copyright Tribune Media Services, Inc.
All rights reserved. Reprinted with permission.
Diagram on page 164 courtesy of the office of FCC Commissioner, Michael J. Copps.

Library of Congress Cataloging-in-Publication Data

Lessig, Lawrence.
Free culture : how big media uses technology and the law to lock down
culture and control creativity / Lawrence Lessig.
p. cm.
Includes index.
ISBN 1-59420-006-8 (hardcover)
1. Intellectual property—United States. 2. Mass media—United States.
3. Technological innovations—United States. 4. Art—United States. I. Title.

KF2979.L47 2004
343.7309'9—dc22   2003063276

This book is printed on acid-free paper. ∞

Printed in the United States of America
1   3   5   7   9   10   8   6   4   2

Designed by Marysarah Quinn

To Eric Eldred—whose work first drew me
to this cause, and for whom
it continues still.

CONTENTS

PREFACE   xiii

INTRODUCTION   1

"PIRACY"   15

  CHAPTER ONE: Creators   21

  CHAPTER TWO: "Mere Copyists"   31

  CHAPTER THREE: Catalogs   48

  CHAPTER FOUR: "Pirates"   53

    Film   53

    Recorded Music   55

    Radio   58

    Cable TV   59

  CHAPTER FIVE: "Piracy"   62

    Piracy I   63

    Piracy II   66

"PROPERTY"   81
  CHAPTER SIX: Founders   85
  CHAPTER SEVEN: Recorders   95
  CHAPTER EIGHT: Transformers   100
  CHAPTER NINE: Collectors   108
  CHAPTER TEN: "Property"   116
    Why Hollywood Is Right   124
    Beginnings   130
    Law: Duration   133
    Law: Scope   136
    Law and Architecture: Reach   139
    Architecture and Law: Force   147
    Market: Concentration   161
    Together   168

PUZZLES   175
  CHAPTER ELEVEN: Chimera   177
  CHAPTER TWELVE: Harms   183
    Constraining Creators   184
    Constraining Innovators   188
    Corrupting Citizens   199

BALANCES   209
  CHAPTER THIRTEEN: Eldred   213
  CHAPTER FOURTEEN: Eldred II   248

CONCLUSION   257

AFTERWORD   273
  Us, Now   276
    Rebuilding Freedoms Previously Presumed:
      Examples   277
    Rebuilding Free Culture: One Idea   282

Them, Soon 287

  1. More Formalities 287
      Registration and Renewal 289
      Marking 290
  2. Shorter Terms 292
  3. Free Use Vs. Fair Use 294
  4. Liberate the Music—Again 296
  5. Fire Lots of Lawyers 304

NOTES 307
ACKNOWLEDGMENTS 331
INDEX 333

PREFACE

At the end of his review of my first book, *Code: And Other Laws of Cyberspace,* David Pogue, a brilliant writer and author of countless technical and computer-related texts, wrote this:

> Unlike actual law, Internet software has no capacity to punish. It doesn't affect people who aren't online (and only a tiny minority of the world population is). And if you don't like the Internet's system, you can always flip off the modem.[1]

Pogue was skeptical of the core argument of the book—that software, or "code," functioned as a kind of law—and his review suggested the happy thought that if life in cyberspace got bad, we could always "drizzle, drazzle, druzzle, drome"-like simply flip a switch and be back home. Turn off the modem, unplug the computer, and any troubles that exist in *that* space wouldn't "affect" us anymore.

Pogue might have been right in 1999—I'm skeptical, but maybe. But even if he was right then, the point is not right now: *Free Culture* is about the troubles the Internet causes even after the modem is turned off. It is an argument about how the battles that now rage regarding life on-line have fundamentally affected "people who aren't online." There is no switch that will insulate us from the Internet's effect.

But unlike *Code*, the argument here is not much about the Internet itself. It is instead about the consequence of the Internet to a part of our tradition that is much more fundamental, and, as hard as this is for a geek-wanna-be to admit, much more important.

That tradition is the way our culture gets made. As I explain in the pages that follow, we come from a tradition of "free culture"—not "free" as in "free beer" (to borrow a phrase from the founder of the free-software movement[2]), but "free" as in "free speech," "free markets," "free trade," "free enterprise," "free will," and "free elections." A free culture supports and protects creators and innovators. It does this directly by granting intellectual property rights. But it does so indirectly by limiting the reach of those rights, to guarantee that follow-on creators and innovators remain *as free as possible* from the control of the past. A free culture is not a culture without property, just as a free market is not a market in which everything is free. The opposite of a free culture is a "permission culture"—a culture in which creators get to create only with the permission of the powerful, or of creators from the past.

If we understood this change, I believe we would resist it. Not "we" on the Left or "you" on the Right, but we who have no stake in the particular industries of culture that defined the twentieth century. Whether you are on the Left or the Right, if you are in this sense disinterested, then the story I tell here will trouble you. For the changes I describe affect values that both sides of our political culture deem fundamental.

We saw a glimpse of this bipartisan outrage in the early summer of 2003. As the FCC considered changes in media ownership rules that would relax limits on media concentration, an extraordinary coalition generated more than 700,000 letters to the FCC opposing the change. As William Safire described marching "uncomfortably alongside CodePink Women for Peace and the National Rifle Association, between liberal Olympia Snowe and conservative Ted Stevens," he formulated perhaps most simply just what was at stake: the concentration of power. And as he asked,

> Does that sound unconservative? Not to me. The concentration of power—political, corporate, media, cultural—should be anathema to conservatives. The diffusion of power through local control, thereby encouraging individual participation, is the essence of federalism and the greatest expression of democracy.[3]

This idea is an element of the argument of *Free Culture*, though my focus is not just on the concentration of power produced by concentrations in ownership, but more importantly, if because less visibly, on the concentration of power produced by a radical change in the effective scope of the law. The law is changing; that change is altering the way our culture gets made; that change should worry you—whether or not you care about the Internet, and whether you're on Safire's left or on his right.

The inspiration for the title and for much of the argument of this book comes from the work of Richard Stallman and the Free Software Foundation. Indeed, as I reread Stallman's own work, especially the essays in *Free Software, Free Society*, I realize that all of the theoretical insights I develop here are insights Stallman described decades ago. One could thus well argue that this work is "merely" derivative.

I accept that criticism, if indeed it is a criticism. The work of a lawyer is always derivative, and I mean to do nothing more in this book than to remind a culture about a tradition that has always been its own. Like Stallman, I defend that tradition on the basis of values. Like Stallman, I believe those are the values of freedom. And like Stallman, I believe those are values of our past that will need to be defended in our future. A free culture has been our past, but it will only be our future if we change the path we are on right now.

Like Stallman's arguments for free software, an argument for free culture stumbles on a confusion that is hard to avoid, and even harder to understand. A free culture is not a culture without property; it is not a culture in which artists don't get paid. A culture without property, or in which creators can't get paid, is anarchy, not freedom. Anarchy is not what I advance here.

Instead, the free culture that I defend in this book is a balance between anarchy and control. A free culture, like a free market, is filled with property. It is filled with rules of property and contract that get enforced by the state. But just as a free market is perverted if its property becomes feudal, so too can a free culture be queered by extremism in the property rights that define it. That is what I fear about our culture today. It is against that extremism that this book is written.

FREE CULTURE

INTRODUCTION

On December 17, 1903, on a windy North Carolina beach for just shy of one hundred seconds, the Wright brothers demonstrated that a heavier-than-air, self-propelled vehicle could fly. The moment was electric and its importance widely understood. Almost immediately, there was an explosion of interest in this newfound technology of manned flight, and a gaggle of innovators began to build upon it.

At the time the Wright brothers invented the airplane, American law held that a property owner presumptively owned not just the surface of his land, but all the land below, down to the center of the earth, and all the space above, to "an indefinite extent, upwards."[1] For many years, scholars had puzzled about how best to interpret the idea that rights in land ran to the heavens. Did that mean that you owned the stars? Could you prosecute geese for their willful and regular trespass?

Then came airplanes, and for the first time, this principle of American law—deep within the foundations of our tradition, and acknowledged by the most important legal thinkers of our past—mattered. If my land reaches to the heavens, what happens when United flies over my field? Do I have the right to banish it from my property? Am I allowed to enter into an exclusive license with Delta Airlines? Could we set up an auction to decide how much these rights are worth?

In 1945, these questions became a federal case. When North Carolina farmers Thomas Lee and Tinie Causby started losing chickens because of low-flying military aircraft (the terrified chickens apparently flew into the barn walls and died), the Causbys filed a lawsuit saying that the government was trespassing on their land. The airplanes, of course, never touched the surface of the Causbys' land. But if, as Blackstone, Kent, and Coke had said, their land reached to "an indefinite extent, upwards," then the government was trespassing on their property, and the Causbys wanted it to stop.

The Supreme Court agreed to hear the Causbys' case. Congress had declared the airways public, but if one's property really extended to the heavens, then Congress's declaration could well have been an unconstitutional "taking" of property without compensation. The Court acknowledged that "it is ancient doctrine that common law ownership of the land extended to the periphery of the universe." But Justice Douglas had no patience for ancient doctrine. In a single paragraph, hundreds of years of property law were erased. As he wrote for the Court,

> [The] doctrine has no place in the modern world. The air is a public highway, as Congress has declared. Were that not true, every transcontinental flight would subject the operator to countless trespass suits. Common sense revolts at the idea. To recognize such private claims to the airspace would clog these highways, seriously interfere with their control and development in the public interest, and transfer into private ownership that to which only the public has a just claim.[2]

"Common sense revolts at the idea."

This is how the law usually works. Not often this abruptly or impatiently, but eventually, this is how it works. It was Douglas's style not to dither. Other justices would have blathered on for pages to reach the conclusion that Douglas holds in a single line: "Common sense revolts at the idea." But whether it takes pages or a few words, it is the special genius of a common law system, as ours is, that the law adjusts to the technologies of the time. And as it adjusts, it changes. Ideas that were as solid as rock in one age crumble in another.

Or at least, this is how things happen when there's no one powerful on the other side of the change. The Causbys were just farmers. And though there were no doubt many like them who were upset by the growing traffic in the air (though one hopes not many chickens flew themselves into walls), the Causbys of the world would find it very hard to unite and stop the idea, and the technology, that the Wright brothers had birthed. The Wright brothers spat airplanes into the technological meme pool; the idea then spread like a virus in a chicken coop; farmers like the Causbys found themselves surrounded by "what seemed reasonable" given the technology that the Wrights had produced. They could stand on their farms, dead chickens in hand, and shake their fists at these newfangled technologies all they wanted. They could call their representatives or even file a lawsuit. But in the end, the force of what seems "obvious" to everyone else—the power of "common sense"—would prevail. Their "private interest" would not be allowed to defeat an obvious public gain.

Edwin Howard Armstrong is one of America's forgotten inventor geniuses. He came to the great American inventor scene just after the titans Thomas Edison and Alexander Graham Bell. But his work in the area of radio technology was perhaps the most important of any single inventor in the first fifty years of radio. He was better educated than Michael Faraday, who as a bookbinder's apprentice had discovered electric induction in 1831. But he had the same intuition about how the world of radio worked, and on at least three occasions, Armstrong invented profoundly important technologies that advanced our understanding of radio.

On the day after Christmas, 1933, four patents were issued to Armstrong for his most significant invention—FM radio. Until then, consumer radio had been amplitude-modulated (AM) radio. The theorists of the day had said that frequency-modulated (FM) radio could never work. They were right about FM radio in a narrow band of spectrum. But Armstrong discovered that frequency-modulated radio in a wide band of spectrum would deliver an astonishing fidelity of sound, with much less transmitter power and static.

On November 5, 1935, he demonstrated the technology at a meeting of the Institute of Radio Engineers at the Empire State Building in New York City. He tuned his radio dial across a range of AM stations, until the radio locked on a broadcast that he had arranged from seventeen miles away. The radio fell totally silent, as if dead, and then with a clarity no one else in that room had ever heard from an electrical device, it produced the sound of an announcer's voice: "This is amateur station W2AG at Yonkers, New York, operating on frequency modulation at two and a half meters."

The audience was hearing something no one had thought possible:

A glass of water was poured before the microphone in Yonkers; it sounded like a glass of water being poured. . . . A paper was crumpled and torn; it sounded like paper and not like a crackling forest fire. . . . Sousa marches were played from records and a piano solo and guitar number were performed. . . . The music was projected with a live-ness rarely if ever heard before from a radio "music box."[3]

As our own common sense tells us, Armstrong had discovered a vastly superior radio technology. But at the time of his invention, Armstrong was working for RCA. RCA was the dominant player in the then dominant AM radio market. By 1935, there were a thousand radio stations across the United States, but the stations in large cities were all owned by a handful of networks.

RCA's president, David Sarnoff, a friend of Armstrong's, was eager that Armstrong discover a way to remove static from AM radio. So Sarnoff was quite excited when Armstrong told him he had a device that removed static from "radio." But when Armstrong demonstrated his invention, Sarnoff was not pleased.

> I thought Armstrong would invent some kind of a filter to remove static from our AM radio. I didn't think he'd start a revolution— start up a whole damn new industry to compete with RCA.[4]

Armstrong's invention threatened RCA's AM empire, so the company launched a campaign to smother FM radio. While FM may have been a superior technology, Sarnoff was a superior tactician. As one author described,

> The forces for FM, largely engineering, could not overcome the weight of strategy devised by the sales, patent, and legal offices to subdue this threat to corporate position. For FM, if allowed to develop unrestrained, posed . . . a complete reordering of radio power . . . and the eventual overthrow of the carefully restricted AM system on which RCA had grown to power.[5]

RCA at first kept the technology in house, insisting that further tests were needed. When, after two years of testing, Armstrong grew impatient, RCA began to use its power with the government to stall FM radio's deployment generally. In 1936, RCA hired the former head of the FCC and assigned him the task of assuring that the FCC assign spectrum in a way that would castrate FM—principally by moving FM radio to a different band of spectrum. At first, these efforts failed. But when Armstrong and the nation were distracted by World War II, RCA's work began to be more successful. Soon after the war ended, the FCC announced a set of policies that would have one clear effect: FM radio would be crippled. As Lawrence Lessing described it,

The series of body blows that FM radio received right after the war, in a series of rulings manipulated through the FCC by the big radio interests, were almost incredible in their force and deviousness.[6]

To make room in the spectrum for RCA's latest gamble, television, FM radio users were to be moved to a totally new spectrum band. The power of FM radio stations was also cut, meaning FM could no longer be used to beam programs from one part of the country to another. (This change was strongly supported by AT&T, because the loss of FM relaying stations would mean radio stations would have to buy wired links from AT&T.) The spread of FM radio was thus choked, at least temporarily.

Armstrong resisted RCA's efforts. In response, RCA resisted Armstrong's patents. After incorporating FM technology into the emerging standard for television, RCA declared the patents invalid—baselessly, and almost fifteen years after they were issued. It thus refused to pay him royalties. For six years, Armstrong fought an expensive war of litigation to defend the patents. Finally, just as the patents expired, RCA offered a settlement so low that it would not even cover Armstrong's lawyers' fees. Defeated, broken, and now broke, in 1954 Armstrong wrote a short note to his wife and then stepped out of a thirteenth-story window to his death.

This is how the law sometimes works. Not often this tragically, and rarely with heroic drama, but sometimes, this is how it works. From the beginning, government and government agencies have been subject to capture. They are more likely captured when a powerful interest is threatened by either a legal or technical change. That powerful interest too often exerts its influence within the government to get the government to protect it. The rhetoric of this protection is of course always public spirited; the reality is something different. Ideas that were as solid as rock in one age, but that, left to themselves, would crumble in another, are sustained through this subtle corruption of our political process. RCA had what the Causbys did not: the power to stifle the effect of technological change.

There's no single inventor of the Internet. Nor is there any good date upon which to mark its birth. Yet in a very short time, the Internet has become part of ordinary American life. According to the Pew Internet and American Life Project, 58 percent of Americans had access to the Internet in 2002, up from 49 percent two years before.[7] That number could well exceed two thirds of the nation by the end of 2004.

As the Internet has been integrated into ordinary life, it has changed things. Some of these changes are technical—the Internet has made communication faster, it has lowered the cost of gathering data, and so on. These technical changes are not the focus of this book. They are important. They are not well understood. But they are the sort of thing that would simply go away if we all just switched the Internet off. They don't affect people who don't use the Internet, or at least they don't affect them directly. They are the proper subject of a book about the Internet. But this is not a book about the Internet.

Instead, this book is about an effect of the Internet beyond the Internet itself: an effect upon how culture is made. My claim is that the Internet has induced an important and unrecognized change in that process. That change will radically transform a tradition that is as old as the Republic itself. Most, if they recognized this change, would reject it. Yet most don't even see the change that the Internet has introduced.

We can glimpse a sense of this change by distinguishing between commercial and noncommercial culture, and by mapping the law's regulation of each. By "commercial culture" I mean that part of our culture that is produced and sold or produced to be sold. By "noncommercial culture" I mean all the rest. When old men sat around parks or on street corners telling stories that kids and others consumed, that was noncommercial culture. When Noah Webster published his "Reader," or Joel Barlow his poetry, that was commercial culture.

At the beginning of our history, and for just about the whole of our tradition, noncommercial culture was essentially unregulated. Of course, if your stories were lewd, or if your song disturbed the peace, then the law might intervene. But the law was never directly concerned with the creation or spread of this form of culture, and it left this culture "free." The ordinary ways in which ordinary individuals shared and transformed their culture—telling stories, reenacting scenes from plays or TV, participating in fan clubs, sharing music, making tapes—were left alone by the law.

The focus of the law was on commercial creativity. At first slightly, then quite extensively, the law protected the incentives of creators by granting them exclusive rights to their creative work, so that they could sell those exclusive rights in a commercial marketplace.[8] This is also, of course, an important part of creativity and culture, and it has become an increasingly important part in America. But in no sense was it dominant within our tradition. It was instead just one part, a controlled part, balanced with the free.

This rough divide between the free and the controlled has now been erased.[9] The Internet has set the stage for this erasure and, pushed by big media, the law has now affected it. For the first time in our tradition, the ordinary ways in which individuals create and share culture fall within the reach of the regulation of the law, which has expanded to draw within its control a vast amount of culture and creativity that it never reached before. The technology that preserved the balance of our history—between uses of our culture that were free and uses of our culture that were only upon permission—has been undone. The consequence is that we are less and less a free culture, more and more a permission culture.

This change gets justified as necessary to protect commercial creativity. And indeed, protectionism is precisely its motivation. But the protectionism that justifies the changes that I will describe below is not the limited and balanced sort that has defined the law in the past. This is not a protectionism to protect artists. It is instead a protectionism to protect certain forms of business. Corporations threatened by the potential of the Internet to change the way both commercial and noncommercial culture are made and shared have united to induce lawmakers to use the law to protect them. It is the story of RCA and Armstrong; it is the dream of the Causbys.

For the Internet has unleashed an extraordinary possibility for many to participate in the process of building and cultivating a culture that reaches far beyond local boundaries. That power has changed the marketplace for making and cultivating culture generally, and that change in turn threatens established content industries. The Internet is thus to the industries that built and distributed content in the twentieth century what FM radio was to AM radio, or what the truck was to the railroad industry of the nineteenth century: the beginning of the end, or at least a substantial transformation. Digital technologies, tied to the Internet, could produce a vastly more competitive and vibrant market for building and cultivating culture; that market could include a much wider and more diverse range of creators; those creators could produce and distribute a much more vibrant range of creativity; and depending upon a few important factors, those creators could earn more on average from this system than creators do today—all so long as the RCAs of our day don't use the law to protect themselves against this competition.

Yet, as I argue in the pages that follow, that is precisely what is happening in our culture today. These modern-day equivalents of the early twentieth-century radio or nineteenth-century railroads are using their power to get the law to protect them against this new, more efficient, more vibrant technology for building culture. They are succeeding in their plan to remake the Internet before the Internet remakes them.

It doesn't seem this way to many. The battles over copyright and the

Internet seem remote to most. To the few who follow them, they seem mainly about a much simpler brace of questions—whether "piracy" will be permitted, and whether "property" will be protected. The "war" that has been waged against the technologies of the Internet—what Motion Picture Association of America (MPAA) president Jack Valenti calls his "own terrorist war"[10]—has been framed as a battle about the rule of law and respect for property. To know which side to take in this war, most think that we need only decide whether we're for property or against it.

If those really were the choices, then I would be with Jack Valenti and the content industry. I, too, am a believer in property, and especially in the importance of what Mr. Valenti nicely calls "creative property." I believe that "piracy" is wrong, and that the law, properly tuned, should punish "piracy," whether on or off the Internet.

But those simple beliefs mask a much more fundamental question and a much more dramatic change. My fear is that unless we come to see this change, the war to rid the world of Internet "pirates" will also rid our culture of values that have been integral to our tradition from the start.

These values built a tradition that, for at least the first 180 years of our Republic, guaranteed creators the right to build freely upon their past, and protected creators and innovators from either state or private control. The First Amendment protected creators against state control. And as Professor Neil Netanel powerfully argues,[11] copyright law, properly balanced, protected creators against private control. Our tradition was thus neither Soviet nor the tradition of patrons. It instead carved out a wide berth within which creators could cultivate and extend our culture.

Yet the law's response to the Internet, when tied to changes in the technology of the Internet itself, has massively increased the effective regulation of creativity in America. To build upon or critique the culture around us one must ask, Oliver Twist–like, for permission first. Permission is, of course, often granted—but it is not often granted to the critical or the independent. We have built a kind of cultural nobility; those within the noble class live easily; those outside it don't. But it is nobility of any form that is alien to our tradition.

The story that follows is about this war. Is it not about the "centrality of technology" to ordinary life. I don't believe in gods, digital or otherwise. Nor is it an effort to demonize any individual or group, for neither do I believe in a devil, corporate or otherwise. It is not a morality tale. Nor is it a call to jihad against an industry.

It is instead an effort to understand a hopelessly destructive war inspired by the technologies of the Internet but reaching far beyond its code. And by understanding this battle, it is an effort to map peace. There is no good reason for the current struggle around Internet technologies to continue. There will be great harm to our tradition and culture if it is allowed to continue unchecked. We must come to understand the source of this war. We must resolve it soon.

Like the Causbys' battle, this war is, in part, about "property." The property of this war is not as tangible as the Causbys', and no innocent chicken has yet to lose its life. Yet the ideas surrounding this "property" are as obvious to most as the Causbys' claim about the sacredness of their farm was to them. We are the Causbys. Most of us take for granted the extraordinarily powerful claims that the owners of "intellectual property" now assert. Most of us, like the Causbys, treat these claims as obvious. And hence we, like the Causbys, object when a new technology interferes with this property. It is as plain to us as it was to them that the new technologies of the Internet are "trespassing" upon legitimate claims of "property." It is as plain to us as it was to them that the law should intervene to stop this trespass.

And thus, when geeks and technologists defend their Armstrong or Wright brothers technology, most of us are simply unsympathetic. Common sense does not revolt. Unlike in the case of the unlucky Causbys, common sense is on the side of the property owners in this war. Unlike the lucky Wright brothers, the Internet has not inspired a revolution on its side.

My hope is to push this common sense along. I have become increasingly amazed by the power of this idea of intellectual property and, more importantly, its power to disable critical thought by policy makers and citizens. There has never been a time in our history when more of our "culture" was as "owned" as it is now. And yet there has never been a time when the concentration of power to control the *uses* of culture has been as unquestioningly accepted as it is now.

The puzzle is, Why?

Is it because we have come to understand a truth about the value and importance of absolute property over ideas and culture? Is it because we have discovered that our tradition of rejecting such an absolute claim was wrong?

Or is it because the idea of absolute property over ideas and culture benefits the RCAs of our time and fits our own unreflective intuitions?

Is the radical shift away from our tradition of free culture an instance of America correcting a mistake from its past, as we did after a bloody war with slavery, and as we are slowly doing with inequality? Or is the radical shift away from our tradition of free culture yet another example of a political system captured by a few powerful special interests?

Does common sense lead to the extremes on this question because common sense actually believes in these extremes? Or does common sense stand silent in the face of these extremes because, as with Armstrong versus RCA, the more powerful side has ensured that it has the more powerful view?

I don't mean to be mysterious. My own views are resolved. I believe it was right for common sense to revolt against the extremism of the Causbys. I believe it would be right for common sense to revolt against the extreme claims made today on behalf of "intellectual property." What the law demands today is increasingly as silly as a sheriff arresting an airplane for trespass. But the consequences of this silliness will be much more profound.

The struggle that rages just now centers on two ideas: "piracy" and "property." My aim in this book's next two parts is to explore these two ideas.

My method is not the usual method of an academic. I don't want to plunge you into a complex argument, buttressed with references to obscure French theorists—however natural that is for the weird sort we academics have become. Instead I begin in each part with a collection of stories that set a context within which these apparently simple ideas can be more fully understood.

The two sections set up the core claim of this book: that while the Internet has indeed produced something fantastic and new, our government, pushed by big media to respond to this "something new," is destroying something very old. Rather than understanding the changes the Internet might permit, and rather than taking time to let "common sense" resolve how best to respond, we are allowing those most threatened by the changes to use their power to change the law—and more importantly, to use their power to change something fundamental about who we have always been.

We allow this, I believe, not because it is right, and not because most of us really believe in these changes. We allow it because the interests most threatened are among the most powerful players in our depressingly compromised process of making law. This book is the story of one more consequence of this form of corruption—a consequence to which most of us remain oblivious.

"PIRACY"

Since the inception of the law regulating creative property, there has been a war against "piracy." The precise contours of this concept, "piracy," are hard to sketch, but the animating injustice is easy to capture. As Lord Mansfield wrote in a case that extended the reach of English copyright law to include sheet music,

> A person may use the copy by playing it, but he has no right to rob the author of the profit, by multiplying copies and disposing of them for his own use.[1]

Today we are in the middle of another "war" against "piracy." The Internet has provoked this war. The Internet makes possible the efficient spread of content. Peer-to-peer (p2p) file sharing is among the most efficient of the efficient technologies the Internet enables. Using distributed intelligence, p2p systems facilitate the easy spread of content in a way unimagined a generation ago.

This efficiency does not respect the traditional lines of copyright. The network doesn't discriminate between the sharing of copyrighted and uncopyrighted content. Thus has there been a vast amount of sharing of copyrighted content. That sharing in turn has excited the war, as copyright owners fear the sharing will "rob the author of the profit."

The warriors have turned to the courts, to the legislatures, and increasingly to technology to defend their "property" against this "piracy." A generation of Americans, the warriors warn, is being raised to believe that "property" should be "free." Forget tattoos, never mind body piercing—our kids are becoming *thieves*!

There's no doubt that "piracy" is wrong, and that pirates should be punished. But before we summon the executioners, we should put this notion of "piracy" in some context. For as the concept is increasingly used, at its core is an extraordinary idea that is almost certainly wrong.

The idea goes something like this:

> Creative work has value; whenever I use, or take, or build upon the creative work of others, I am taking from them something of value. Whenever I take something of value from someone else, I should have their permission. The taking of something of value from someone else without permission is wrong. It is a form of piracy.

This view runs deep within the current debates. It is what NYU law professor Rochelle Dreyfuss criticizes as the "if value, then right" theory of creative property[2]—if there is value, then someone must have a right to that value. It is the perspective that led a composers' rights organization, ASCAP, to sue the Girl Scouts for failing to pay for the songs that girls sang around Girl Scout campfires.[3] There was "value" (the songs) so there must have been a "right"—even against the Girl Scouts.

This idea is certainly a possible understanding of how creative property should work. It might well be a possible design for a system of law protecting creative property. But the "if value, then right" theory of creative property has never been America's theory of creative property. It has never taken hold within our law.

Instead, in our tradition, intellectual property is an instrument. It sets the groundwork for a richly creative society but remains subservient to the value of creativity. The current debate has this turned around. We have become so concerned with protecting the instrument that we are losing sight of the value.

The source of this confusion is a distinction that the law no longer takes care to draw—the distinction between republishing someone's work on the one hand and building upon or transforming that work on the other. Copyright law at its birth had only publishing as its concern; copyright law today regulates both.

Before the technologies of the Internet, this conflation didn't matter all that much. The technologies of publishing were expensive; that meant the vast majority of publishing was commercial. Commercial entities could bear the burden of the law—even the burden of the Byzantine complexity that copyright law has become. It was just one more expense of doing business.

But with the birth of the Internet, this natural limit to the reach of the law has disappeared. The law controls not just the creativity of commercial creators but effectively that of anyone. Although that expansion would not matter much if copyright law regulated only "copying," when the law regulates as broadly and obscurely as it does, the extension matters a lot. The burden of this law now vastly outweighs any original benefit—certainly as it affects noncommercial creativity, and increasingly as it affects commercial creativity as well. Thus, as we'll see more clearly in the chapters below, the law's role is less and less to support creativity, and more and more to protect certain industries against competition. Just at the time digital technology could unleash an extraordinary range of commercial and noncommercial creativity, the law burdens this creativity with insanely complex and vague rules and with the threat of obscenely severe penalties. We may be seeing, as Richard Florida writes, the "Rise of the Creative Class."[4] Unfortunately, we are also seeing an extraordinary rise of regulation of this creative class.

These burdens make no sense in our tradition. We should begin by understanding that tradition a bit more and by placing in their proper context the current battles about behavior labeled "piracy."

CHAPTER ONE: Creators

In 1928, a cartoon character was born. An early Mickey Mouse made his debut in May of that year, in a silent flop called *Plane Crazy*. In November, in New York City's Colony Theater, in the first widely distributed cartoon synchronized with sound, *Steamboat Willie* brought to life the character that would become Mickey Mouse.

Synchronized sound had been introduced to film a year earlier in the movie *The Jazz Singer*. That success led Walt Disney to copy the technique and mix sound with cartoons. No one knew whether it would work or, if it did work, whether it would win an audience. But when Disney ran a test in the summer of 1928, the results were unambiguous. As Disney describes that first experiment,

> A couple of my boys could read music, and one of them could play a mouth organ. We put them in a room where they could not see the screen and arranged to pipe their sound into the room where our wives and friends were going to see the picture.

The boys worked from a music and sound-effects score. After several false starts, sound and action got off with the gun. The mouth organist played the tune, the rest of us in the sound department bammed tin pans and blew slide whistles on the beat. The synchronization was pretty close.

The effect on our little audience was nothing less than electric. They responded almost instinctively to this union of sound and motion. I thought they were kidding me. So they put me in the audience and ran the action again. It was terrible, but it was wonderful! And it was something new![1]

Disney's then partner, and one of animation's most extraordinary talents, Ub Iwerks, put it more strongly: "I have never been so thrilled in my life. Nothing since has ever equaled it."

Disney had created something very new, based upon something relatively new. Synchronized sound brought life to a form of creativity that had rarely—except in Disney's hands—been anything more than filler for other films. Throughout animation's early history, it was Disney's invention that set the standard that others struggled to match. And quite often, Disney's great genius, his spark of creativity, was built upon the work of others.

This much is familiar. What you might not know is that 1928 also marks another important transition. In that year, a comic (as opposed to cartoon) genius created his last independently produced silent film. That genius was Buster Keaton. The film was *Steamboat Bill, Jr.*

Keaton was born into a vaudeville family in 1895. In the era of silent film, he had mastered using broad physical comedy as a way to spark uncontrollable laughter from his audience. *Steamboat Bill, Jr.* was a classic of this form, famous among film buffs for its incredible stunts. The film was classic Keaton—wildly popular and among the best of its genre.

Steamboat Bill, Jr. appeared before Disney's cartoon *Steamboat Willie.* The coincidence of titles is not coincidental. Steamboat Willie is a direct cartoon parody of Steamboat Bill,[2] and both are built upon a common song as a source. It is not just from the invention of synchronized sound in *The Jazz Singer* that we get *Steamboat Willie*. It is also from Buster Keaton's invention of Steamboat Bill, Jr., itself inspired by the song "Steamboat Bill," that we get Steamboat Willie, and then from Steamboat Willie, Mickey Mouse.

This "borrowing" was nothing unique, either for Disney or for the industry. Disney was always parroting the feature-length mainstream films of his day.[3] So did many others. Early cartoons are filled with knockoffs—slight variations on winning themes; retellings of ancient stories. The key to success was the brilliance of the differences. With Disney, it was sound that gave his animation its spark. Later, it was the quality of his work relative to the production-line cartoons with which he competed. Yet these additions were built upon a base that was borrowed. Disney added to the work of others before him, creating something new out of something just barely old.

Sometimes this borrowing was slight. Sometimes it was significant. Think about the fairy tales of the Brothers Grimm. If you're as oblivious as I was, you're likely to think that these tales are happy, sweet stories, appropriate for any child at bedtime. In fact, the Grimm fairy tales are, well, for us, grim. It is a rare and perhaps overly ambitious parent who would dare to read these bloody, moralistic stories to his or her child, at bedtime or anytime.

Disney took these stories and retold them in a way that carried them into a new age. He animated the stories, with both characters and light. Without removing the elements of fear and danger altogether, he made funny what was dark and injected a genuine emotion of compassion where before there was fear. And not just with the work of the Brothers Grimm. Indeed, the catalog of Disney work drawing upon the work of others is astonishing when set together: *Snow White* (1937), *Fantasia* (1940), *Pinocchio* (1940), *Dumbo* (1941), *Bambi* (1942), *Song of the South* (1946), *Cinderella* (1950), *Alice in Wonderland* (1951), *Robin Hood* (1952), *Peter Pan* (1953), *Lady and the Tramp*

(1955), *Mulan* (1998), *Sleeping Beauty* (1959), *101 Dalmatians* (1961), *The Sword in the Stone* (1963), and *The Jungle Book* (1967)—not to mention a recent example that we should perhaps quickly forget, *Treasure Planet* (2003). In all of these cases, Disney (or Disney, Inc.) ripped creativity from the culture around him, mixed that creativity with his own extraordinary talent, and then burned that mix into the soul of his culture. Rip, mix, and burn.

This is a kind of creativity. It is a creativity that we should remember and celebrate. There are some who would say that there is no creativity except this kind. We don't need to go that far to recognize its importance. We could call this "Disney creativity," though that would be a bit misleading. It is, more precisely, "Walt Disney creativity"—a form of expression and genius that builds upon the culture around us and makes it something different.

In 1928, the culture that Disney was free to draw upon was relatively fresh. The public domain in 1928 was not very old and was therefore quite vibrant. The average term of copyright was just around thirty years—for that minority of creative work that was in fact copyrighted.[4] That means that for thirty years, on average, the authors or copyright holders of a creative work had an "exclusive right" to control certain uses of the work. To use this copyrighted work in limited ways required the permission of the copyright owner.

At the end of a copyright term, a work passes into the public domain. No permission is then needed to draw upon or use that work. No permission and, hence, no lawyers. The public domain is a "lawyer-free zone." Thus, most of the content from the nineteenth century was free for Disney to use and build upon in 1928. It was free for anyone—whether connected or not, whether rich or not, whether approved or not—to use and build upon.

This is the ways things always were—until quite recently. For most of our history, the public domain was just over the horizon. From 1790 until 1978, the average copyright term was never more than thirty-two years, meaning that most culture just a generation and a half old was free for anyone to build upon without the permission of anyone else. Today's equivalent would be for creative work from the 1960s and 1970s to now be free for the next Walt Disney to build upon without permission. Yet today, the public domain is presumptive only for content from before the Great Depression.

Of course, Walt Disney had no monopoly on "Walt Disney creativity." Nor does America. The norm of free culture has, until recently, and except within totalitarian nations, been broadly exploited and quite universal.

Consider, for example, a form of creativity that seems strange to many Americans but that is inescapable within Japanese culture: *manga,* or comics. The Japanese are fanatics about comics. Some 40 percent of publications are comics, and 30 percent of publication revenue derives from comics. They are everywhere in Japanese society, at every magazine stand, carried by a large proportion of commuters on Japan's extraordinary system of public transportation.

Americans tend to look down upon this form of culture. That's an unattractive characteristic of ours. We're likely to misunderstand much about manga, because few of us have ever read anything close to the stories that these "graphic novels" tell. For the Japanese, manga cover every aspect of social life. For us, comics are "men in tights." And anyway, it's not as if the New York subways are filled with readers of Joyce or even Hemingway. People of different cultures distract themselves in different ways, the Japanese in this interestingly different way.

But my purpose here is not to understand manga. It is to describe a variant on manga that from a lawyer's perspective is quite odd, but from a Disney perspective is quite familiar.

This is the phenomenon of *doujinshi*. Doujinshi are also comics, but they are a kind of copycat comic. A rich ethic governs the creation of doujinshi. It is not doujinshi if it is *just* a copy; the artist must make a contribution to the art he copies, by transforming it either subtly or significantly. A doujinshi comic can thus take a mainstream comic and develop it differently—with a different story line. Or the comic can keep the character in character but change its look slightly. There is no formula for what makes the doujinshi sufficiently "different." But they must be different if they are to be considered true doujinshi. Indeed, there are committees that review doujinshi for inclusion within shows and reject any copycat comic that is merely a copy.

These copycat comics are not a tiny part of the manga market. They are huge. More than 33,000 "circles" of creators from across Japan produce these bits of Walt Disney creativity. More than 450,000 Japanese come together twice a year, in the largest public gathering in the country, to exchange and sell them. This market exists in parallel to the mainstream commercial manga market. In some ways, it obviously competes with that market, but there is no sustained effort by those who control the commercial manga market to shut the doujinshi market down. It flourishes, despite the competition and despite the law.

The most puzzling feature of the doujinshi market, for those trained in the law, at least, is that it is allowed to exist at all. Under Japanese copyright law, which in this respect (on paper) mirrors American copyright law, the doujinshi market is an illegal one. Doujinshi are plainly "derivative works." There is no general practice by doujinshi artists of securing the permission of the manga creators. Instead, the practice is simply to take and modify the creations of others, as Walt Disney did with *Steamboat Bill, Jr.* Under both Japanese and American law, that "taking" without the permission of the original copyright owner is illegal. It is an infringement of the original copyright to make a copy or a derivative work without the original copyright owner's permission.

Yet this illegal market exists and indeed flourishes in Japan, and in the view of many, it is precisely because it exists that Japanese manga flourish. As American graphic novelist Judd Winick said to me, "The early days of comics in America are very much like what's going on in Japan now. . . . American comics were born out of copying each other. . . . That's how [the artists] learn to draw—by going into comic books and not tracing them, but looking at them and copying them" and building from them.[5]

American comics now are quite different, Winick explains, in part because of the legal difficulty of adapting comics the way doujinshi are allowed. Speaking of Superman, Winick told me, "there are these rules and you have to stick to them." There are things Superman "cannot" do. "As a creator, it's frustrating having to stick to some parameters which are fifty years old."

The norm in Japan mitigates this legal difficulty. Some say it is precisely the benefit accruing to the Japanese manga market that explains the mitigation. Temple University law professor Salil Mehra, for example, hypothesizes that the manga market accepts these technical violations because they spur the manga market to be more wealthy and productive. Everyone would be worse off if doujinshi were banned, so the law does not ban doujinshi.[6]

The problem with this story, however, as Mehra plainly acknowledges, is that the mechanism producing this laissez faire response is not clear. It may well be that the market as a whole is better off if doujinshi are permitted rather than banned, but that doesn't explain why individual copyright owners don't sue nonetheless. If the law has no general exception for doujinshi, and indeed in some cases individual manga artists have sued doujinshi artists, why is there not a more general pattern of blocking this "free taking" by the doujinshi culture?

I spent four wonderful months in Japan, and I asked this question as often as I could. Perhaps the best account in the end was offered by a friend from a major Japanese law firm. "We don't have enough lawyers," he told me one afternoon. There "just aren't enough resources to prosecute cases like this."

This is a theme to which we will return: that regulation by law is a function of both the words on the books and the costs of making those words have effect. For now, focus on the obvious question that is begged: Would Japan be better off with more lawyers? Would manga be richer if doujinshi artists were regularly prosecuted? Would the Japanese gain something important if they could end this practice of uncompensated sharing? Does piracy here hurt the victims of the piracy, or does it help them? Would lawyers fighting this piracy help their clients or hurt them?

Let's pause for a moment.

If you're like I was a decade ago, or like most people are when they first start thinking about these issues, then just about now you should be puzzled about something you hadn't thought through before.

We live in a world that celebrates "property." I am one of those celebrants. I believe in the value of property in general, and I also believe in the value of that weird form of property that lawyers call "intellectual property."[7] A large, diverse society cannot survive without property; a large, diverse, and modern society cannot flourish without intellectual property.

But it takes just a second's reflection to realize that there is plenty of value out there that "property" doesn't capture. I don't mean "money can't buy you love," but rather, value that is plainly part of a process of production, including commercial as well as noncommercial production. If Disney animators had stolen a set of pencils to draw Steamboat Willie, we'd have no hesitation in condemning that taking as wrong—even though trivial, even if unnoticed. Yet there was nothing wrong, at least under the law of the day, with Disney's taking from Buster Keaton or from the Brothers Grimm. There was nothing wrong with the taking from Keaton because Disney's use would have been considered "fair." There was nothing wrong with the taking from the Grimms because the Grimms' work was in the public domain.

Thus, even though the things that Disney took—or more generally, the things taken by anyone exercising Walt Disney creativity—are valuable, our tradition does not treat those takings as wrong. Some things remain free for the taking within a free culture, and that freedom is good.

The same with the doujinshi culture. If a doujinshi artist broke into a publisher's office and ran off with a thousand copies of his latest work—or even one copy—without paying, we'd have no hesitation in saying the artist was wrong. In addition to having trespassed, he would have stolen something of value. The law bans that stealing in whatever form, whether large or small.

Yet there is an obvious reluctance, even among Japanese lawyers, to say that the copycat comic artists are "stealing." This form of Walt Disney creativity is seen as fair and right, even if lawyers in particular find it hard to say why.

It's the same with a thousand examples that appear everywhere once you begin to look. Scientists build upon the work of other scientists without asking or paying for the privilege. ("Excuse me, Professor Einstein, but may I have permission to use your theory of relativity to show that you were wrong about quantum physics?") Acting companies perform adaptations of the works of Shakespeare without securing permission from anyone. (Does *anyone* believe Shakespeare would be better spread within our culture if there were a central Shakespeare rights clearinghouse that all productions of Shakespeare must appeal to first?) And Hollywood goes through cycles with a certain kind of movie: five asteroid films in the late 1990s; two volcano disaster films in 1997.

Creators here and everywhere are always and at all times building upon the creativity that went before and that surrounds them now. That building is always and everywhere at least partially done without permission and without compensating the original creator. No society, free or controlled, has ever demanded that every use be paid for or that permission for Walt Disney creativity must always be sought. Instead, every society has left a certain bit of its culture free for the taking—free societies more fully than unfree, perhaps, but all societies to some degree.

The hard question is therefore not *whether* a culture is free. All cultures are free to some degree. The hard question instead is "*How* free is this culture?" How much, and how broadly, is the culture free for others to take and build upon? Is that freedom limited to party members? To members of the royal family? To the top ten corporations on the New York Stock Exchange? Or is that freedom spread broadly? To artists generally, whether affiliated with the Met or not? To musicians generally, whether white or not? To filmmakers generally, whether affiliated with a studio or not?

Free cultures are cultures that leave a great deal open for others to build upon; unfree, or permission, cultures leave much less. Ours was a free culture. It is becoming much less so.

CHAPTER TWO: "Mere Copyists"

In 1839, Louis Daguerre invented the first practical technology for producing what we would call "photographs." Appropriately enough, they were called "daguerreotypes." The process was complicated and expensive, and the field was thus limited to professionals and a few zealous and wealthy amateurs. (There was even an American Daguerre Association that helped regulate the industry, as do all such associations, by keeping competition down so as to keep prices up.)

Yet despite high prices, the demand for daguerreotypes was strong. This pushed inventors to find simpler and cheaper ways to make "automatic pictures." William Talbot soon discovered a process for making "negatives." But because the negatives were glass, and had to be kept wet, the process still remained expensive and cumbersome. In the 1870s, dry plates were developed, making it easier to separate the taking of a picture from its developing. These were still plates of glass, and thus it was still not a process within reach of most amateurs.

The technological change that made mass photography possible didn't happen until 1888, and was the creation of a single man. George

Eastman, himself an amateur photographer, was frustrated by the technology of photographs made with plates. In a flash of insight (so to speak), Eastman saw that if the film could be made to be flexible, it could be held on a single spindle. That roll could then be sent to a developer, driving the costs of photography down substantially. By lowering the costs, Eastman expected he could dramatically broaden the population of photographers.

Eastman developed flexible, emulsion-coated paper film and placed rolls of it in small, simple cameras: the Kodak. The device was marketed on the basis of its simplicity. "You press the button and we do the rest."[1] As he described in *The Kodak Primer*:

> The principle of the Kodak system is the separation of the work that any person whomsoever can do in making a photograph, from the work that only an expert can do. . . . We furnish anybody, man, woman or child, who has sufficient intelligence to point a box straight and press a button, with an instrument which altogether removes from the practice of photography the necessity for exceptional facilities or, in fact, any special knowledge of the art. It can be employed without preliminary study, without a darkroom and without chemicals.[2]

For $25, anyone could make pictures. The camera came preloaded with film, and when it had been used, the camera was returned to an Eastman factory, where the film was developed. Over time, of course, the cost of the camera and the ease with which it could be used both improved. Roll film thus became the basis for the explosive growth of popular photography. Eastman's camera first went on sale in 1888; one year later, Kodak was printing more than six thousand negatives a day. From 1888 through 1909, while industrial production was rising by 4.7 percent, photographic equipment and material sales increased by 11 percent.[3] Eastman Kodak's sales during the same period experienced an average annual increase of over 17 percent.[4]

The real significance of Eastman's invention, however, was not economic. It was social. Professional photography gave individuals a glimpse of places they would never otherwise see. Amateur photography gave them the ability to record their own lives in a way they had never been able to do before. As author Brian Coe notes, "For the first time the snapshot album provided the man on the street with a permanent record of his family and its activities. . . . For the first time in history there exists an authentic visual record of the appearance and activities of the common man made without [literary] interpretation or bias."[5]

In this way, the Kodak camera and film were technologies of expression. The pencil or paintbrush was also a technology of expression, of course. But it took years of training before they could be deployed by amateurs in any useful or effective way. With the Kodak, expression was possible much sooner and more simply. The barrier to expression was lowered. Snobs would sneer at its "quality"; professionals would discount it as irrelevant. But watch a child study how best to frame a picture and you get a sense of the experience of creativity that the Kodak enabled. Democratic tools gave ordinary people a way to express themselves more easily than any tools could have before.

What was required for this technology to flourish? Obviously, Eastman's genius was an important part. But also important was the legal environment within which Eastman's invention grew. For early in the history of photography, there was a series of judicial decisions that could well have changed the course of photography substantially. Courts were asked whether the photographer, amateur or professional, required permission before he could capture and print whatever image he wanted. Their answer was no.[6]

The arguments in favor of requiring permission will sound surprisingly familiar. The photographer was "taking" something from the person or building whose photograph he shot—pirating something of value. Some even thought he was taking the target's soul. Just as Disney was not free to take the pencils that his animators used to draw

Mickey, so, too, should these photographers not be free to take images that they thought valuable.

On the other side was an argument that should be familiar, as well. Sure, there may be something of value being used. But citizens should have the right to capture at least those images that stand in public view. (Louis Brandeis, who would become a Supreme Court Justice, thought the rule should be different for images from private spaces.[7]) It may be that this means that the photographer gets something for nothing. Just as Disney could take inspiration from *Steamboat Bill, Jr.* or the Brothers Grimm, the photographer should be free to capture an image without compensating the source.

Fortunately for Mr. Eastman, and for photography in general, these early decisions went in favor of the pirates. In general, no permission would be required before an image could be captured and shared with others. Instead, permission was presumed. Freedom was the default. (The law would eventually craft an exception for famous people: commercial photographers who snap pictures of famous people for commercial purposes have more restrictions than the rest of us. But in the ordinary case, the image can be captured without clearing the rights to do the capturing.[8])

We can only speculate about how photography would have developed had the law gone the other way. If the presumption had been against the photographer, then the photographer would have had to demonstrate permission. Perhaps Eastman Kodak would have had to demonstrate permission, too, before it developed the film upon which images were captured. After all, if permission were not granted, then Eastman Kodak would be benefiting from the "theft" committed by the photographer. Just as Napster benefited from the copyright infringements committed by Napster users, Kodak would be benefiting from the "image-right" infringement of its photographers. We could imagine the law then requiring that some form of permission be demonstrated before a company developed pictures. We could imagine a system developing to demonstrate that permission.

But though we could imagine this system of permission, it would be very hard to see how photography could have flourished as it did if the requirement for permission had been built into the rules that govern it. Photography would have existed. It would have grown in importance over time. Professionals would have continued to use the technology as they did—since professionals could have more easily borne the burdens of the permission system. But the spread of photography to ordinary people would not have occurred. Nothing like that growth would have been realized. And certainly, nothing like that growth in a democratic technology of expression would have been realized.

If you drive through San Francisco's Presidio, you might see two gaudy yellow school buses painted over with colorful and striking images, and the logo "Just Think!" in place of the name of a school. But there's little that's "just" cerebral in the projects that these busses enable. These buses are filled with technologies that teach kids to tinker with film. Not the film of Eastman. Not even the film of your VCR. Rather the "film" of digital cameras. Just Think! is a project that enables kids to make films, as a way to understand and critique the filmed culture that they find all around them. Each year, these busses travel to more than thirty schools and enable three hundred to five hundred children to learn something about media by doing something with media. By doing, they think. By tinkering, they learn.

These buses are not cheap, but the technology they carry is increasingly so. The cost of a high-quality digital video system has fallen dramatically. As one analyst puts it, "Five years ago, a good real-time digital video editing system cost $25,000. Today you can get professional quality for $595."[9] These buses are filled with technology that would have cost hundreds of thousands just ten years ago. And it is now feasible to imagine not just buses like this, but classrooms across the country where kids are learning more and more of something teachers call "media literacy."

"Media literacy," as Dave Yanofsky, the executive director of Just Think!, puts it, "is the ability . . . to understand, analyze, and deconstruct media images. Its aim is to make [kids] literate about the way media works, the way it's constructed, the way it's delivered, and the way people access it."

This may seem like an odd way to think about "literacy." For most people, literacy is about reading and writing. Faulkner and Hemingway and noticing split infinitives are the things that "literate" people know about.

Maybe. But in a world where children see on average 390 hours of television commercials per year, or between 20,000 and 45,000 commercials generally,[10] it is increasingly important to understand the "grammar" of media. For just as there is a grammar for the written word, so, too, is there one for media. And just as kids learn how to write by writing lots of terrible prose, kids learn how to write media by constructing lots of (at least at first) terrible media.

A growing field of academics and activists sees this form of literacy as crucial to the next generation of culture. For though anyone who has written understands how difficult writing is—how difficult it is to sequence the story, to keep a reader's attention, to craft language to be understandable—few of us have any real sense of how difficult media is. Or more fundamentally, few of us have a sense of how media works, how it holds an audience or leads it through a story, how it triggers emotion or builds suspense.

It took filmmaking a generation before it could do these things well. But even then, the knowledge was in the filming, not in writing about the film. The skill came from experiencing the making of a film, not from reading a book about it. One learns to write by writing and then reflecting upon what one has written. One learns to write with images by making them and then reflecting upon what one has created.

This grammar has changed as media has changed. When it was just film, as Elizabeth Daley, executive director of the University of Southern California's Annenberg Center for Communication and dean of the

USC School of Cinema-Television, explained to me, the grammar was about "the placement of objects, color, . . . rhythm, pacing, and texture."[11] But as computers open up an interactive space where a story is "played" as well as experienced, that grammar changes. The simple control of narrative is lost, and so other techniques are necessary. Author Michael Crichton had mastered the narrative of science fiction. But when he tried to design a computer game based on one of his works, it was a new craft he had to learn. How to lead people through a game without their feeling they have been led was not obvious, even to a wildly successful author.[12]

This skill is precisely the craft a filmmaker learns. As Daley describes, "people are very surprised about how they are led through a film. [I]t is perfectly constructed to keep you from seeing it, so you have no idea. If a filmmaker succeeds you do not know how you were led." If you know you were led through a film, the film has failed.

Yet the push for an expanded literacy—one that goes beyond text to include audio and visual elements—is not about making better film directors. The aim is not to improve the profession of filmmaking at all. Instead, as Daley explained,

> From my perspective, probably the most important digital divide is not access to a box. It's the ability to be empowered with the language that that box works in. Otherwise only a very few people can write with this language, and all the rest of us are reduced to being read-only.

"Read-only." Passive recipients of culture produced elsewhere. Couch potatoes. Consumers. This is the world of media from the twentieth century.

The twenty-first century could be different. This is the crucial point: It could be both read and write. Or at least reading and better understanding the craft of writing. Or best, reading and understanding the tools that enable the writing to lead or mislead. The aim of any literacy, and this literacy in particular, is to "empower people to choose the appropriate language for what they need to create or express."[13] It is to enable students "to communicate in the language of the twenty-first century."[14]

As with any language, this language comes more easily to some than to others. It doesn't necessarily come more easily to those who excel in written language. Daley and Stephanie Barish, director of the Institute for Multimedia Literacy at the Annenberg Center, describe one particularly poignant example of a project they ran in a high school. The high school was a very poor inner-city Los Angeles school. In all the traditional measures of success, this school was a failure. But Daley and Barish ran a program that gave kids an opportunity to use film to express meaning about something the students know something about—gun violence.

The class was held on Friday afternoons, and it created a relatively new problem for the school. While the challenge in most classes was getting the kids to come, the challenge in this class was keeping them away. The "kids were showing up at 6 A.M. and leaving at 5 at night," said Barish. They were working harder than in any other class to do what education should be about—learning how to express themselves.

Using whatever "free web stuff they could find," and relatively simple tools to enable the kids to mix "image, sound, and text," Barish said this class produced a series of projects that showed something about gun violence that few would otherwise understand. This was an issue close to the lives of these students. The project "gave them a tool and empowered them to be able to both understand it and talk about it," Barish explained. That tool succeeded in creating expression—far more successfully and powerfully than could have been created using only text. "If you had said to these students, 'you have to do it in text,' they would've just thrown their hands up and gone and done something else," Barish described, in part, no doubt, because expressing themselves in text is not something these students can do well. Yet neither is text a form in which *these* ideas can be expressed well. The power of this message depended upon its connection to this form of expression.

"But isn't education about teaching kids to write?" I asked. In part, of course, it is. But why are we teaching kids to write? Education, Daley explained, is about giving students a way of "constructing meaning." To say that that means just writing is like saying teaching writing is only about teaching kids how to spell. Text is one part—and increasingly, not the most powerful part—of constructing meaning. As Daley explained in the most moving part of our interview,

> What you want is to give these students ways of constructing meaning. If all you give them is text, they're not going to do it. Because they can't. You know, you've got Johnny who can look at a video, he can play a video game, he can do graffiti all over your walls, he can take your car apart, and he can do all sorts of other things. He just can't read your text. So Johnny comes to school and you say, "Johnny, you're illiterate. Nothing you can do matters." Well, Johnny then has two choices: He can dismiss you or he [can] dismiss himself. If his ego is healthy at all, he's going to dismiss you. [But i]nstead, if you say, "Well, with all these things that you can do, let's talk about this issue. Play for me music that you think reflects that, or show me images that you think reflect that, or draw for me something that reflects that." Not by giving a kid a video camera and . . . saying, "Let's go have fun with the video camera and make a little movie." But instead, really help you take these elements that you understand, that are your language, and construct meaning about the topic. . . .
>
> That empowers enormously. And then what happens, of course, is eventually, as it has happened in all these classes, they bump up against the fact, "I need to explain this and I really need to write something." And as one of the teachers told Stephanie, they would rewrite a paragraph 5, 6, 7, 8 times, till they got it right.
>
> Because they needed to. There was a reason for doing it. They needed to say something, as opposed to just jumping through your hoops. They actually needed to use a language that they

didn't speak very well. But they had come to understand that they had a lot of power with this language."

When two planes crashed into the World Trade Center, another into the Pentagon, and a fourth into a Pennsylvania field, all media around the world shifted to this news. Every moment of just about every day for that week, and for weeks after, television in particular, and media generally, retold the story of the events we had just witnessed. The telling was a retelling, because we had seen the events that were described. The genius of this awful act of terrorism was that the delayed second attack was perfectly timed to assure that the whole world would be watching.

These retellings had an increasingly familiar feel. There was music scored for the intermissions, and fancy graphics that flashed across the screen. There was a formula to interviews. There was "balance," and seriousness. This was news choreographed in the way we have increasingly come to expect it, "news as entertainment," even if the entertainment is tragedy.

But in addition to this produced news about the "tragedy of September 11," those of us tied to the Internet came to see a very different production as well. The Internet was filled with accounts of the same events. Yet these Internet accounts had a very different flavor. Some people constructed photo pages that captured images from around the world and presented them as slide shows with text. Some offered open letters. There were sound recordings. There was anger and frustration. There were attempts to provide context. There was, in short, an extraordinary worldwide barn raising, in the sense Mike Godwin uses the term in his book *Cyber Rights,* around a news event that had captured the attention of the world. There was ABC and CBS, but there was also the Internet.

I don't mean simply to praise the Internet—though I do think the people who supported this form of speech should be praised. I mean instead to point to a significance in this form of speech. For like a Kodak, the Internet enables people to capture images. And like in a movie by a student on the "Just Think!" bus, the visual images could be mixed with sound or text.

But unlike any technology for simply capturing images, the Internet allows these creations to be shared with an extraordinary number of people, practically instantaneously. This is something new in our tradition—not just that culture can be captured mechanically, and obviously not just that events are commented upon critically, but that this mix of captured images, sound, and commentary can be widely spread practically instantaneously.

September 11 was not an aberration. It was a beginning. Around the same time, a form of communication that has grown dramatically was just beginning to come into public consciousness: the Web-log, or blog. The blog is a kind of public diary, and within some cultures, such as in Japan, it functions very much like a diary. In those cultures, it records private facts in a public way—it's a kind of electronic *Jerry Springer*, available anywhere in the world.

But in the United States, blogs have taken on a very different character. There are some who use the space simply to talk about their private life. But there are many who use the space to engage in public discourse. Discussing matters of public import, criticizing others who are mistaken in their views, criticizing politicians about the decisions they make, offering solutions to problems we all see: blogs create the sense of a virtual public meeting, but one in which we don't all hope to be there at the same time and in which conversations are not necessarily linked. The best of the blog entries are relatively short; they point directly to words used by others, criticizing with or adding to them. They are arguably the most important form of unchoreographed public discourse that we have.

That's a strong statement. Yet it says as much about our democracy as it does about blogs. This is the part of America that is most difficult for those of us who love America to accept: Our democracy has atrophied. Of course we have elections, and most of the time the courts allow those elections to count. A relatively small number of people vote in those elections. The cycle of these elections has become totally professionalized and routinized. Most of us think this is democracy.

But democracy has never just been about elections. Democracy means rule by the people, but rule means something more than mere elections. In our tradition, it also means control through reasoned discourse. This was the idea that captured the imagination of Alexis de Tocqueville, the nineteenth-century French lawyer who wrote the most important account of early "Democracy in America." It wasn't popular elections that fascinated him—it was the jury, an institution that gave ordinary people the right to choose life or death for other citizens. And most fascinating for him was that the jury didn't just vote about the outcome they would impose. They deliberated. Members argued about the "right" result; they tried to persuade each other of the "right" result, and in criminal cases at least, they had to agree upon a unanimous result for the process to come to an end.[15]

Yet even this institution flags in American life today. And in its place, there is no systematic effort to enable citizen deliberation. Some are pushing to create just such an institution.[16] And in some towns in New England, something close to deliberation remains. But for most of us for most of the time, there is no time or place for "democratic deliberation" to occur.

More bizarrely, there is generally not even permission for it to occur. We, the most powerful democracy in the world, have developed a strong norm against talking about politics. It's fine to talk about politics with people you agree with. But it is rude to argue about politics with people you disagree with. Political discourse becomes isolated, and isolated discourse becomes more extreme.[17] We say what our friends want to hear, and hear very little beyond what our friends say.

Enter the blog. The blog's very architecture solves one part of this problem. People post when they want to post, and people read when they want to read. The most difficult time is synchronous time. Technologies that enable asynchronous communication, such as e-mail, increase the opportunity for communication. Blogs allow for public discourse without the public ever needing to gather in a single public place.

But beyond architecture, blogs also have solved the problem of norms. There's no norm (yet) in blog space not to talk about politics. Indeed, the space is filled with political speech, on both the right and the left. Some of the most popular sites are conservative or libertarian, but there are many of all political stripes. And even blogs that are not political cover political issues when the occasion merits.

The significance of these blogs is tiny now, though not so tiny. The name Howard Dean may well have faded from the 2004 presidential race but for blogs. Yet even if the number of readers is small, the reading is having an effect.

One direct effect is on stories that had a different life cycle in the mainstream media. The Trent Lott affair is an example. When Lott "misspoke" at a party for Senator Strom Thurmond, essentially praising Thurmond's segregationist policies, he calculated correctly that this story would disappear from the mainstream press within forty-eight hours. It did. But he didn't calculate its life cycle in blog space. The bloggers kept researching the story. Over time, more and more instances of the same "misspeaking" emerged. Finally, the story broke back into the mainstream press. In the end, Lott was forced to resign as senate majority leader.[18]

This different cycle is possible because the same commercial pressures don't exist with blogs as with other ventures. Television and newspapers are commercial entities. They must work to keep attention. If they lose readers, they lose revenue. Like sharks, they must move on.

But bloggers don't have a similar constraint. They can obsess, they can focus, they can get serious. If a particular blogger writes a particularly interesting story, more and more people link to that story. And as the number of links to a particular story increases, it rises in the ranks of stories. People read what is popular; what is popular has been selected by a very democratic process of peer-generated rankings.

There's a second way, as well, in which blogs have a different cycle from the mainstream press. As Dave Winer, one of the fathers of this movement and a software author for many decades, told me, another difference is the absence of a financial "conflict of interest." "I think you have to take the conflict of interest" out of journalism, Winer told me. "An amateur journalist simply doesn't have a conflict of interest, or the conflict of interest is so easily disclosed that you know you can sort of get it out of the way."

These conflicts become more important as media becomes more concentrated (more on this below). A concentrated media can hide more from the public than an unconcentrated media can—as CNN admitted it did after the Iraq war because it was afraid of the consequences to its own employees.[19] It also needs to sustain a more coherent account. (In the middle of the Iraq war, I read a post on the Internet from someone who was at that time listening to a satellite uplink with a reporter in Iraq. The New York headquarters was telling the reporter over and over that her account of the war was too bleak: She needed to offer a more optimistic story. When she told New York that wasn't warranted, they told her that *they* were writing "the story.")

Blog space gives amateurs a way to enter the debate—"amateur" not in the sense of inexperienced, but in the sense of an Olympic athlete, meaning not paid by anyone to give their reports. It allows for a much broader range of input into a story, as reporting on the Columbia disaster revealed, when hundreds from across the southwest United States turned to the Internet to retell what they had seen.[20] And it drives readers to read across the range of accounts and "triangulate," as Winer puts it, the truth. Blogs, Winer says, are "communicating directly with our constituency, and the middle man is out of it"—with all the benefits, and costs, that might entail.

Winer is optimistic about the future of journalism infected with blogs. "It's going to become an essential skill," Winer predicts, for public figures and increasingly for private figures as well. It's not clear that "journalism" is happy about this—some journalists have been told to curtail their blogging.[21] But it is clear that we are still in transition. "A lot of what we are doing now is warm-up exercises," Winer told me. There is a lot that must mature before this space has its mature effect. And as the inclusion of content in this space is the least infringing use of the Internet (meaning infringing on copyright), Winer said, "we will be the last thing that gets shut down."

This speech affects democracy. Winer thinks that happens because "you don't have to work for somebody who controls, [for] a gate-keeper." That is true. But it affects democracy in another way as well. As more and more citizens express what they think, and defend it in writing, that will change the way people understand public issues. It is easy to be wrong and misguided in your head. It is harder when the product of your mind can be criticized by others. Of course, it is a rare human who admits that he has been persuaded that he is wrong. But it is even rarer for a human to ignore when he has been proven wrong. The writing of ideas, arguments, and criticism improves democracy. Today there are probably a couple of million blogs where such writing happens. When there are ten million, there will be something extraordinary to report.

John Seely Brown is the chief scientist of the Xerox Corporation. His work, as his Web site describes it, is "human learning and . . . the creation of knowledge ecologies for creating . . . innovation."

Brown thus looks at these technologies of digital creativity a bit differently from the perspectives I've sketched so far. I'm sure he would be excited about any technology that might improve democracy. But his real excitement comes from how these technologies affect learning.

As Brown believes, we learn by tinkering. When "a lot of us grew up," he explains, that tinkering was done "on motorcycle engines, lawn-mower engines, automobiles, radios, and so on." But digital technologies enable a different kind of tinkering—with abstract ideas though in concrete form. The kids at Just Think! not only think about how a commercial portrays a politician; using digital technology, they can take the commercial apart and manipulate it, tinker with it to see how it does what it does. Digital technologies launch a kind of bricolage, or "free collage," as Brown calls it. Many get to add to or transform the tinkering of many others.

The best large-scale example of this kind of tinkering so far is free software or open-source software (FS/OSS). FS/OSS is software whose source code is shared. Anyone can download the technology that makes a FS/OSS program run. And anyone eager to learn how a particular bit of FS/OSS technology works can tinker with the code.

This opportunity creates a "completely new kind of learning platform," as Brown describes. "As soon as you start doing that, you . . . unleash a free collage on the community, so that other people can start looking at your code, tinkering with it, trying it out, seeing if they can improve it." Each effort is a kind of apprenticeship. "Open source becomes a major apprenticeship platform."

In this process, "the concrete things you tinker with are abstract. They are code." Kids are "shifting to the ability to tinker in the abstract, and this tinkering is no longer an isolated activity that you're doing in your garage. You are tinkering with a community platform. . . . You are tinkering with other people's stuff. The more you tinker the more you improve." The more you improve, the more you learn.

This same thing happens with content, too. And it happens in the same collaborative way when that content is part of the Web. As Brown puts it, "the Web [is] the first medium that truly honors multiple forms of intelligence." Earlier technologies, such as the typewriter or word processors, helped amplify text. But the Web amplifies much more than text. "The Web . . . says if you are musical, if you are artistic, if you are visual, if you are interested in film . . . [then] there is a lot you can start to do on this medium. [It] can now amplify and honor these multiple forms of intelligence."

Brown is talking about what Elizabeth Daley, Stephanie Barish, and Just Think! teach: that this tinkering with culture teaches as well as creates. It develops talents differently, and it builds a different kind of recognition.

Yet the freedom to tinker with these objects is not guaranteed. Indeed, as we'll see through the course of this book, that freedom is increasingly highly contested. While there's no doubt that your father had the right to tinker with the car engine, there's great doubt that your child will have the right to tinker with the images she finds all around. The law and, increasingly, technology interfere with a freedom that technology, and curiosity, would otherwise ensure.

These restrictions have become the focus of researchers and scholars. Professor Ed Felten of Princeton (whom we'll see more of in chapter 10) has developed a powerful argument in favor of the "right to tinker" as it applies to computer science and to knowledge in general.[22] But Brown's concern is earlier, or younger, or more fundamental. It is about the learning that kids can do, or can't do, because of the law.

"This is where education in the twenty-first century is going," Brown explains. We need to "understand how kids who grow up digital think and want to learn."

"Yet," as Brown continued, and as the balance of this book will evince, "we are building a legal system that completely suppresses the natural tendencies of today's digital kids. . . . We're building an architecture that unleashes 60 percent of the brain [and] a legal system that closes down that part of the brain."

We're building a technology that takes the magic of Kodak, mixes moving images and sound, and adds a space for commentary and an opportunity to spread that creativity everywhere. But we're building the law to close down that technology.

"No way to run a culture," as Brewster Kahle, whom we'll meet in chapter 9, quipped to me in a rare moment of despondence.

CHAPTER THREE: Catalogs

In the fall of 2002, Jesse Jordan of Oceanside, New York, enrolled as a freshman at Rensselaer Polytechnic Institute, in Troy, New York. His major at RPI was information technology. Though he is not a programmer, in October Jesse decided to begin to tinker with search engine technology that was available on the RPI network.

RPI is one of America's foremost technological research institutions. It offers degrees in fields ranging from architecture and engineering to information sciences. More than 65 percent of its five thousand undergraduates finished in the top 10 percent of their high school class. The school is thus a perfect mix of talent and experience to imagine and then build, a generation for the network age.

RPI's computer network links students, faculty, and administration to one another. It also links RPI to the Internet. Not everything available on the RPI network is available on the Internet. But the network is designed to enable students to get access to the Internet, as well as more intimate access to other members of the RPI community.

Search engines are a measure of a network's intimacy. Google brought the Internet much closer to all of us by fantastically improving the quality of search on the network. Specialty search engines can do this even better. The idea of "intranet" search engines, search engines that search within the network of a particular institution, is to provide users of that institution with better access to material from that institution. Businesses do this all the time, enabling employees to have access to material that people outside the business can't get. Universities do it as well.

These engines are enabled by the network technology itself. Microsoft, for example, has a network file system that makes it very easy for search engines tuned to that network to query the system for information about the publicly (within that network) available content. Jesse's search engine was built to take advantage of this technology. It used Microsoft's network file system to build an index of all the files available within the RPI network.

Jesse's wasn't the first search engine built for the RPI network. Indeed, his engine was a simple modification of engines that others had built. His single most important improvement over those engines was to fix a bug within the Microsoft file-sharing system that could cause a user's computer to crash. With the engines that existed before, if you tried to access a file through a Windows browser that was on a computer that was off-line, your computer could crash. Jesse modified the system a bit to fix that problem, by adding a button that a user could click to see if the machine holding the file was still on-line.

Jesse's engine went on-line in late October. Over the following six months, he continued to tweak it to improve its functionality. By March, the system was functioning quite well. Jesse had more than one million files in his directory, including every type of content that might be on users' computers.

Thus the index his search engine produced included pictures, which students could use to put on their own Web sites; copies of notes or research; copies of information pamphlets; movie clips that students might have created; university brochures—basically anything that users of the RPI network made available in a public folder of their computer.

But the index also included music files. In fact, one quarter of the files that Jesse's search engine listed were music files. But that means, of course, that three quarters were not, and—so that this point is absolutely clear—Jesse did nothing to induce people to put music files in their public folders. He did nothing to target the search engine to these files. He was a kid tinkering with a Google-like technology at a university where he was studying information science, and hence, tinkering was the aim. Unlike Google, or Microsoft, for that matter, he made no money from this tinkering; he was not connected to any business that would make any money from this experiment. He was a kid tinkering with technology in an environment where tinkering with technology was precisely what he was supposed to do.

On April 3, 2003, Jesse was contacted by the dean of students at RPI. The dean informed Jesse that the Recording Industry Association of America, the RIAA, would be filing a lawsuit against him and three other students whom he didn't even know, two of them at other universities. A few hours later, Jesse was served with papers from the suit. As he read these papers and watched the news reports about them, he was increasingly astonished.

"It was absurd," he told me. "I don't think I did anything wrong. . . . I don't think there's anything wrong with the search engine that I ran or . . . what I had done to it. I mean, I hadn't modified it in any way that promoted or enhanced the work of pirates. I just modified the search engine in a way that would make it easier to use"—again, a *search engine*, which Jesse had not himself built, using the Windows file-sharing system, which Jesse had not himself built, to enable members of the RPI community to get access to content, which Jesse had not himself created or posted, and the vast majority of which had nothing to do with music.

But the RIAA branded Jesse a pirate. They claimed he operated a network and had therefore "willfully" violated copyright laws. They demanded that he pay them the damages for his wrong. For cases of "willful infringement," the Copyright Act specifies something lawyers call "statutory damages." These damages permit a copyright owner to claim $150,000 per infringement. As the RIAA alleged more than one hundred specific copyright infringements, they therefore demanded that Jesse pay them at least $15,000,000.

Similar lawsuits were brought against three other students: one other student at RPI, one at Michigan Technical University, and one at Princeton. Their situations were similar to Jesse's. Though each case was different in detail, the bottom line in each was exactly the same: huge demands for "damages" that the RIAA claimed it was entitled to. If you added up the claims, these four lawsuits were asking courts in the United States to award the plaintiffs close to $100 *billion*—six times the *total* profit of the film industry in 2001.[1]

Jesse called his parents. They were supportive but a bit frightened. An uncle was a lawyer. He began negotiations with the RIAA. They demanded to know how much money Jesse had. Jesse had saved $12,000 from summer jobs and other employment. They demanded $12,000 to dismiss the case.

The RIAA wanted Jesse to admit to doing something wrong. He refused. They wanted him to agree to an injunction that would essentially make it impossible for him to work in many fields of technology for the rest of his life. He refused. They made him understand that this process of being sued was not going to be pleasant. (As Jesse's father recounted to me, the chief lawyer on the case, Matt Oppenheimer, told Jesse, "You don't want to pay another visit to a dentist like me.") And throughout, the RIAA insisted it would not settle the case until it took every penny Jesse had saved.

Jesse's family was outraged at these claims. They wanted to fight. But Jesse's uncle worked to educate the family about the nature of the American legal system. Jesse could fight the RIAA. He might even win. But the cost of fighting a lawsuit like this, Jesse was told, would be at least $250,000. If he won, he would not recover that money. If he won, he would have a piece of paper saying he had won, and a piece of paper saying he and his family were bankrupt.

So Jesse faced a mafia-like choice: $250,000 and a chance at winning, or $12,000 and a settlement.

The recording industry insists this is a matter of law and morality. Let's put the law aside for a moment and think about the morality. Where is the morality in a lawsuit like this? What is the virtue in scapegoatism? The RIAA is an extraordinarily powerful lobby. The president of the RIAA is reported to make more than $1 million a year. Artists, on the other hand, are not well paid. The average recording artist makes $45,900.[2] There are plenty of ways for the RIAA to affect and direct policy. So where is the morality in taking money from a student for running a search engine?[3]

On June 23, Jesse wired his savings to the lawyer working for the RIAA. The case against him was then dismissed. And with this, this kid who had tinkered a computer into a $15 million lawsuit became an activist:

> I was definitely not an activist [before]. I never really meant to be an activist. . . . [But] I've been pushed into this. In no way did I ever foresee anything like this, but I think it's just completely absurd what the RIAA has done.

Jesse's parents betray a certain pride in their reluctant activist. As his father told me, Jesse "considers himself very conservative, and so do I. . . . He's not a tree hugger. . . . I think it's bizarre that they would pick on him. But he wants to let people know that they're sending the wrong message. And he wants to correct the record."

CHAPTER FOUR: "Pirates"

If "piracy" means using the creative property of others without their permission—if "if value, then right" is true—then the history of the content industry is a history of piracy. Every important sector of "big media" today—film, records, radio, and cable TV—was born of a kind of piracy so defined. The consistent story is how last generation's pirates join this generation's country club—until now.

Film

The film industry of Hollywood was built by fleeing pirates.[1] Creators and directors migrated from the East Coast to California in the early twentieth century in part to escape controls that patents granted the inventor of filmmaking, Thomas Edison. These controls were exercised through a monopoly "trust," the Motion Pictures Patents Company, and were based on Thomas Edison's creative property—patents. Edison formed the MPPC to exercise the rights this creative property gave him, and the MPPC was serious about the control it demanded. As one commentator tells one part of the story,

> A January 1909 deadline was set for all companies to comply with the license. By February, unlicensed outlaws, who referred to themselves as independents protested the trust and carried on business without submitting to the Edison monopoly. In the summer of 1909 the independent movement was in full-swing, with producers and theater owners using illegal equipment and imported film stock to create their own underground market.
>
> With the country experiencing a tremendous expansion in the number of nickelodeons, the Patents Company reacted to the independent movement by forming a strong-arm subsidiary known as the General Film Company to block the entry of non-licensed independents. With coercive tactics that have become legendary, General Film confiscated unlicensed equipment, discontinued product supply to theaters which showed unlicensed films, and effectively monopolized distribution with the acquisition of all U.S. film exchanges, except for the one owned by the independent William Fox who defied the Trust even after his license was revoked.[2]

The Napsters of those days, the "independents," were companies like Fox. And no less than today, these independents were vigorously resisted. "Shooting was disrupted by machinery stolen, and 'accidents' resulting in loss of negatives, equipment, buildings and sometimes life and limb frequently occurred."[3] That led the independents to flee the East Coast. California was remote enough from Edison's reach that film-makers there could pirate his inventions without fear of the law. And the leaders of Hollywood filmmaking, Fox most prominently, did just that.

Of course, California grew quickly, and the effective enforcement of federal law eventually spread west. But because patents grant the patent holder a truly "limited" monopoly (just seventeen years at that time), by the time enough federal marshals appeared, the patents had expired. A new industry had been born, in part from the piracy of Edison's creative property.

Recorded Music

The record industry was born of another kind of piracy, though to see how requires a bit of detail about the way the law regulates music.

At the time that Edison and Henri Fourneaux invented machines for reproducing music (Edison the phonograph, Fourneaux the player piano), the law gave composers the exclusive right to control copies of their music and the exclusive right to control public performances of their music. In other words, in 1900, if I wanted a copy of Phil Russel's 1899 hit "Happy Mose," the law said I would have to pay for the right to get a copy of the musical score, and I would also have to pay for the right to perform it publicly.

But what if I wanted to record "Happy Mose," using Edison's phonograph or Fourneaux's player piano? Here the law stumbled. It was clear enough that I would have to buy any copy of the musical score that I performed in making this recording. And it was clear enough that I would have to pay for any public performance of the work I was recording. But it wasn't totally clear that I would have to pay for a "public performance" if I recorded the song in my own house (even today, you don't owe the Beatles anything if you sing their songs in the shower), or if I recorded the song from memory (copies in your brain are not—yet—regulated by copyright law). So if I simply sang the song into a recording device in the privacy of my own home, it wasn't clear that I owed the composer anything. And more importantly, it wasn't clear whether I owed the composer anything if I then made copies of those recordings. Because of this gap in the law, then, I could effectively pirate someone else's song without paying its composer anything.

The composers (and publishers) were none too happy about

this capacity to pirate. As South Dakota senator Alfred Kittredge put it,

> Imagine the injustice of the thing. A composer writes a song or an opera. A publisher buys at great expense the rights to the same and copyrights it. Along come the phonographic companies and companies who cut music rolls and deliberately steal the work of the brain of the composer and publisher without any regard for [their] rights.[4]

The innovators who developed the technology to record other people's works were "sponging upon the toil, the work, the talent, and genius of American composers,"[5] and the "music publishing industry" was thereby "at the complete mercy of this one pirate."[6] As John Philip Sousa put it, in as direct a way as possible, "When they make money out of my pieces, I want a share of it."[7]

These arguments have familiar echoes in the wars of our day. So, too, do the arguments on the other side. The innovators who developed the player piano argued that "it is perfectly demonstrable that the introduction of automatic music players has not deprived any composer of anything he had before their introduction." Rather, the machines increased the sales of sheet music.[8] In any case, the innovators argued, the job of Congress was "to consider first the interest of [the public], whom they represent, and whose servants they are." "All talk about 'theft,'" the general counsel of the American Graphophone Company wrote, "is the merest claptrap, for there exists no property in ideas musical, literary or artistic, except as defined by statute."[9]

The law soon resolved this battle in favor of the composer *and* the recording artist. Congress amended the law to make sure that composers would be paid for the "mechanical reproductions" of their music. But rather than simply granting the composer complete control over the right to make mechanical reproductions, Congress gave recording artists a right to record the music, at a price set by Congress, once the composer allowed it to be recorded once. This is the part of copyright law that makes cover songs possible. Once a composer authorizes a recording of his song, others are free to record the same song, so long as they pay the original composer a fee set by the law.

American law ordinarily calls this a "compulsory license," but I will refer to it as a "statutory license." A statutory license is a license whose key terms are set by law. After Congress's amendment of the Copyright Act in 1909, record companies were free to distribute copies of recordings so long as they paid the composer (or copyright holder) the fee set by the statute.

This is an exception within the law of copyright. When John Grisham writes a novel, a publisher is free to publish that novel only if Grisham gives the publisher permission. Grisham, in turn, is free to charge whatever he wants for that permission. The price to publish Grisham is thus set by Grisham, and copyright law ordinarily says you have no permission to use Grisham's work except with permission of Grisham.

But the law governing recordings gives recording artists less. And thus, in effect, the law *subsidizes* the recording industry through a kind of piracy—by giving recording artists a weaker right than it otherwise gives creative authors. The Beatles have less control over their creative work than Grisham does. And the beneficiaries of this less control are the recording industry and the public. The recording industry gets something of value for less than it otherwise would pay; the public gets access to a much wider range of musical creativity. Indeed, Congress was quite explicit about its reasons for granting this right. Its fear was the monopoly power of rights holders, and that that power would stifle follow-on creativity.[10]

While the recording industry has been quite coy about this recently, historically it has been quite a supporter of the statutory license for records. As a 1967 report from the House Committee on the Judiciary relates,

> the record producers argued vigorously that the compulsory license system must be retained. They asserted that the record in-

dustry is a half-billion-dollar business of great economic importance in the United States and throughout the world; records today are the principal means of disseminating music, and this creates special problems, since performers need unhampered access to musical material on nondiscriminatory terms. Historically, the record producers pointed out, there were no recording rights before 1909 and the 1909 statute adopted the compulsory license as a deliberate anti-monopoly condition on the grant of these rights. They argue that the result has been an outpouring of recorded music, with the public being given lower prices, improved quality, and a greater choice.[11]

By limiting the rights musicians have, by partially pirating their creative work, the record producers, and the public, benefit.

Radio

Radio was also born of piracy.

When a radio station plays a record on the air, that constitutes a "public performance" of the composer's work.[12] As I described above, the law gives the composer (or copyright holder) an exclusive right to public performances of his work. The radio station thus owes the composer money for that performance.

But when the radio station plays a record, it is not only performing a copy of the *composer's* work. The radio station is also performing a copy of the *recording artist's* work. It's one thing to have "Happy Birthday" sung on the radio by the local children's choir; it's quite another to have it sung by the Rolling Stones or Lyle Lovett. The recording artist is adding to the value of the composition performed on the radio station. And if the law were perfectly consistent, the radio station would have to pay the recording artist for his work, just as it pays the composer of the music for his work.

But it doesn't. Under the law governing radio performances, the radio station does not have to pay the recording artist. The radio station need only pay the composer. The radio station thus gets a bit of something for nothing. It gets to perform the recording artist's work for free, even if it must pay the composer something for the privilege of playing the song.

This difference can be huge. Imagine you compose a piece of music. Imagine it is your first. You own the exclusive right to authorize public performances of that music. So if Madonna wants to sing your song in public, she has to get your permission.

Imagine she does sing your song, and imagine she likes it a lot. She then decides to make a recording of your song, and it becomes a top hit. Under our law, every time a radio station plays your song, you get some money. But Madonna gets nothing, save the indirect effect on the sale of her CDs. The public performance of her recording is not a "protected" right. The radio station thus gets to *pirate* the value of Madonna's work without paying her anything.

No doubt, one might argue that, on balance, the recording artists benefit. On average, the promotion they get is worth more than the performance rights they give up. Maybe. But even if so, the law ordinarily gives the creator the right to make this choice. By making the choice for him or her, the law gives the radio station the right to take something for nothing.

Cable TV

Cable TV was also born of a kind of piracy.

When cable entrepreneurs first started wiring communities with cable television in 1948, most refused to pay broadcasters for the content that they echoed to their customers. Even when the cable companies started selling access to television broadcasts, they refused to pay for what they sold. Cable companies were thus Napsterizing broadcasters' content, but more egregiously than anything Napster ever did—Napster never charged for the content it enabled others to give away.

Broadcasters and copyright owners were quick to attack this theft. Rosel Hyde, chairman of the FCC, viewed the practice as a kind of "unfair and potentially destructive competition."[13] There may have been a "public interest" in spreading the reach of cable TV, but as Douglas Anello, general counsel to the National Association of Broadcasters, asked Senator Quentin Burdick during testimony, "Does public interest dictate that you use somebody else's property?"[14] As another broadcaster put it,

> The extraordinary thing about the CATV business is that it is the only business I know of where the product that is being sold is not paid for.[15]

Again, the demand of the copyright holders seemed reasonable enough:

> All we are asking for is a very simple thing, that people who now take our property for nothing pay for it. We are trying to stop piracy and I don't think there is any lesser word to describe it. I think there are harsher words which would fit it.[16]

These were "free-ride[rs]," Screen Actor's Guild president Charlton Heston said, who were "depriving actors of compensation."[17]

But again, there was another side to the debate. As Assistant Attorney General Edwin Zimmerman put it,

> Our point here is that unlike the problem of whether you have any copyright protection at all, the problem here is whether copyright holders who are already compensated, who already have a monopoly, should be permitted to extend that monopoly. . . . The

question here is how much compensation they should have and how far back they should carry their right to compensation.[18]

Copyright owners took the cable companies to court. Twice the Supreme Court held that the cable companies owed the copyright owners nothing.

It took Congress almost thirty years before it resolved the question of whether cable companies had to pay for the content they "pirated." In the end, Congress resolved this question in the same way that it resolved the question about record players and player pianos. Yes, cable companies would have to pay for the content that they broadcast; but the price they would have to pay was not set by the copyright owner. The price was set by law, so that the broadcasters couldn't exercise veto power over the emerging technologies of cable. Cable companies thus built their empire in part upon a "piracy" of the value created by broadcasters' content.

These separate stories sing a common theme. If "piracy" means using value from someone else's creative property without permission from that creator—as it is increasingly described today[19]— then *every* industry affected by copyright today is the product and beneficiary of a certain kind of piracy. Film, records, radio, cable TV. . . . The list is long and could well be expanded. Every generation welcomes the pirates from the last. Every generation—until now.

CHAPTER FIVE: "Piracy"

There is piracy of copyrighted material. Lots of it. This piracy comes in many forms. The most significant is commercial piracy, the unauthorized taking of other people's content within a commercial context. Despite the many justifications that are offered in its defense, this taking is wrong. No one should condone it, and the law should stop it.

But as well as copy-shop piracy, there is another kind of "taking" that is more directly related to the Internet. That taking, too, seems wrong to many, and it is wrong much of the time. Before we paint this taking "piracy," however, we should understand its nature a bit more. For the harm of this taking is significantly more ambiguous than outright copying, and the law should account for that ambiguity, as it has so often done in the past.

Piracy I

All across the world, but especially in Asia and Eastern Europe, there are businesses that do nothing but take others people's copyrighted content, copy it, and sell it—all without the permission of a copyright owner. The recording industry estimates that it loses about $4.6 billion every year to physical piracy[1] (that works out to one in three CDs sold worldwide). The MPAA estimates that it loses $3 billion annually worldwide to piracy.

This is piracy plain and simple. Nothing in the argument of this book, nor in the argument that most people make when talking about the subject of this book, should draw into doubt this simple point: This piracy is wrong.

Which is not to say that excuses and justifications couldn't be made for it. We could, for example, remind ourselves that for the first one hundred years of the American Republic, America did not honor foreign copyrights. We were born, in this sense, a pirate nation. It might therefore seem hypocritical for us to insist so strongly that other developing nations treat as wrong what we, for the first hundred years of our existence, treated as right.

That excuse isn't terribly strong. Technically, our law did not ban the taking of foreign works. It explicitly limited itself to American works. Thus the American publishers who published foreign works without the permission of foreign authors were not violating any rule. The copy shops in Asia, by contrast, are violating Asian law. Asian law does protect foreign copyrights, and the actions of the copy shops violate that law. So the wrong of piracy that they engage in is not just a moral wrong, but a legal wrong, and not just an internationally legal wrong, but a locally legal wrong as well.

True, these local rules have, in effect, been imposed upon these countries. No country can be part of the world economy and choose not to protect copyright internationally. We may have been born a pirate nation, but we will not allow any other nation to have a similar childhood.

If a country is to be treated as a sovereign, however, then its laws are its laws regardless of their source. The international law under which these nations live gives them some opportunities to escape the burden of intellectual property law.[2] In my view, more developing nations should take advantage of that opportunity, but when they don't, then their laws should be respected. And under the laws of these nations, this piracy is wrong.

Alternatively, we could try to excuse this piracy by noting that in any case, it does no harm to the industry. The Chinese who get access to American CDs at 50 cents a copy are not people who would have bought those American CDs at $15 a copy. So no one really has any less money than they otherwise would have had.[3]

This is often true (though I have friends who have purchased many thousands of pirated DVDs who certainly have enough money to pay for the content they have taken), and it does mitigate to some degree the harm caused by such taking. Extremists in this debate love to say, "You wouldn't go into Barnes & Noble and take a book off of the shelf without paying; why should it be any different with on-line music?" The difference is, of course, that when you take a book from Barnes & Noble, it has one less book to sell. By contrast, when you take an MP3 from a computer network, there is not one less CD that can be sold. The physics of piracy of the intangible are different from the physics of piracy of the tangible.

This argument is still very weak. However, although copyright is a property right of a very special sort, it *is* a property right. Like all property rights, the copyright gives the owner the right to decide the terms under which content is shared. If the copyright owner doesn't want to sell, she doesn't have to. There are exceptions: important statutory licenses that apply to copyrighted content regardless of the wish of the copyright owner. Those licenses give people the right to "take" copyrighted content whether or not the copyright owner wants to sell. But where the law does not give people the right to take content, it is wrong to take that content even if the wrong does no harm. If we have a property system, and that system is properly balanced to the technology of a time, then it is wrong to take property without the permission of a property owner. That is exactly what "property" means.

Finally, we could try to excuse this piracy with the argument that the piracy actually helps the copyright owner. When the Chinese "steal" Windows, that makes the Chinese dependent on Microsoft. Microsoft loses the value of the software that was taken. But it gains users who are used to life in the Microsoft world. Over time, as the nation grows more wealthy, more and more people will buy software rather than steal it. And hence over time, because that buying will benefit Microsoft, Microsoft benefits from the piracy. If instead of pirating Microsoft Windows, the Chinese used the free GNU/Linux operating system, then these Chinese users would not eventually be buying Microsoft. Without piracy, then, Microsoft would lose.

This argument, too, is somewhat true. The addiction strategy is a good one. Many businesses practice it. Some thrive because of it. Law students, for example, are given free access to the two largest legal databases. The companies marketing both hope the students will become so used to their service that they will want to use it and not the other when they become lawyers (and must pay high subscription fees).

Still, the argument is not terribly persuasive. We don't give the alcoholic a defense when he steals his first beer, merely because that will make it more likely that he will buy the next three. Instead, we ordinarily allow businesses to decide for themselves when it is best to give their product away. If Microsoft fears the competition of GNU/Linux, then Microsoft can give its product away, as it did, for example, with Internet Explorer to fight Netscape. A property right means giving the property owner the right to say who gets access to what—at least ordinarily. And if the law properly balances the rights of the copyright owner with the rights of access, then violating the law is still wrong.

Thus, while I understand the pull of these justifications for piracy, and I certainly see the motivation, in my view, in the end, these efforts at justifying commercial piracy simply don't cut it. This kind of piracy is rampant and just plain wrong. It doesn't transform the content it steals; it doesn't transform the market it competes in. It merely gives someone access to something that the law says he should not have. Nothing has changed to draw that law into doubt. This form of piracy is flat out wrong.

But as the examples from the four chapters that introduced this part suggest, even if some piracy is plainly wrong, not all "piracy" is. Or at least, not all "piracy" is wrong if that term is understood in the way it is increasingly used today. Many kinds of "piracy" are useful and productive, to produce either new content or new ways of doing business. Neither our tradition nor any tradition has ever banned all "piracy" in that sense of the term.

This doesn't mean that there are no questions raised by the latest piracy concern, peer-to-peer file sharing. But it does mean that we need to understand the harm in peer-to-peer sharing a bit more before we condemn it to the gallows with the charge of piracy.

For (1) like the original Hollywood, p2p sharing escapes an overly controlling industry; and (2) like the original recording industry, it simply exploits a new way to distribute content; but (3) unlike cable TV, no one is selling the content that is shared on p2p services.

These differences distinguish p2p sharing from true piracy. They should push us to find a way to protect artists while enabling this sharing to survive.

Piracy II

The key to the "piracy" that the law aims to quash is a use that "rob[s] the author of [his] profit."[4] This means we must determine whether and how much p2p sharing harms before we know how strongly the law should seek to either prevent it or find an alternative to assure the author of his profit.

Peer-to-peer sharing was made famous by Napster. But the inventors of the Napster technology had not made any major technological innovations. Like every great advance in innovation on the Internet (and, arguably, off the Internet as well[5]), Shawn Fanning and crew had simply put together components that had been developed independently.

The result was spontaneous combustion. Launched in July 1999, Napster amassed over 10 million users within nine months. After eighteen months, there were close to 80 million registered users of the system.[6] Courts quickly shut Napster down, but other services emerged to take its place. (Kazaa is currently the most popular p2p service. It boasts over 100 million members.) These services' systems are different architecturally, though not very different in function: Each enables users to make content available to any number of other users. With a p2p system, you can share your favorite songs with your best friend—or your 20,000 best friends.

According to a number of estimates, a huge proportion of Americans have tasted file-sharing technology. A study by Ipsos-Insight in September 2002 estimated that 60 million Americans had downloaded music—28 percent of Americans older than 12.[7] A survey by the NPD group quoted in *The New York Times* estimated that 43 million citizens used file-sharing networks to exchange content in May 2003.[8] The vast majority of these are not kids. Whatever the actual figure, a massive quantity of content is being "taken" on these networks. The ease and inexpensiveness of file-sharing networks have inspired millions to enjoy music in a way that they hadn't before.

Some of this enjoying involves copyright infringement. Some of it does not. And even among the part that is technically copyright infringement, calculating the actual harm to copyright owners is more complicated than one might think. So consider—a bit more carefully than the polarized voices around this debate usually do—the kinds of sharing that file sharing enables, and the kinds of harm it entails.

File sharers share different kinds of content. We can divide these different kinds into four types.

A. There are some who use sharing networks as substitutes for purchasing content. Thus, when a new Madonna CD is released, rather than buying the CD, these users simply take it. We might quibble about whether everyone who takes it would actually have bought it if sharing didn't make it available for free. Most probably wouldn't have, but clearly there are some who would. The latter are the target of category A: users who download instead of purchasing.

B. There are some who use sharing networks to sample music before purchasing it. Thus, a friend sends another friend an MP3 of an artist he's not heard of. The other friend then buys CDs by that artist. This is a kind of targeted advertising, quite likely to succeed. If the friend recommending the album gains nothing from a bad recommendation, then one could expect that the recommendations will actually be quite good. The net effect of this sharing could increase the quantity of music purchased.

C. There are many who use sharing networks to get access to copyrighted content that is no longer sold or that they would not have purchased because the transaction costs off the Net are too high. This use of sharing networks is among the most rewarding for many. Songs that were part of your childhood but have long vanished from the marketplace magically appear again on the network. (One friend told me that when she discovered Napster, she spent a solid weekend "recalling" old songs. She was astonished at the range and mix of content that was available.) For content not sold, this is still technically a violation of copyright, though because the copyright owner is not selling the content anymore, the economic harm is zero—the same harm that occurs when I sell my collection of 1960s 45-rpm records to a local collector.

D. Finally, there are many who use sharing networks to get access to content that is not copyrighted or that the copyright owner wants to give away.

How do these different types of sharing balance out?

Let's start with some simple but important points. From the perspective of the law, only type D sharing is clearly legal. From the perspective of economics, only type A sharing is clearly harmful.[9] Type B sharing is illegal but plainly beneficial. Type C sharing is illegal, yet good for society (since more exposure to music is good) and harmless to the artist (since the work is not otherwise available). So how sharing matters on balance is a hard question to answer—and certainly much more difficult than the current rhetoric around the issue suggests.

Whether on balance sharing is harmful depends importantly on how harmful type A sharing is. Just as Edison complained about Hollywood, composers complained about piano rolls, recording artists complained about radio, and broadcasters complained about cable TV, the music industry complains that type A sharing is a kind of "theft" that is "devastating" the industry.

While the numbers do suggest that sharing is harmful, how harmful is harder to reckon. It has long been the recording industry's practice to blame technology for any drop in sales. The history of cassette recording is a good example. As a study by Cap Gemini Ernst & Young put it, "Rather than exploiting this new, popular technology, the labels fought it."[10] The labels claimed that every album taped was an album unsold, and when record sales fell by 11.4 percent in 1981, the industry claimed that its point was proved. Technology was the problem, and banning or regulating technology was the answer.

Yet soon thereafter, and before Congress was given an opportunity to enact regulation, MTV was launched, and the industry had a record turnaround. "In the end," Cap Gemini concludes, "the 'crisis' . . . was not the fault of the tapers—who did not [stop after MTV came into being]—but had to a large extent resulted from stagnation in musical innovation at the major labels."[11]

But just because the industry was wrong before does not mean it is wrong today. To evaluate the real threat that p2p sharing presents to the industry in particular, and society in general—or at least the society that inherits the tradition that gave us the film industry, the record industry, the radio industry, cable TV, and the VCR—the question is not simply whether type A sharing is harmful. The question is also *how* harmful type A sharing is, and how beneficial the other types of sharing are.

We start to answer this question by focusing on the net harm, from the standpoint of the industry as a whole, that sharing networks cause. The "net harm" to the industry as a whole is the amount by which type A sharing exceeds type B. If the record companies sold more records through sampling than they lost through substitution, then sharing networks would actually benefit music companies on balance. They would therefore have little *static* reason to resist them.

Could that be true? Could the industry as a whole be gaining because of file sharing? Odd as that might sound, the data about CD sales actually suggest it might be close.

In 2002, the RIAA reported that CD sales had fallen by 8.9 percent, from 882 million to 803 million units; revenues fell 6.7 percent.[12] This confirms a trend over the past few years. The RIAA blames Internet piracy for the trend, though there are many other causes that could account for this drop. SoundScan, for example, reports a more than 20 percent drop in the number of CDs released since 1999. That no doubt accounts for some of the decrease in sales. Rising prices could account for at least some of the loss. "From 1999 to 2001, the average price of a CD rose 7.2 percent, from $13.04 to $14.19."[13] Competition from other forms of media could also account for some of the decline. As Jane Black of *BusinessWeek* notes, "The soundtrack to the film *High Fidelity* has a list price of $18.98. You could get the whole movie [on DVD] for $19.99."[14]

But let's assume the RIAA is right, and all of the decline in CD sales is because of Internet sharing. Here's the rub: In the same period that the RIAA estimates that 803 million CDs were sold, the RIAA estimates that 2.1 billion CDs were downloaded for free. Thus, although 2.6 times the total number of CDs sold were downloaded for free, sales revenue fell by just 6.7 percent.

There are too many different things happening at the same time to explain these numbers definitively, but one conclusion is unavoidable: The recording industry constantly asks, "What's the difference between downloading a song and stealing a CD?"—but their own numbers reveal the difference. If I steal a CD, then there is one less CD to sell. Every taking is a lost sale. But on the basis of the numbers the RIAA provides, it is absolutely clear that the same is not true of downloads. If every download were a lost sale—if every use of Kazaa "rob[bed]" the author of [his] profit"—then the industry would have suffered a 100 percent drop in sales last year, not a 7 percent drop. If 2.6 times the number of CDs sold were downloaded for free, and yet sales revenue dropped by just 6.7 percent, then there is a huge difference between "downloading a song and stealing a CD."

These are the harms—alleged and perhaps exaggerated but, let's assume, real. What of the benefits? File sharing may impose costs on the recording industry. What value does it produce in addition to these costs?

One benefit is type C sharing—making available content that is technically still under copyright but is no longer commercially available. This is not a small category of content. There are millions of tracks that are no longer commercially available.[15] And while it's conceivable that some of this content is not available because the artist producing the content doesn't want it to be made available, the vast majority of it is unavailable solely because the publisher or the distributor has decided it no longer makes economic sense *to the company* to make it available.

In real space—long before the Internet—the market had a simple response to this problem: used book and record stores. There are thousands of used book and used record stores in America today.[16] These stores buy content from owners, then sell the content they buy. And under American copyright law, when they buy and sell this content, *even if the content is still under copyright,* the copyright owner doesn't get a dime. Used book and record stores are commercial entities; their owners make money from the content they sell; but as with cable companies before statutory licensing, they don't have to pay the copyright owner for the content they sell.

Type C sharing, then, is very much like used book stores or used record stores. It is different, of course, because the person making the content available isn't making money from making the content available. It is also different, of course, because in real space, when I sell a record, I don't have it anymore, while in cyberspace, when someone shares my 1949 recording of Bernstein's "Two Love Songs," I still have it. That difference would matter economically if the owner of the 1949 copyright were selling the record in competition to my sharing. But we're talking about the class of content that is not currently commercially available. The Internet is making it available, through cooperative sharing, without competing with the market.

It may well be, all things considered, that it would be better if the copyright owner got something from this trade. But just because it may well be better, it doesn't follow that it would be good to ban used book stores. Or put differently, if you think that type C sharing should be stopped, do you think that libraries and used book stores should be shut as well?

Finally, and perhaps most importantly, file-sharing networks enable type D sharing to occur—the sharing of content that copyright owners want to have shared or for which there is no continuing copyright. This sharing clearly benefits authors and society. Science fiction author Cory Doctorow, for example, released his first novel, *Down and Out in the Magic Kingdom,* both free on-line and in bookstores on the same day. His (and his publisher's) thinking was that the on-line distribution would be a great advertisement for the "real" book. People would read part on-line, and then decide whether they liked the book or not. If they liked it, they would be more likely to buy it. Doctorow's content is type D content. If sharing networks enable his work to be spread, then both he and society are better off. (Actually, much better off: It is a great book!)

Likewise for work in the public domain: This sharing benefits society with no legal harm to authors at all. If efforts to solve the problem of type A sharing destroy the opportunity for type D sharing, then we lose something important in order to protect type A content.

The point throughout is this: While the recording industry understandably says, "This is how much we've lost," we must also ask, "How much has society gained from p2p sharing? What are the efficiencies? What is the content that otherwise would be unavailable?"

For unlike the piracy I described in the first section of this chapter, much of the "piracy" that file sharing enables is plainly legal and good. And like the piracy I described in chapter 4, much of this piracy is motivated by a new way of spreading content caused by changes in the technology of distribution. Thus, consistent with the tradition that gave us Hollywood, radio, the recording industry, and cable TV, the question we should be asking about file sharing is how best to preserve its benefits while minimizing (to the extent possible) the wrongful harm it causes artists. The question is one of balance. The law should seek that balance, and that balance will be found only with time.

"But isn't the war just a war against illegal sharing? Isn't the target just what you call type A sharing?"

You would think. And we should hope. But so far, it is not. The effect of the war purportedly on type A sharing alone has been felt far beyond that one class of sharing. That much is obvious from the Napster case itself. When Napster told the district court that it had developed a technology to block the transfer of 99.4 percent of identified infringing material, the district court told counsel for Napster 99.4 percent was not good enough. Napster had to push the infringements "down to zero."[17]

If 99.4 percent is not good enough, then this is a war on file-sharing technologies, not a war on copyright infringement. There is no way to assure that a p2p system is used 100 percent of the time in compliance with the law, any more than there is a way to assure that 100 percent of VCRs or 100 percent of Xerox machines or 100 percent of handguns are used in compliance with the law. Zero tolerance means zero p2p. The court's ruling means that we as a society must lose the benefits of p2p, even for the totally legal and beneficial uses they serve, simply to assure that there are zero copyright infringements caused by p2p.

Zero tolerance has not been our history. It has not produced the content industry that we know today. The history of American law has been a process of balance. As new technologies changed the way content was distributed, the law adjusted, after some time, to the new technology. In this adjustment, the law sought to ensure the legitimate rights of creators while protecting innovation. Sometimes this has meant more rights for creators. Sometimes less.

So, as we've seen, when "mechanical reproduction" threatened the interests of composers, Congress balanced the rights of composers against the interests of the recording industry. It granted rights to composers, but also to the recording artists: Composers were to be paid, but at a price set by Congress. But when radio started broadcasting the recordings made by these recording artists, and they complained to Congress that their "creative property" was not being respected (since the radio station did not have to pay them for the creativity it broadcast), Congress rejected their claim. An indirect benefit was enough.

Cable TV followed the pattern of record albums. When the courts rejected the claim that cable broadcasters had to pay for the content they rebroadcast, Congress responded by giving broadcasters a right to compensation, but at a level set by the law. It likewise gave cable companies the right to the content, so long as they paid the statutory price.

This compromise, like the compromise affecting records and player pianos, served two important goals—indeed, the two central goals of any copyright legislation. First, the law assured that new innovators would have the freedom to develop new ways to deliver content. Second, the law assured that copyright holders would be paid for the content that was distributed. One fear was that if Congress simply required cable TV to pay copyright holders whatever they demanded for their content, then copyright holders associated with broadcasters would use their power to stifle this new technology, cable. But if Congress had permitted cable to use broadcasters' content for free, then it would have unfairly subsidized cable. Thus Congress chose a path that would assure *compensation* without giving the past (broadcasters) control over the future (cable).

In the same year that Congress struck this balance, two major producers and distributors of film content filed a lawsuit against another technology, the video tape recorder (VTR, or as we refer to them today, VCRs) that Sony had produced, the Betamax. Disney's and Universal's claim against Sony was relatively simple: Sony produced a device, Disney and Universal claimed, that enabled consumers to engage in copyright infringement. Because the device that Sony built had a "record" button, the device could be used to record copyrighted movies and shows. Sony was therefore benefiting from the copyright infringement of its customers. It should therefore, Disney and Universal claimed, be partially liable for that infringement.

There was something to Disney's and Universal's claim. Sony did decide to design its machine to make it very simple to record television shows. It could have built the machine to block or inhibit any direct copying from a television broadcast. Or possibly, it could have built the machine to copy only if there were a special "copy me" signal on the line. It was clear that there were many television shows that did not grant anyone permission to copy. Indeed, if anyone had asked, no doubt the majority of shows would not have authorized copying. And in the face of this obvious preference, Sony could have designed its system to minimize the opportunity for copyright infringement. It did not, and for that, Disney and Universal wanted to hold it responsible for the architecture it chose.

MPAA president Jack Valenti became the studios' most vocal champion. Valenti called VCRs "tapeworms." He warned, "When there are 20, 30, 40 million of these VCRs in the land, we will be invaded by millions of 'tapeworms,' eating away at the very heart and essence of the most precious asset the copyright owner has, his copyright."[18] "One does not have to be trained in sophisticated marketing and creative judgment," he told Congress, "to understand the devastation on the after-theater marketplace caused by the hundreds of millions of tapings that will adversely impact on the future of the creative community in this country. It is simply a question of basic economics and plain common sense."[19] Indeed, as surveys would later show, 45 percent of VCR owners had movie libraries of ten videos or more[20]—a use the Court would later hold was not "fair." By "allowing VCR owners to copy freely by the means of an exemption from copyright infringement without creating a mechanism to compensate copyright owners," Valenti testified, Congress would "take from the owners the very essence of their property: the exclusive right to control who may use their work, that is, who may copy it and thereby profit from its reproduction."[21]

It took eight years for this case to be resolved by the Supreme Court. In the interim, the Ninth Circuit Court of Appeals, which includes Hollywood in its jurisdiction—leading Judge Alex Kozinski, who sits on that court, refers to it as the "Hollywood Circuit"—held that Sony would be liable for the copyright infringement made possible by its machines. Under the Ninth Circuit's rule, this totally familiar technology—which Jack Valenti had called "the Boston Strangler of the American film industry" (worse yet, it was a *Japanese* Boston Strangler of the American film industry)—was an illegal technology.[22]

But the Supreme Court reversed the decision of the Ninth Circuit.

And in its reversal, the Court clearly articulated its understanding of when and whether courts should intervene in such disputes. As the Court wrote,

> Sound policy, as well as history, supports our consistent deference to Congress when major technological innovations alter the market for copyrighted materials. Congress has the constitutional authority and the institutional ability to accommodate fully the varied permutations of competing interests that are inevitably implicated by such new technology.[23]

Congress was asked to respond to the Supreme Court's decision. But as with the plea of recording artists about radio broadcasts, Congress ignored the request. Congress was convinced that American film got enough, this "taking" notwithstanding.

If we put these cases together, a pattern is clear:

CASE	WHOSE VALUE WAS "PIRATED"	RESPONSE OF THE COURTS	RESPONSE OF CONGRESS
Recordings	Composers	No protection	Statutory license
Radio	Recording artists	N/A	Nothing
Cable TV	Broadcasters	No protection	Statutory license
VCR	Film creators	No protection	Nothing

In each case throughout our history, a new technology changed the way content was distributed.[24] In each case, throughout our history, that change meant that someone got a "free ride" on someone else's work.

In *none* of these cases did either the courts or Congress eliminate all free riding. In *none* of these cases did the courts or Congress insist that the law should assure that the copyright holder get all the value that his copyright created. In every case, the copyright owners complained of "piracy." In every case, Congress acted to recognize some of the legitimacy in the behavior of the "pirates." In each case, Congress allowed some new technology to benefit from content made before. It balanced the interests at stake.

When you think across these examples, and the other examples that make up the first four chapters of this section, this balance makes sense. Was Walt Disney a pirate? Would doujinshi be better if creators had to ask permission? Should tools that enable others to capture and spread images as a way to cultivate or criticize our culture be better regulated? Is it really right that building a search engine should expose you to $15 million in damages? Would it have been better if Edison had controlled film? Should every cover band have to hire a lawyer to get permission to record a song?

We could answer yes to each of these questions, but our tradition has answered no. In our tradition, as the Supreme Court has stated, copyright "has never accorded the copyright owner complete control over all possible uses of his work."[25] Instead, the particular uses that the law regulates have been defined by balancing the good that comes from granting an exclusive right against the burdens such an exclusive right creates. And this balancing has historically been done *after* a technology has matured, or settled into the mix of technologies that facilitate the distribution of content.

We should be doing the same thing today. The technology of the Internet is changing quickly. The way people connect to the Internet (wires vs. wireless) is changing very quickly. No doubt the network should not become a tool for "stealing" from artists. But neither should the law become a tool to entrench one particular way in which artists (or more accurately, distributors) get paid. As I describe in some detail in the last chapter of this book, we should be securing income to artists while we allow the market to secure the most efficient way to promote and distribute content. This will require changes in the law, at least in the interim. These changes should be designed to balance the protection of the law against the strong public interest that innovation continue.

This is especially true when a new technology enables a vastly superior mode of distribution. And this p2p has done. P2p technologies can be ideally efficient in moving content across a widely diverse network. Left to develop, they could make the network vastly more efficient. Yet these "potential public benefits," as John Schwartz writes in *The New York Times,* "could be delayed in the P2P fight."[26]

Yet when anyone begins to talk about "balance," the copyright warriors raise a different argument. "All this hand waving about balance and incentives," they say, "misses a fundamental point. Our content," the warriors insist, "is our *property.* Why should we wait for Congress to 'rebalance' our property rights? Do you have to wait before calling the police when your car has been stolen? And why should Congress deliberate at all about the merits of this theft? Do we ask whether the car thief had a good use for the car before we arrest him?"

"It is *our property,*" the warriors insist. "And it should be protected just as any other property is protected."

"PROPERTY"

The copyright warriors are right: A copyright is a kind of property. It can be owned and sold, and the law protects against its theft. Ordinarily, the copyright owner gets to hold out for any price he wants. Markets reckon the supply and demand that partially determine the price she can get.

But in ordinary language, to call a copyright a "property" right is a bit misleading, for the property of copyright is an odd kind of property. Indeed, the very idea of property in any idea or any expression is very odd. I understand what I am taking when I take the picnic table you put in your backyard. I am taking a thing, the picnic table, and after I take it, you don't have it. But what am I taking when I take the good *idea* you had to put a picnic table in the backyard—by, for example, going to Sears, buying a table, and putting it in my backyard? What is the thing I am taking then?

The point is not just about the thingness of picnic tables versus ideas, though that's an important difference. The point instead is that in the ordinary case—indeed, in practically every case except for a narrow range of exceptions—ideas released to the world are free. I don't take anything from you when I copy the way you dress—though I might seem weird if I did it every day, and especially weird if you are a woman. Instead, as Thomas Jefferson said (and as is especially true when I copy the way someone else dresses), "He who receives an idea from me, receives instruction himself without lessening mine; as he who lights his taper at mine, receives light without darkening me."[1]

The exceptions to free use are ideas and expressions within the reach of the law of patent and copyright, and a few other domains that I won't discuss here. Here the law says you can't take my idea or expression without my permission: The law turns the intangible into property.

But how, and to what extent, and in what form—the details, in other words—matter. To get a good sense of how this practice of turning the intangible into property emerged, we need to place this "property" in its proper context.[2]

My strategy in doing this will be the same as my strategy in the preceding part. I offer four stories to help put the idea of "copyright material is property" in context. Where did the idea come from? What are its limits? How does it function in practice? After these stories, the significance of this true statement—"copyright material is property"—will be a bit more clear, and its implications will be revealed as quite different from the implications that the copyright warriors would have us draw.

CHAPTER SIX: Founders

William Shakespeare wrote *Romeo and Juliet* in 1595. The play was first published in 1597. It was the eleventh major play that Shakespeare had written. He would continue to write plays through 1613, and the plays that he wrote have continued to define Anglo-American culture ever since. So deeply have the works of a sixteenth-century writer seeped into our culture that we often don't even recognize their source. I once overheard someone commenting on Kenneth Branagh's adaptation of Henry V: "I liked it, but Shakespeare is so full of clichés."

In 1774, almost 180 years after *Romeo and Juliet* was written, the "copy-right" for the work was still thought by many to be the exclusive right of a single London publisher, Jacob Tonson.[1] Tonson was the most prominent of a small group of publishers called the Conger[2] who controlled bookselling in England during the eighteenth century. The Conger claimed a perpetual right to control the "copy" of books that they had acquired from authors. That perpetual right meant that no one else could publish copies of a book to which they held the copyright. Prices of the classics were thus kept high; competition to produce better or cheaper editions was eliminated.

Now, there's something puzzling about the year 1774 to anyone who knows a little about copyright law. The better-known year in the history of copyright is 1710, the year that the British Parliament adopted the first "copyright" act. Known as the Statute of Anne, the act stated that all published works would get a copyright term of fourteen years, renewable once if the author was alive, and that all works already published by 1710 would get a single term of twenty-one additional years.[3] Under this law, *Romeo and Juliet* should have been free in 1731. So why was there any issue about it still being under Tonson's control in 1774?

The reason is that the English hadn't yet agreed on what a "copyright" was—indeed, no one had. At the time the English passed the Statute of Anne, there was no other legislation governing copyrights. The last law regulating publishers, the Licensing Act of 1662, had expired in 1695. That law gave publishers a monopoly over publishing, as a way to make it easier for the Crown to control what was published. But after it expired, there was no positive law that said that the publishers, or "Stationers," had an exclusive right to print books.

There was no *positive* law, but that didn't mean that there was no law. The Anglo-American legal tradition looks to both the words of legislatures and the words of judges to know the rules that are to govern how people are to behave. We call the words from legislatures "positive law." We call the words from judges "common law." The common law sets the background against which legislatures legislate; the legislature, ordinarily, can trump that background only if it passes a law to displace it. And so the real question after the licensing statutes had expired was whether the common law protected a copyright, independent of any positive law.

This question was important to the publishers, or "booksellers," as they were called, because there was growing competition from foreign publishers. The Scottish, in particular, were increasingly publishing and exporting books to England. That competition reduced the profits of the Conger, which reacted by demanding that Parliament pass a law to again give them exclusive control over publishing. That demand ultimately resulted in the Statute of Anne.

The Statute of Anne granted the author or "proprietor" of a book an exclusive right to print that book. In an important limitation, however, and to the horror of the booksellers, the law gave the bookseller that right for a limited term. At the end of that term, the copyright "expired," and the work would then be free and could be published by anyone. Or so the legislature is thought to have believed.

Now, the thing to puzzle about for a moment is this: Why would Parliament limit the exclusive right? Not why would they limit it to the particular limit they set, but why would they limit the right *at all?*

For the booksellers, and the authors whom they represented, had a very strong claim. Take *Romeo and Juliet* as an example: That play was written by Shakespeare. It was his genius that brought it into the world. He didn't take anybody's property when he created this play (that's a controversial claim, but never mind), and by his creating this play, he didn't make it any harder for others to craft a play. So why is it that the law would ever allow someone else to come along and take Shakespeare's play without his, or his estate's, permission? What reason is there to allow someone else to "steal" Shakespeare's work?

The answer comes in two parts. We first need to see something special about the notion of "copyright" that existed at the time of the Statute of Anne. Second, we have to see something important about "booksellers."

First, about copyright. In the last three hundred years, we have come to apply the concept of "copyright" ever more broadly. But in 1710, it wasn't so much a concept as it was a very particular right. The copyright was born as a very specific set of restrictions: It forbade others from reprinting a book. In 1710, the "copy-right" was a right to use a particular machine to replicate a particular work. It did not go beyond that very narrow right. It did not control any more generally how a work could be *used.* Today the right includes a large collection of restrictions on the freedom of others: It grants the author the exclusive right to copy, the exclusive right to distribute, the exclusive right to perform, and so on.

So, for example, even if the copyright to Shakespeare's works were perpetual, all that would have meant under the original meaning of the term was that no one could reprint Shakespeare's work without the permission of the Shakespeare estate. It would not have controlled anything, for example, about how the work could be performed, whether the work could be translated, or whether Kenneth Branagh would be allowed to make his films. The "copy-right" was only an exclusive right to print—no less, of course, but also no more.

Even that limited right was viewed with skepticism by the British. They had had a long and ugly experience with "exclusive rights," especially "exclusive rights" granted by the Crown. The English had fought a civil war in part about the Crown's practice of handing out monopolies—especially monopolies for works that already existed. King Henry VIII granted a patent to print the Bible and a monopoly to Darcy to print playing cards. The English Parliament began to fight back against this power of the Crown. In 1656, it passed the Statute of Monopolies, limiting monopolies to patents for new inventions. And by 1710, Parliament was eager to deal with the growing monopoly in publishing.

Thus the "copy-right," when viewed as a monopoly right, was naturally viewed as a right that should be limited. (However convincing the claim that "it's my property, and I should have it forever," try sounding convincing when uttering, "It's my monopoly, and I should have it forever.") The state would protect the exclusive right, but only so long as it benefited society. The British saw the harms from special-interest favors; they passed a law to stop them.

Second, about booksellers. It wasn't just that the copyright was a monopoly. It was also that it was a monopoly held by the booksellers. Booksellers sound quaint and harmless to us. They were not viewed as harmless in seventeenth-century England. Members of the Conger were increasingly seen as monopolists of the worst kind—tools of the Crown's repression, selling the liberty of England to guarantee themselves a monopoly profit. The attacks against these monopolists were harsh: Milton described them as "old patentees and monopolizers in the trade of book-selling"; they were "men who do not therefore labour in an honest profession to which learning is indetted."[4]

Many believed the power the booksellers exercised over the spread of knowledge was harming that spread, just at the time the Enlightenment was teaching the importance of education and knowledge spread generally. The idea that knowledge should be free was a hallmark of the time, and these powerful commercial interests were interfering with that idea.

To balance this power, Parliament decided to increase competition among booksellers, and the simplest way to do that was to spread the wealth of valuable books. Parliament therefore limited the term of copyrights, and thereby guaranteed that valuable books would become open to any publisher to publish after a limited time. Thus the setting of the term for existing works to just twenty-one years was a compromise to fight the power of the booksellers. The limitation on terms was an indirect way to assure competition among publishers, and thus the construction and spread of culture.

When 1731 (1710 + 21) came along, however, the booksellers were getting anxious. They saw the consequences of more competition, and like every competitor, they didn't like them. At first booksellers simply ignored the Statute of Anne, continuing to insist on the perpetual right to control publication. But in 1735 and 1737, they tried to persuade Parliament to extend their terms. Twenty-one years was not enough, they said; they needed more time.

Parliament rejected their requests. As one pamphleteer put it, in words that echo today,

I see no Reason for granting a further Term now, which will not hold as well for granting it again and again, as often as the Old ones Expire; so that should this Bill pass, it will in Effect be establishing a perpetual Monopoly, a Thing deservedly odious in the Eye of the Law; it will be a great Cramp to Trade, a Discouragement to Learning, no Benefit to the Authors, but a general Tax on the Publick; and all this only to increase the private Gain of the Booksellers.[5]

Having failed in Parliament, the publishers turned to the courts in a series of cases. Their argument was simple and direct: The Statute of Anne gave authors certain protections through positive law, but those protections were not intended as replacements for the common law. Instead, they were intended simply to supplement the common law. Under common law, it was already wrong to take another person's creative "property" and use it without his permission. The Statute of Anne, the booksellers argued, didn't change that. Therefore, just because the protections of the Statute of Anne expired, that didn't mean the protections of the common law expired: Under the common law they had the right to ban the publication of a book, even if its Statute of Anne copyright had expired. This, they argued, was the only way to protect authors.

This was a clever argument, and one that had the support of some of the leading jurists of the day. It also displayed extraordinary chutzpah. Until then, as law professor Raymond Patterson has put it, "The publishers . . . had as much concern for authors as a cattle rancher has for cattle."[6] The bookseller didn't care squat for the rights of the author. His concern was the monopoly profit that the author's work gave.

The booksellers' argument was not accepted without a fight. The hero of this fight was a Scottish bookseller named Alexander Donaldson.[7]

Donaldson was an outsider to the London Conger. He began his career in Edinburgh in 1750. The focus of his business was inexpensive reprints "of standard works whose copyright term had expired," at least under the Statute of Anne.[8] Donaldson's publishing house prospered and became "something of a center for literary Scotsmen." "[A]mong them," Professor Mark Rose writes, was "the young James Boswell who, together with his friend Andrew Erskine, published an anthology of contemporary Scottish poems with Donaldson."[9]

When the London booksellers tried to shut down Donaldson's shop in Scotland, he responded by moving his shop to London, where he sold inexpensive editions "of the most popular English books, in defiance of the supposed common law right of Literary Property."[10] His books undercut the Conger prices by 30 to 50 percent, and he rested his right to compete upon the ground that, under the Statute of Anne, the works he was selling had passed out of protection.

The London booksellers quickly brought suit to block "piracy" like Donaldson's. A number of actions were successful against the "pirates," the most important early victory being *Millar v. Taylor*.

Millar was a bookseller who in 1729 had purchased the rights to James Thomson's poem "The Seasons." Millar complied with the requirements of the Statute of Anne, and therefore received the full protection of the statute. After the term of copyright ended, Robert Taylor began printing a competing volume. Millar sued, claiming a perpetual common law right, the Statute of Anne notwithstanding.[11]

Astonishingly to modern lawyers, one of the greatest judges in English history, Lord Mansfield, agreed with the booksellers. Whatever protection the Statute of Anne gave booksellers, it did not, he held, extinguish any common law right. The question was whether the common law would protect the author against subsequent "pirates." Mansfield's answer was yes: The common law would bar Taylor from reprinting Thomson's poem without Millar's permission. That common law rule thus effectively gave the booksellers a perpetual right to control the publication of any book assigned to them.

Considered as a matter of abstract justice—reasoning as if justice were just a matter of logical deduction from first principles—Mansfield's conclusion might make some sense. But what it ignored was the larger issue that Parliament had struggled with in 1710: How best to limit the monopoly power of publishers? Parliament's strategy was to offer a term for existing works that was long enough to buy peace in 1710, but short enough to assure that culture would pass into competition within a reasonable period of time. Within twenty-one years, Parliament believed, Britain would mature from the controlled culture that the Crown coveted to the free culture that we inherited.

The fight to defend the limits of the Statute of Anne was not to end there, however, and it is here that Donaldson enters the mix.

Millar died soon after his victory, so his case was not appealed. His estate sold Thomson's poems to a syndicate of printers that included Thomas Beckett.[12] Donaldson then released an unauthorized edition of Thomson's works. Beckett, on the strength of the decision in *Millar*, got an injunction against Donaldson. Donaldson appealed the case to the House of Lords, which functioned much like our own Supreme Court. In February of 1774, that body had the chance to interpret the meaning of Parliament's limits from sixty years before.

As few legal cases ever do, *Donaldson* v. *Beckett* drew an enormous amount of attention throughout Britain. Donaldson's lawyers argued that whatever rights may have existed under the common law, the Statute of Anne terminated those rights. After passage of the Statute of Anne, the only legal protection for an exclusive right to control publication came from that statute. Thus, they argued, after the term specified in the Statute of Anne expired, works that had been protected by the statute were no longer protected.

The House of Lords was an odd institution. Legal questions were presented to the House and voted upon first by the "law lords," members of special legal distinction who functioned much like the Justices in our Supreme Court. Then, after the law lords voted, the House of Lords generally voted.

The reports about the law lords' votes are mixed. On some counts, it looks as if perpetual copyright prevailed. But there is no ambiguity about how the House of Lords voted as whole. By a two-to-one majority (22 to 11) they voted to reject the idea of perpetual copyrights. Whatever one's understanding of the common law, now a copyright was fixed for a limited time, after which the work protected by copyright passed into the public domain.

"The public domain." Before the case of *Donaldson* v. *Beckett,* there was no clear idea of a public domain in England. Before 1774, there was a strong argument that common law copyrights were perpetual. After 1774, the public domain was born. For the first time in Anglo-American history, the legal control over creative works expired, and the greatest works in English history—including those of Shakespeare, Bacon, Milton, Johnson, and Bunyan—were free of legal restraint.

It is hard for us to imagine, but this decision by the House of Lords fueled an extraordinarily popular and political reaction. In Scotland, where most of the "pirate publishers" did their work, people celebrated the decision in the streets. As the *Edinburgh Advertiser* reported, "No private cause has so much engrossed the attention of the public, and none has been tried before the House of Lords in the decision of which so many individuals were interested." "Great rejoicing in Edinburgh upon victory over literary property: bonfires and illuminations."[13]

In London, however, at least among publishers, the reaction was equally strong in the opposite direction. The *Morning Chronicle* reported:

> By the above decision . . . near 200,000 pounds worth of what was honestly purchased at public sale, and which was yesterday thought property is now reduced to nothing. The Booksellers of London and Westminster, many of whom sold estates and houses to purchase Copy-right, are in a manner ruined, and those who after many years industry thought they had acquired a competency to provide for their families now find themselves without a shilling to devise to their successors. [14]

"Ruined" is a bit of an exaggeration. But it is not an exaggeration to say that the change was profound. The decision of the House of Lords meant that the booksellers could no longer control how culture in England would grow and develop. Culture in England was thereafter *free*. Not in the sense that copyrights would not be respected, for of course, for a limited time after a work was published, the bookseller had an exclusive right to control the publication of that book. And not in the sense that books could be stolen, for even after a copyright expired, you still had to buy the book from someone. But *free* in the sense that the culture and its growth would no longer be controlled by a small group of publishers. As every free market does, this free market of free culture would grow as the consumers and producers chose. English culture would develop as the many English readers chose to let it develop—chose in the books they bought and wrote; chose in the memes they repeated and endorsed. Chose in a *competitive context*, not a context in which the choices about what culture is available to people and how they get access to it are made by the few despite the wishes of the many.

At least, this was the rule in a world where the Parliament is antimonopoly, resistant to the protectionist pleas of publishers. In a world where the Parliament is more pliant, free culture would be less protected.

CHAPTER SEVEN: Recorders

Jon Else is a filmmaker. He is best known for his documentaries and has been very successful in spreading his art. He is also a teacher, and as a teacher myself, I envy the loyalty and admiration that his students feel for him. (I met, by accident, two of his students at a dinner party. He was their god.)

Else worked on a documentary that I was involved in. At a break, he told me a story about the freedom to create with film in America today.

In 1990, Else was working on a documentary about Wagner's Ring Cycle. The focus was stagehands at the San Francisco Opera. Stagehands are a particularly funny and colorful element of an opera. During a show, they hang out below the stage in the grips' lounge and in the lighting loft. They make a perfect contrast to the art on the stage.

During one of the performances, Else was shooting some stagehands playing checkers. In one corner of the room was a television set. Playing on the television set, while the stagehands played checkers and the opera company played Wagner, was *The Simpsons*. As Else judged it, this touch of cartoon helped capture the flavor of what was special about the scene.

Years later, when he finally got funding to complete the film, Else attempted to clear the rights for those few seconds of *The Simpsons*. For of course, those few seconds are copyrighted; and of course, to use copyrighted material you need the permission of the copyright owner, unless "fair use" or some other privilege applies.

Else called *Simpsons* creator Matt Groening's office to get permission. Groening approved the shot. The shot was a four-and-a-half-second image on a tiny television set in the corner of the room. How could it hurt? Groening was happy to have it in the film, but he told Else to contact Gracie Films, the company that produces the program.

Gracie Films was okay with it, too, but they, like Groening, wanted to be careful. So they told Else to contact Fox, Gracie's parent company. Else called Fox and told them about the clip in the corner of the one room shot of the film. Matt Groening had already given permission, Else said. He was just confirming the permission with Fox.

Then, as Else told me, "two things happened. First we discovered . . . that Matt Groening doesn't own his own creation—or at least that someone [at Fox] believes he doesn't own his own creation." And second, Fox "wanted ten thousand dollars as a licensing fee for us to use this four-point-five seconds of . . . entirely unsolicited *Simpsons* which was in the corner of the shot."

Else was certain there was a mistake. He worked his way up to someone he thought was a vice president for licensing, Rebecca Herrera. He explained to her, "There must be some mistake here. . . . We're asking for your educational rate on this." That was the educational rate, Herrera told Else. A day or so later, Else called again to confirm what he had been told.

"I wanted to make sure I had my facts straight," he told me. "Yes, you have your facts straight," she said. It would cost $10,000 to use the clip of *The Simpsons* in the corner of a shot in a documentary film about

Wagner's Ring Cycle. And then, astonishingly, Herrera told Else, "And if you quote me, I'll turn you over to our attorneys." As an assistant to Herrera told Else later on, "They don't give a shit. They just want the money."

Else didn't have the money to buy the right to replay what was playing on the television backstage at the San Francisco Opera. To reproduce this reality was beyond the documentary filmmaker's budget. At the very last minute before the film was to be released, Else digitally replaced the shot with a clip from another film that he had worked on, *The Day After Trinity,* from ten years before.

There's no doubt that someone, whether Matt Groening or Fox, owns the copyright to *The Simpsons.* That copyright is their property. To use that copyrighted material thus sometimes requires the permission of the copyright owner. If the use that Else wanted to make of the *Simpsons* copyright were one of the uses restricted by the law, then he would need to get the permission of the copyright owner before he could use the work in that way. And in a free market, it is the owner of the copyright who gets to set the price for any use that the law says the owner gets to control.

For example, "public performance" is a use of *The Simpsons* that the copyright owner gets to control. If you take a selection of favorite episodes, rent a movie theater, and charge for tickets to come see "My Favorite *Simpsons,*" then you need to get permission from the copyright owner. And the copyright owner (rightly, in my view) can charge whatever she wants—$10 or $1,000,000. That's her right, as set by the law.

But when lawyers hear this story about Jon Else and Fox, their first thought is "fair use."[1] Else's use of just 4.5 seconds of an indirect shot of a *Simpsons* episode is clearly a fair use of *The Simpsons*—and fair use does not require the permission of anyone.

So I asked Else why he didn't just rely upon "fair use." Here's his reply:

> The *Simpsons* fiasco was for me a great lesson in the gulf be-
> tween what lawyers find irrelevant in some abstract sense, and
> what is crushingly relevant in practice to those of us actually
> trying to make and broadcast documentaries. I never had any
> doubt that it was "clearly fair use" in an absolute legal sense. But
> I couldn't rely on the concept in any concrete way. Here's why:
>
> 1. Before our films can be broadcast, the network requires
> that we buy Errors and Omissions insurance. The carriers re-
> quire a detailed "visual cue sheet" listing the source and licens-
> ing status of each shot in the film. They take a dim view of
> "fair use," and a claim of "fair use" can grind the application
> process to a halt.
>
> 2. I probably never should have asked Matt Groening in the
> first place. But I knew (at least from folklore) that Fox had a
> history of tracking down and stopping unlicensed *Simpsons*
> usage, just as George Lucas had a very high profile litigating
> *Star Wars* usage. So I decided to play by the book, thinking
> that we would be granted free or cheap license to four seconds
> of *Simpsons*. As a documentary producer working to exhaus-
> tion on a shoestring, the last thing I wanted was to risk legal
> trouble, even nuisance legal trouble, and even to defend a
> principle.
>
> 3. I did, in fact, speak with one of your colleagues at Stanford
> Law School . . . who confirmed that it was fair use. He also
> confirmed that Fox would "depose and litigate you to within
> an inch of your life," regardless of the merits of my claim. He
> made clear that it would boil down to who had the bigger le-
> gal department and the deeper pockets, me or them.

4. The question of fair use usually comes up at the end of the project, when we are up against a release deadline and out of money.

In theory, fair use means you need no permission. The theory therefore supports free culture and insulates against a permission culture. But in practice, fair use functions very differently. The fuzzy lines of the law, tied to the extraordinary liability if lines are crossed, means that the effective fair use for many types of creators is slight. The law has the right aim; practice has defeated the aim.

This practice shows just how far the law has come from its eighteenth-century roots. The law was born as a shield to protect publishers' profits against the unfair competition of a pirate. It has matured into a sword that interferes with any use, transformative or not.

CHAPTER EIGHT: Transformers

In 1993, Alex Alben was a lawyer working at Starwave, Inc. Starwave was an innovative company founded by Microsoft cofounder Paul Allen to develop digital entertainment. Long before the Internet became popular, Starwave began investing in new technology for delivering entertainment in anticipation of the power of networks.

Alben had a special interest in new technology. He was intrigued by the emerging market for CD-ROM technology—not to distribute film, but to do things with film that otherwise would be very difficult. In 1993, he launched an initiative to develop a product to build retrospectives on the work of particular actors. The first actor chosen was Clint Eastwood. The idea was to showcase all of the work of Eastwood, with clips from his films and interviews with figures important to his career.

At that time, Eastwood had made more than fifty films, as an actor and as a director. Alben began with a series of interviews with Eastwood, asking him about his career. Because Starwave produced those interviews, it was free to include them on the CD.

That alone would not have made a very interesting product, so Starwave wanted to add content from the movies in Eastwood's career: posters, scripts, and other material relating to the films Eastwood made. Most of his career was spent at Warner Brothers, and so it was relatively easy to get permission for that content.

Then Alben and his team decided to include actual film clips. "Our goal was that we were going to have a clip from every one of Eastwood's films," Alben told me. It was here that the problem arose. "No one had ever really done this before," Alben explained. "No one had ever tried to do this in the context of an artistic look at an actor's career."

Alben brought the idea to Michael Slade, the CEO of Starwave. Slade asked, "Well, what will it take?"

Alben replied, "Well, we're going to have to clear rights from everyone who appears in these films, and the music and everything else that we want to use in these film clips." Slade said, "Great! Go for it."[1]

The problem was that neither Alben nor Slade had any idea what clearing those rights would mean. Every actor in each of the films could have a claim to royalties for the reuse of that film. But CD-ROMs had not been specified in the contracts for the actors, so there was no clear way to know just what Starwave was to do.

I asked Alben how he dealt with the problem. With an obvious pride in his resourcefulness that obscured the obvious bizarreness of his tale, Alben recounted just what they did:

So we very mechanically went about looking up the film clips. We made some artistic decisions about what film clips to include—of course we were going to use the "Make my day" clip from *Dirty Harry*. But you then need to get the guy on the ground who's wiggling under the gun and you need to get his permission. And then you have to decide what you are going to pay him.

We decided that it would be fair if we offered them the day-player rate for the right to reuse that performance. We're talking about a clip of less than a minute, but to reuse that performance in the CD-ROM the rate at the time was about $600.

So we had to identify the people—some of them were hard to identify because in Eastwood movies you can't tell who's the guy crashing through the glass—is it the actor or is it the stuntman? And then we just, we put together a team, my assistant and some others, and we just started calling people.

Some actors were glad to help—Donald Sutherland, for example, followed up himself to be sure that the rights had been cleared. Others were dumbfounded at their good fortune. Alben would ask, "Hey, can I pay you $600 or maybe if you were in two films, you know, $1,200?" And they would say, "Are you for real? Hey, I'd love to get $1,200." And some of course were a bit difficult (estranged ex-wives, in particular). But eventually, Alben and his team had cleared the rights to this retrospective CD-ROM on Clint Eastwood's career.

It was one *year* later—"and even then we weren't sure whether we were totally in the clear."

Alben is proud of his work. The project was the first of its kind and the only time he knew of that a team had undertaken such a massive project for the purpose of releasing a retrospective.

Everyone thought it would be too hard. Everyone just threw up their hands and said, "Oh, my gosh, a film, it's so many copyrights, there's the music, there's the screenplay, there's the director, there's the actors." But we just broke it down. We just put it into its constituent parts and said, "Okay, there's this many actors, this many directors, . . . this many musicians," and we just went at it very systematically and cleared the rights.

And no doubt, the product itself was exceptionally good. Eastwood loved it, and it sold very well.

But I pressed Alben about how weird it seems that it would have to take a year's work simply to clear rights. No doubt Alben had done this efficiently, but as Peter Drucker has famously quipped, "There is nothing so useless as doing efficiently that which should not be done at all."[2] Did it make sense, I asked Alben, that this is the way a new work has to be made?

For, as he acknowledged, "very few . . . have the time and resources, and the will to do this," and thus, very few such works would ever be made. Does it make sense, I asked him, from the standpoint of what anybody really thought they were ever giving rights for originally, that you would have to go clear rights for these kinds of clips?

> I don't think so. When an actor renders a performance in a movie, he or she gets paid very well. . . . And then when 30 seconds of that performance is used in a new product that is a retrospective of somebody's career, I don't think that that person . . . should be compensated for that.

Or at least, is this *how* the artist should be compensated? Would it make sense, I asked, for there to be some kind of statutory license that someone could pay and be free to make derivative use of clips like this? Did it really make sense that a follow-on creator would have to track down every artist, actor, director, musician, and get explicit permission from each? Wouldn't a lot more be created if the legal part of the creative process could be made to be more clean?

> Absolutely. I think that if there were some fair-licensing mechanism—where you weren't subject to hold-ups and you weren't subject to estranged former spouses—you'd see a lot more of this work, because it wouldn't be so daunting to try to put together a

retrospective of someone's career and meaningfully illustrate it with lots of media from that person's career. You'd build in a cost as the producer of one of these things. You'd build in a cost of paying X dollars to the talent that performed. But it would be a known cost. That's the thing that trips everybody up and makes this kind of product hard to get off the ground. If you knew I have a hundred minutes of film in this product and it's going to cost me X, then you build your budget around it, and you can get investments and everything else that you need to produce it. But if you say, "Oh, I want a hundred minutes of something and I have no idea what it's going to cost me, and a certain number of people are going to hold me up for money," then it becomes difficult to put one of these things together.

Alben worked for a big company. His company was backed by some of the richest investors in the world. He therefore had authority and access that the average Web designer would not have. So if it took him a year, how long would it take someone else? And how much creativity is never made just because the costs of clearing the rights are so high?

These costs are the burdens of a kind of regulation. Put on a Republican hat for a moment, and get angry for a bit. The government defines the scope of these rights, and the scope defined determines how much it's going to cost to negotiate them. (Remember the idea that land runs to the heavens, and imagine the pilot purchasing fly-through rights as he negotiates to fly from Los Angeles to San Francisco.) These rights might well have once made sense; but as circumstances change, they make no sense at all. Or at least, a well-trained, regulation-minimizing Republican should look at the rights and ask, "Does this still make sense?"

I've seen the flash of recognition when people get this point, but only a few times. The first was at a conference of federal judges in California. The judges were gathered to discuss the emerging topic of cyber-law. I was asked to be on the panel. Harvey Saferstein, a well-respected lawyer from an L.A. firm, introduced the panel with a video that he and a friend, Robert Fairbank, had produced.

The video was a brilliant collage of film from every period in the twentieth century, all framed around the idea of a *60 Minutes* episode. The execution was perfect, down to the sixty-minute stopwatch. The judges loved every minute of it.

When the lights came up, I looked over to my copanelist, David Nimmer, perhaps the leading copyright scholar and practitioner in the nation. He had an astonished look on his face, as he peered across the room of over 250 well-entertained judges. Taking an ominous tone, he began his talk with a question: "Do you know how many federal laws were just violated in this room?"

For of course, the two brilliantly talented creators who made this film hadn't done what Alben did. They hadn't spent a year clearing the rights to these clips; technically, what they had done violated the law. Of course, it wasn't as if they or anyone were going to be prosecuted for this violation (the presence of 250 judges and a gaggle of federal marshals notwithstanding). But Nimmer was making an important point: A year before anyone would have heard of the word Napster, and two years before another member of our panel, David Boies, would defend Napster before the Ninth Circuit Court of Appeals, Nimmer was trying to get the judges to see that the law would not be friendly to the capacities that this technology would enable. Technology means you can now do amazing things easily; but you couldn't easily do them legally.

We live in a "cut and paste" culture enabled by technology. Anyone building a presentation knows the extraordinary freedom that the cut and paste architecture of the Internet created—in a second you can find just about any image you want; in another second, you can have it planted in your presentation.

But presentations are just a tiny beginning. Using the Internet and its archives, musicians are able to string together mixes of sound never before imagined; filmmakers are able to build movies out of clips on computers around the world. An extraordinary site in Sweden takes images of politicians and blends them with music to create biting political commentary. A site called Camp Chaos has produced some of the most biting criticism of the record industry that there is through the mixing of Flash! and music.

All of these creations are technically illegal. Even if the creators wanted to be "legal," the cost of complying with the law is impossibly high. Therefore, for the law-abiding sorts, a wealth of creativity is never made. And for that part that is made, if it doesn't follow the clearance rules, it doesn't get released.

To some, these stories suggest a solution: Let's alter the mix of rights so that people are free to build upon our culture. Free to add or mix as they see fit. We could even make this change without necessarily requiring that the "free" use be free as in "free beer." Instead, the system could simply make it easy for follow-on creators to compensate artists without requiring an army of lawyers to come along: a rule, for example, that says "the royalty owed the copyright owner of an unregistered work for the derivative reuse of his work will be a flat 1 percent of net revenues, to be held in escrow for the copyright owner." Under this rule, the copyright owner could benefit from some royalty, but he would not have the benefit of a full property right (meaning the right to name his own price) unless he registers the work.

Who could possibly object to this? And what reason would there be for objecting? We're talking about work that is not now being made; which if made, under this plan, would produce new income for artists. What reason would anyone have to oppose it?

In February 2003, DreamWorks studios announced an agreement with Mike Myers, the comic genius of *Saturday Night Live* and Austin Powers. According to the announcement, Myers and Dream-

Works would work together to form a "unique filmmaking pact." Under the agreement, DreamWorks "will acquire the rights to existing motion picture hits and classics, write new storylines and—with the use of state-of-the-art digital technology—insert Myers and other actors into the film, thereby creating an entirely new piece of entertainment."

The announcement called this "film sampling." As Myers explained, "Film Sampling is an exciting way to put an original spin on existing films and allow audiences to see old movies in a new light. Rap artists have been doing this for years with music and now we are able to take that same concept and apply it to film." Steven Spielberg is quoted as saying, "If anyone can create a way to bring old films to new audiences, it is Mike."

Spielberg is right. Film sampling by Myers will be brilliant. But if you don't think about it, you might miss the truly astonishing point about this announcement. As the vast majority of our film heritage remains under copyright, the real meaning of the DreamWorks announcement is just this: It is Mike Myers and only Mike Myers who is free to sample. Any general freedom to build upon the film archive of our culture, a freedom in other contexts presumed for us all, is now a privilege reserved for the funny and famous—and presumably rich.

This privilege becomes reserved for two sorts of reasons. The first continues the story of the last chapter: the vagueness of "fair use." Much of "sampling" should be considered "fair use." But few would rely upon so weak a doctrine to create. That leads to the second reason that the privilege is reserved for the few: The costs of negotiating the legal rights for the creative reuse of content are astronomically high. These costs mirror the costs with fair use: You either pay a lawyer to defend your fair use rights or pay a lawyer to track down permissions so you don't have to rely upon fair use rights. Either way, the creative process is a process of paying lawyers—again a privilege, or perhaps a curse, reserved for the few.

CHAPTER NINE: Collectors

In April 1996, millions of "bots"—computer codes designed to "spider," or automatically search the Internet and copy content—began running across the Net. Page by page, these bots copied Internet-based information onto a small set of computers located in a basement in San Francisco's Presidio. Once the bots finished the whole of the Internet, they started again. Over and over again, once every two months, these bits of code took copies of the Internet and stored them.

By October 2001, the bots had collected more than five years of copies. And at a small announcement in Berkeley, California, the archive that these copies created, the Internet Archive, was opened to the world. Using a technology called "the Way Back Machine," you could enter a Web page, and see all of its copies going back to 1996, as well as when those pages changed.

This is the thing about the Internet that Orwell would have appreciated. In the dystopia described in *1984,* old newspapers were constantly updated to assure that the current view of the world, approved of by the government, was not contradicted by previous news reports.

Thousands of workers constantly reedited the past, meaning there was no way ever to know whether the story you were reading today was the story that was printed on the date published on the paper.

It's the same with the Internet. If you go to a Web page today, there's no way for you to know whether the content you are reading is the same as the content you read before. The page may seem the same, but the content could easily be different. The Internet is Orwell's library—constantly updated, without any reliable memory.

Until the Way Back Machine, at least. With the Way Back Machine, and the Internet Archive underlying it, you can see what the Internet was. You have the power to see what you remember. More importantly, perhaps, you also have the power to find what you don't remember and what others might prefer you forget.[1]

We take it for granted that we can go back to see what we remember reading. Think about newspapers. If you wanted to study the reaction of your hometown newspaper to the race riots in Watts in 1965, or to Bull Connor's water cannon in 1963, you could go to your public library and look at the newspapers. Those papers probably exist on microfiche. If you're lucky, they exist in paper, too. Either way, you are free, using a library, to go back and remember—not just what it is convenient to remember, but remember something close to the truth.

It is said that those who fail to remember history are doomed to repeat it. That's not quite correct. We *all* forget history. The key is whether we have a way to go back to rediscover what we forget. More directly, the key is whether an objective past can keep us honest. Libraries help do that, by collecting content and keeping it, for schoolchildren, for researchers, for grandma. A free society presumes this knowedge.

The Internet was an exception to this presumption. Until the Internet Archive, there was no way to go back. The Internet was the quintessentially transitory medium. And yet, as it becomes more important in forming and reforming society, it becomes more and more important to maintain in some historical form. It's just bizarre to think that we have scads of archives of newspapers from tiny towns around the world, yet there is but one copy of the Internet—the one kept by the Internet Archive.

Brewster Kahle is the founder of the Internet Archive. He was a very successful Internet entrepreneur after he was a successful computer researcher. In the 1990s, Kahle decided he had had enough business success. It was time to become a different kind of success. So he launched a series of projects designed to archive human knowledge. The Internet Archive was just the first of the projects of this Andrew Carnegie of the Internet. By December of 2002, the archive had over 10 billion pages, and it was growing at about a billion pages a month.

The Way Back Machine is the largest archive of human knowledge in human history. At the end of 2002, it held "two hundred and thirty terabytes of material"—and was "ten times larger than the Library of Congress." And this was just the first of the archives that Kahle set out to build. In addition to the Internet Archive, Kahle has been constructing the Television Archive. Television, it turns out, is even more ephemeral than the Internet. While much of twentieth-century culture was constructed through television, only a tiny proportion of that culture is available for anyone to see today. Three hours of news are recorded each evening by Vanderbilt University—thanks to a specific exemption in the copyright law. That content is indexed, and is available to scholars for a very low fee. "But other than that, [television] is almost unavailable," Kahle told me. "If you were Barbara Walters you could get access to [the archives], but if you are just a graduate student?" As Kahle put it,

Do you remember when Dan Quayle was interacting with Murphy Brown? Remember that back and forth surreal experience of a politician interacting with a fictional television character? If you were a graduate student wanting to study that, and you wanted to get those original back and forth exchanges between the two, the

60 Minutes episode that came out after it . . . it would be almost impossible. . . . Those materials are almost unfindable. . . .

Why is that? Why is it that the part of our culture that is recorded in newspapers remains perpetually accessible, while the part that is recorded on videotape is not? How is it that we've created a world where researchers trying to understand the effect of media on nineteenth-century America will have an easier time than researchers trying to understand the effect of media on twentieth-century America?

In part, this is because of the law. Early in American copyright law, copyright owners were required to deposit copies of their work in libraries. These copies were intended both to facilitate the spread of knowledge and to assure that a copy of the work would be around once the copyright expired, so that others might access and copy the work.

These rules applied to film as well. But in 1915, the Library of Congress made an exception for film. Film could be copyrighted so long as such deposits were made. But the filmmaker was then allowed to borrow back the deposits—for an unlimited time at no cost. In 1915 alone, there were more than 5,475 films deposited and "borrowed back." Thus, when the copyrights to films expire, there is no copy held by any library. The copy exists—if it exists at all—in the library archive of the film company.[2]

The same is generally true about television. Television broadcasts were originally not copyrighted—there was no way to capture the broadcasts, so there was no fear of "theft." But as technology enabled capturing, broadcasters relied increasingly upon the law. The law required they make a copy of each broadcast for the work to be "copyrighted." But those copies were simply kept by the broadcasters. No library had any right to them; the government didn't demand them. The content of this part of American culture is practically invisible to anyone who would look.

Kahle was eager to correct this. Before September 11, 2001, he and his allies had started capturing television. They selected twenty stations from around the world and hit the Record button. After September 11, Kahle, working with dozens of others, selected twenty stations from around the world and, beginning October 11, 2001, made their coverage during the week of September 11 available free on-line. Anyone could see how news reports from around the world covered the events of that day.

Kahle had the same idea with film. Working with Rick Prelinger, whose archive of film includes close to 45,000 "ephemeral films" (meaning films other than Hollywood movies, films that were never copyrighted), Kahle established the Movie Archive. Prelinger let Kahle digitize 1,300 films in this archive and post those films on the Internet to be downloaded for free. Prelinger's is a for-profit company. It sells copies of these films as stock footage. What he has discovered is that after he made a significant chunk available for free, his stock footage sales went up dramatically. People could easily find the material they wanted to use. Some downloaded that material and made films on their own. Others purchased copies to enable other films to be made. Either way, the archive enabled access to this important part of our culture. Want to see a copy of the "Duck and Cover" film that instructed children how to save themselves in the middle of nuclear attack? Go to archive.org, and you can download the film in a few minutes—for free.

Here again, Kahle is providing access to a part of our culture that we otherwise could not get easily, if at all. It is yet another part of what defines the twentieth century that we have lost to history. The law doesn't require these copies to be kept by anyone, or to be deposited in an archive by anyone. Therefore, there is no simple way to find them.

The key here is access, not price. Kahle wants to enable free access to this content, but he also wants to enable others to sell access to it. His aim is to ensure competition in access to this important part of our culture. Not during the commercial life of a bit of creative property, but during a second life that all creative property has—a noncommercial life.

For here is an idea that we should more clearly recognize. Every bit of creative property goes through different "lives." In its first life, if the creator is lucky, the content is sold. In such cases the commercial market is successful for the creator. The vast majority of creative property doesn't enjoy such success, but some clearly does. For that content, commercial life is extremely important. Without this commercial market, there would be, many argue, much less creativity.

After the commercial life of creative property has ended, our tradition has always supported a second life as well. A newspaper delivers the news every day to the doorsteps of America. The very next day, it is used to wrap fish or to fill boxes with fragile gifts or to build an archive of knowledge about our history. In this second life, the content can continue to inform even if that information is no longer sold.

The same has always been true about books. A book goes out of print very quickly (the average today is after about a year [3]). After it is out of print, it can be sold in used book stores without the copyright owner getting anything and stored in libraries, where many get to read the book, also for free. Used book stores and libraries are thus the second life of a book. That second life is extremely important to the spread and stability of culture.

Yet increasingly, any assumption about a stable second life for creative property does not hold true with the most important components of popular culture in the twentieth and twenty-first centuries. For these—television, movies, music, radio, the Internet—there is no guarantee of a second life. For these sorts of culture, it is as if we've replaced libraries with Barnes & Noble superstores. With this culture, what's accessible is nothing but what a certain limited market demands. Beyond that, culture disappears.

For most of the twentieth century, it was economics that made this so. It would have been insanely expensive to collect and make accessible all television and film and music: The cost of analog copies is extraordinarily high. So even though the law in principle would have restricted the ability of a Brewster Kahle to copy culture generally, the real restriction was economics. The market made it impossibly difficult to do anything about this ephemeral culture; the law had little practical effect.

Perhaps the single most important feature of the digital revolution is that for the first time since the Library of Alexandria, it is feasible to imagine constructing archives that hold all culture produced or distributed publicly. Technology makes it possible to imagine an archive of all books published, and increasingly makes it possible to imagine an archive of all moving images and sound.

The scale of this potential archive is something we've never imagined before. The Brewster Kahles of our history have dreamed about it; but we are for the first time at a point where that dream is possible. As Kahle describes,

> It looks like there's about two to three million recordings of music. Ever. There are about a hundred thousand theatrical releases of movies, . . . and about one to two million movies [distributed] during the twentieth century. There are about twenty-six million different titles of books. All of these would fit on computers that would fit in this room and be able to be afforded by a small company. So we're at a turning point in our history. Universal access is the goal. And the opportunity of leading a different life, based on this, is . . . thrilling. It could be one of the things humankind would be most proud of. Up there with the Library of Alexandria, putting a man on the moon, and the invention of the printing press.

Kahle is not the only librarian. The Internet Archive is not the only archive. But Kahle and the Internet Archive suggest what the future of libraries or archives could be. *When* the commercial life of creative property ends, I don't know. But it does. And whenever it does, Kahle and his archive hint at a world where this knowledge, and culture, remains perpetually available. Some will draw upon it to understand it;

some to criticize it. Some will use it, as Walt Disney did, to re-create the past for the future. These technologies promise something that had become unimaginable for much of our past—a future *for* our past. The technology of digital arts could make the dream of the Library of Alexandria real again.

Technologists have thus removed the economic costs of building such an archive. But lawyers' costs remain. For as much as we might like to call these "archives," as warm as the idea of a "library" might seem, the "content" that is collected in these digital spaces is also someone's "property." And the law of property restricts the freedoms that Kahle and others would exercise.

CHAPTER TEN: "Property"

Jack Valenti has been the president of the Motion Picture Association of America since 1966. He first came to Washington, D.C., with Lyndon Johnson's administration—literally. The famous picture of Johnson's swearing-in on Air Force One after the assassination of President Kennedy has Valenti in the background. In his almost forty years of running the MPAA, Valenti has established himself as perhaps the most prominent and effective lobbyist in Washington.

The MPAA is the American branch of the international Motion Picture Association. It was formed in 1922 as a trade association whose goal was to defend American movies against increasing domestic criticism. The organization now represents not only filmmakers but producers and distributors of entertainment for television, video, and cable. Its board is made up of the chairmen and presidents of the seven major producers and distributors of motion picture and television programs in the United States: Walt Disney, Sony Pictures Entertainment, MGM, Paramount Pictures, Twentieth Century Fox, Universal Studios, and Warner Brothers.

Valenti is only the third president of the MPAA. No president before him has had as much influence over that organization, or over Washington. As a Texan, Valenti has mastered the single most important political skill of a Southerner—the ability to appear simple and slow while hiding a lightning-fast intellect. To this day, Valenti plays the simple, humble man. But this Harvard MBA, and author of four books, who finished high school at the age of fifteen and flew more than fifty combat missions in World War II, is no Mr. Smith. When Valenti went to Washington, he mastered the city in a quintessentially Washingtonian way.

In defending artistic liberty and the freedom of speech that our culture depends upon, the MPAA has done important good. In crafting the MPAA rating system, it has probably avoided a great deal of speech-regulating harm. But there is an aspect to the organization's mission that is both the most radical and the most important. This is the organization's effort, epitomized in Valenti's every act, to redefine the meaning of "creative property."

In 1982, Valenti's testimony to Congress captured the strategy perfectly:

> No matter the lengthy arguments made, no matter the charges and the counter-charges, no matter the tumult and the shouting, reasonable men and women will keep returning to the fundamental issue, the central theme which animates this entire debate: *Creative property owners must be accorded the same rights and protection resident in all other property owners in the nation.* That is the issue. That is the question. And that is the rostrum on which this entire hearing and the debates to follow must rest.[1]

The strategy of this rhetoric, like the strategy of most of Valenti's rhetoric, is brilliant and simple and brilliant because simple. The "central theme" to which "reasonable men and women" will return is this: "Creative property owners must be accorded the same rights and protections resident in all other property owners in the nation." There are no second-class citizens, Valenti might have continued. There should be no second-class property owners.

This claim has an obvious and powerful intuitive pull. It is stated with such clarity as to make the idea as obvious as the notion that we use elections to pick presidents. But in fact, there is no more extreme a claim made by *anyone* who is serious in this debate than this claim of Valenti's. Jack Valenti, however sweet and however brilliant, is perhaps the nation's foremost extremist when it comes to the nature and scope of "creative property." His views have *no* reasonable connection to our actual legal tradition, even if the subtle pull of his Texan charm has slowly redefined that tradition, at least in Washington.

While "creative property" is certainly "property" in a nerdy and precise sense that lawyers are trained to understand,[2] it has never been the case, nor should it be, that "creative property owners" have been "accorded the same rights and protection resident in all other property owners." Indeed, if creative property owners were given the same rights as all other property owners, that would effect a radical, and radically undesirable, change in our tradition.

Valenti knows this. But he speaks for an industry that cares squat for our tradition and the values it represents. He speaks for an industry that is instead fighting to restore the tradition that the British overturned in 1710. In the world that Valenti's changes would create, a powerful few would exercise powerful control over how our creative culture would develop.

I have two purposes in this chapter. The first is to convince you that, historically, Valenti's claim is absolutely wrong. The second is to convince you that it would be terribly wrong for us to reject our history. We have always treated rights in creative property differently from the rights resident in all other property owners. They have never been the same. And they should never be the same, because, however counterintuitive this may seem, to make them the same would be to fundamentally weaken the opportunity for new creators to create. Creativity depends upon the owners of creativity having less than perfect control.

Organizations such as the MPAA, whose board includes the most powerful of the old guard, have little interest, their rhetoric notwithstanding, in assuring that the new can displace them. No organization does. No person does. (Ask me about tenure, for example.) But what's good for the MPAA is not necessarily good for America. A society that defends the ideals of free culture must preserve precisely the opportunity for new creativity to threaten the old.

To get just a hint that there is something fundamentally wrong in Valenti's argument, we need look no further than the United States Constitution itself.

The framers of our Constitution loved "property." Indeed, so strongly did they love property that they built into the Constitution an important requirement. If the government takes your property—if it condemns your house, or acquires a slice of land from your farm—it is required, under the Fifth Amendment's "Takings Clause," to pay you "just compensation" for that taking. The Constitution thus guarantees that property is, in a certain sense, sacred. It cannot *ever* be taken from the property owner unless the government pays for the privilege.

Yet the very same Constitution speaks very differently about what Valenti calls "creative property." In the clause granting Congress the power to create "creative property," the Constitution *requires* that after a "limited time," Congress take back the rights that it has granted and set the "creative property" free to the public domain. Yet when Congress does this, when the expiration of a copyright term "takes" your copyright and turns it over to the public domain, Congress does not have any obligation to pay "just compensation" for this "taking." Instead, the same Constitution that requires compensation for your land requires that you lose your "creative property" right without any compensation at all.

The Constitution thus on its face states that these two forms of property are not to be accorded the same rights. They are plainly to be treated differently. Valenti is therefore not just asking for a change in our tradition when he argues that creative-property owners should be accorded the same rights as every other property-right owner. He is effectively arguing for a change in our Constitution itself.

Arguing for a change in our Constitution is not necessarily wrong. There was much in our original Constitution that was plainly wrong. The Constitution of 1789 entrenched slavery; it left senators to be appointed rather than elected; it made it possible for the electoral college to produce a tie between the president and his own vice president (as it did in 1800). The framers were no doubt extraordinary, but I would be the first to admit that they made big mistakes. We have since rejected some of those mistakes; no doubt there could be others that we should reject as well. So my argument is not simply that because Jefferson did it, we should, too.

Instead, my argument is that because Jefferson did it, we should at least try to understand *why*. Why did the framers, fanatical property types that they were, reject the claim that creative property be given the same rights as all other property? Why did they require that for creative property there must be a public domain?

To answer this question, we need to get some perspective on the history of these "creative property" rights, and the control that they enabled. Once we see clearly how differently these rights have been defined, we will be in a better position to ask the question that should be at the core of this war: Not *whether* creative property should be protected, but how. Not *whether* we will enforce the rights the law gives to creative-property owners, but what the particular mix of rights ought to be. Not *whether* artists should be paid, but whether institutions designed to assure that artists get paid need also control how culture develops.

To answer these questions, we need a more general way to talk about how property is protected. More precisely, we need a more general way than the narrow language of the law allows. In *Code and Other Laws of Cyberspace,* I used a simple model to capture this more general perspective. For any particular right or regulation, this model asks how four different modalities of regulation interact to support or weaken the right or regulation. I represented it with this diagram:

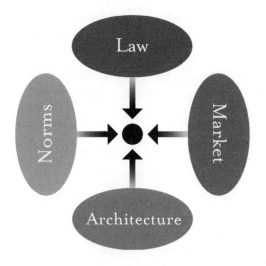

At the center of this picture is a regulated dot: the individual or group that is the target of regulation, or the holder of a right. (In each case throughout, we can describe this either as regulation or as a right. For simplicity's sake, I will speak only of regulations.) The ovals represent four ways in which the individual or group might be regulated—either constrained or, alternatively, enabled. Law is the most obvious constraint (to lawyers, at least). It constrains by threatening punishments after the fact if the rules set in advance are violated. So if, for example, you willfully infringe Madonna's copyright by copying a song from her latest CD and posting it on the Web, you can be punished with a $150,000 fine. The fine is an ex post punishment for violating an ex ante rule. It is imposed by the state.

Norms are a different kind of constraint. They, too, punish an individual for violating a rule. But the punishment of a norm is imposed by a community, not (or not only) by the state. There may be no law against spitting, but that doesn't mean you won't be punished if you spit on the ground while standing in line at a movie. The punishment might not be harsh, though depending upon the community, it could easily be more harsh than many of the punishments imposed by the state. The mark of the difference is not the severity of the rule, but the source of the enforcement.

The market is a third type of constraint. Its constraint is effected through conditions: You can do X if you pay Y; you'll be paid M if you do N. These constraints are obviously not independent of law or norms—it is property law that defines what must be bought if it is to be taken legally; it is norms that say what is appropriately sold. But given a set of norms, and a background of property and contract law, the market imposes a simultaneous constraint upon how an individual or group might behave.

Finally, and for the moment, perhaps, most mysteriously, "architecture"—the physical world as one finds it—is a constraint on behavior. A fallen bridge might constrain your ability to get across a river. Railroad tracks might constrain the ability of a community to integrate its social life. As with the market, architecture does not effect its constraint through ex post punishments. Instead, also as with the market, architecture effects its constraint through simultaneous conditions. These conditions are imposed not by courts enforcing contracts, or by police punishing theft, but by nature, by "architecture." If a 500-pound boulder blocks your way, it is the law of gravity that enforces this constraint. If a $500 airplane ticket stands between you and a flight to New York, it is the market that enforces this constraint.

So the first point about these four modalities of regulation is obvious: They interact. Restrictions imposed by one might be reinforced by another. Or restrictions imposed by one might be undermined by another.

The second point follows directly: If we want to understand the effective freedom that anyone has at a given moment to do any particular thing, we have to consider how these four modalities interact. Whether or not there are other constraints (there may well be; my claim is not about comprehensiveness), these four are among the most significant, and any regulator (whether controlling or freeing) must consider how these four in particular interact.

So, for example, consider the "freedom" to drive a car at a high speed. That freedom is in part restricted by laws: speed limits that say how fast you can drive in particular places at particular times. It is in part restricted by architecture: speed bumps, for example, slow most rational drivers; governors in buses, as another example, set the maximum rate at which the driver can drive. The freedom is in part restricted by the market: Fuel efficiency drops as speed increases, thus the price of gasoline indirectly constrains speed. And finally, the norms of a community may or may not constrain the freedom to speed. Drive at 50 mph by a school in your own neighborhood and you're likely to be punished by the neighbors. The same norm wouldn't be as effective in a different town, or at night.

The final point about this simple model should also be fairly clear: While these four modalities are analytically independent, law has a special role in affecting the three.[3] The law, in other words, sometimes operates to increase or decrease the constraint of a particular modality. Thus, the law might be used to increase taxes on gasoline, so as to increase the incentives to drive more slowly. The law might be used to mandate more speed bumps, so as to increase the difficulty of driving rapidly. The law might be used to fund ads that stigmatize reckless driving. Or the law might be used to require that other laws be more

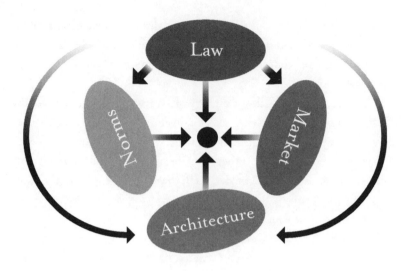

strict—a federal requirement that states decrease the speed limit, for example—so as to decrease the attractiveness of fast driving.

These constraints can thus change, and they can be changed. To understand the effective protection of liberty or protection of property at any particular moment, we must track these changes over time. A restriction imposed by one modality might be erased by another. A freedom enabled by one modality might be displaced by another.[4]

Why Hollywood Is Right

The most obvious point that this model reveals is just why, or just how, Hollywood is right. The copyright warriors have rallied Congress and the courts to defend copyright. This model helps us see why that rallying makes sense.

Let's say this is the picture of copyright's regulation before the Internet:

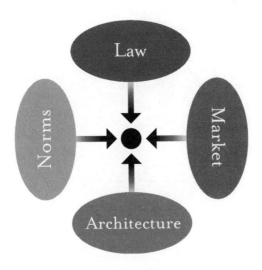

There is balance between law, norms, market, and architecture. The law limits the ability to copy and share content, by imposing penalties on those who copy and share content. Those penalties are reinforced by technologies that make it hard to copy and share content (architecture) and expensive to copy and share content (market). Finally, those penalties are mitigated by norms we all recognize—kids, for example, taping other kids' records. These uses of copyrighted material may well be infringement, but the norms of our society (before the Internet, at least) had no problem with this form of infringement.

Enter the Internet, or, more precisely, technologies such as MP3s and p2p sharing. Now the constraint of architecture changes dramatically, as does the constraint of the market. And as both the market and architecture relax the regulation of copyright, norms pile on. The happy balance (for the warriors, at least) of life before the Internet becomes an effective state of anarchy after the Internet.

Thus the sense of, and justification for, the warriors' response. Technology has changed, the warriors say, and the effect of this change, when ramified through the market and norms, is that a balance of protection for the copyright owners' rights has been lost. This is Iraq

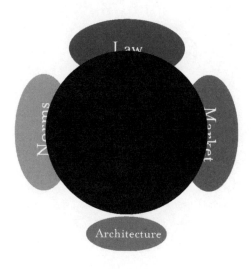

after the fall of Saddam, but this time no government is justifying the looting that results.

Neither this analysis nor the conclusions that follow are new to the warriors. Indeed, in a "White Paper" prepared by the Commerce Department (one heavily influenced by the copyright warriors) in 1995, this mix of regulatory modalities had already been identified and the strategy to respond already mapped. In response to the changes the Internet had effected, the White Paper argued (1) Congress should strengthen intellectual property law, (2) businesses should adopt innovative marketing techniques, (3) technologists should push to develop code to protect copyrighted material, and (4) educators should educate kids to better protect copyright.

This mixed strategy is just what copyright needed—if it was to preserve the particular balance that existed before the change induced by the Internet. And it's just what we should expect the content industry to push for. It is as American as apple pie to consider the happy life you have as an entitlement, and to look to the law to protect it if something comes along to change that happy life. Homeowners living in a flood plain have no hesitation appealing to the government to rebuild (and rebuild again) when a flood (architecture) wipes away their property (law). Farmers have no hesitation appealing to the government to bail them out when a virus (architecture) devastates their crop. Unions have no hesitation appealing to the government to bail them out when imports (market) wipe out the U.S. steel industry.

Thus, there's nothing wrong or surprising in the content industry's campaign to protect itself from the harmful consequences of a technological innovation. And I would be the last person to argue that the changing technology of the Internet has not had a profound effect on the content industry's way of doing business, or as John Seely Brown describes it, its "architecture of revenue."

But just because a particular interest asks for government support, it doesn't follow that support should be granted. And just because technology has weakened a particular way of doing business, it doesn't follow that the government should intervene to support that old way of doing business. Kodak, for example, has lost perhaps as much as 20 percent of their traditional film market to the emerging technologies of digital cameras.[5] Does anyone believe the government should ban digital cameras just to support Kodak? Highways have weakened the freight business for railroads. Does anyone think we should ban trucks from roads *for the purpose of* protecting the railroads? Closer to the subject of this book, remote channel changers have weakened the "stickiness" of television advertising (if a boring commercial comes on the TV, the remote makes it easy to surf), and it may well be that this change has weakened the television advertising market. But does anyone believe we should regulate remotes to reinforce commercial television? (Maybe by limiting them to function only once a second, or to switch to only ten channels within an hour?)

The obvious answer to these obviously rhetorical questions is no. In a free society, with a free market, supported by free enterprise and free trade, the government's role is not to support one way of doing business against others. Its role is not to pick winners and protect them against loss. If the government did this generally, then we would never have any progress. As Microsoft chairman Bill Gates wrote in 1991, in a memo criticizing software patents, "established companies have an interest in excluding future competitors."[6] And relative to a startup, established companies also have the means. (Think RCA and FM radio.) A world in which competitors with new ideas must fight not only the market but also the government is a world in which competitors with new ideas will not succeed. It is a world of stasis and increasingly concentrated stagnation. It is the Soviet Union under Brezhnev.

Thus, while it is understandable for industries threatened with new technologies that change the way they do business to look to the government for protection, it is the special duty of policy makers to guarantee that that protection not become a deterrent to progress. It is the duty of policy makers, in other words, to assure that the changes they create, in response to the request of those hurt by changing technology, are changes that preserve the incentives and opportunities for innovation and change.

In the context of laws regulating speech—which include, obviously, copyright law—that duty is even stronger. When the industry complaining about changing technologies is asking Congress to respond in a way that burdens speech and creativity, policy makers should be especially wary of the request. It is always a bad deal for the government to get into the business of regulating speech markets. The risks and dangers of that game are precisely why our framers created the First Amendment to our Constitution: "Congress shall make no law . . . abridging the freedom of speech." So when Congress is being asked to pass laws that would "abridge" the freedom of speech, it should ask—carefully—whether such regulation is justified.

My argument just now, however, has nothing to do with whether the changes that are being pushed by the copyright warriors are "justified." My argument is about their effect. For before we get to the question of justification, a hard question that depends a great deal upon your values, we should first ask whether we understand the effect of the changes the content industry wants.

Here's the metaphor that will capture the argument to follow.

In 1873, the chemical DDT was first synthesized. In 1948, Swiss chemist Paul Hermann Müller won the Nobel Prize for his work demonstrating the insecticidal properties of DDT. By the 1950s, the insecticide was widely used around the world to kill disease-carrying pests. It was also used to increase farm production.

No one doubts that killing disease-carrying pests or increasing crop production is a good thing. No one doubts that the work of Müller was important and valuable and probably saved lives, possibly millions.

But in 1962, Rachel Carson published *Silent Spring*, which argued that DDT, whatever its primary benefits, was also having unintended environmental consequences. Birds were losing the ability to reproduce. Whole chains of the ecology were being destroyed.

No one set out to destroy the environment. Paul Müller certainly did not aim to harm any birds. But the effort to solve one set of problems produced another set which, in the view of some, was far worse than the problems that were originally attacked. Or more accurately, the problems DDT caused were worse than the problems it solved, at least when considering the other, more environmentally friendly ways to solve the problems that DDT was meant to solve.

It is to this image precisely that Duke University law professor James Boyle appeals when he argues that we need an "environmentalism" for culture.[7] His point, and the point I want to develop in the balance of this chapter, is not that the aims of copyright are flawed. Or that authors should not be paid for their work. Or that music should be given away "for free." The point is that some of the ways in which we might protect authors will have unintended consequences for the cultural environment, much like DDT had for the natural environment. And just as criticism of DDT is not an endorsement of malaria or an attack on farmers, so, too, is criticism of one particular set of regulations protecting copyright not an endorsement of anarchy or an attack on authors. It is an environment of creativity that we seek, and we should be aware of our actions' effects on the environment.

My argument, in the balance of this chapter, tries to map exactly this effect. No doubt the technology of the Internet has had a dramatic effect on the ability of copyright owners to protect their content. But there should also be little doubt that when you add together the changes in copyright law over time, plus the change in technology that the Internet is undergoing just now, the net effect of these changes will not be only that copyrighted work is effectively protected. Also, and generally missed, the net effect of this massive increase in protection will be devastating to the environment for creativity.

In a line: To kill a gnat, we are spraying DDT with consequences for free culture that will be far more devastating than that this gnat will be lost.

Beginnings

America copied English copyright law. Actually, we copied and improved English copyright law. Our Constitution makes the purpose of "creative property" rights clear; its express limitations reinforce the English aim to avoid overly powerful publishers.

The power to establish "creative property" rights is granted to Congress in a way that, for our Constitution, at least, is very odd. Article I, section 8, clause 8 of our Constitution states that:

> Congress has the power to promote the Progress of Science and useful Arts, by securing for limited Times to Authors and Inventors the exclusive Right to their respective Writings and Discoveries.

We can call this the "Progress Clause," for notice what this clause does not say. It does not say Congress has the power to grant "creative property rights." It says that Congress has the power *to promote progress*. The grant of power is its purpose, and its purpose is a public one, not the purpose of enriching publishers, nor even primarily the purpose of rewarding authors.

The Progress Clause expressly limits the term of copyrights. As we saw in chapter 6, the English limited the term of copyright so as to assure that a few would not exercise disproportionate control over culture by exercising disproportionate control over publishing. We can assume the framers followed the English for a similar purpose. Indeed, unlike the English, the framers reinforced that objective, by requiring that copyrights extend "to Authors" only.

The design of the Progress Clause reflects something about the Constitution's design in general. To avoid a problem, the framers built structure. To prevent the concentrated power of publishers, they built a structure that kept copyrights away from publishers and kept them short. To prevent the concentrated power of a church, they banned the federal government from establishing a church. To prevent concentrating power in the federal government, they built structures to reinforce the power of the states—including the Senate, whose members were at the time selected by the states, and an electoral college, also selected by the states, to select the president. In each case, a *structure* built checks and balances into the constitutional frame, structured to prevent otherwise inevitable concentrations of power.

I doubt the framers would recognize the regulation we call "copyright" today. The scope of that regulation is far beyond anything they ever considered. To begin to understand what they did, we need to put our "copyright" in context: We need to see how it has changed in the 210 years since they first struck its design.

Some of these changes come from the law: some in light of changes in technology, and some in light of changes in technology given a particular concentration of market power. In terms of our model, we started here:

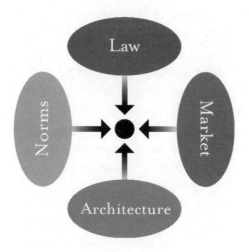

We will end here:

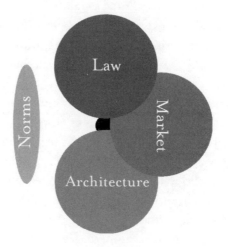

Let me explain how.

Law: Duration

When the first Congress enacted laws to protect creative property, it faced the same uncertainty about the status of creative property that the English had confronted in 1774. Many states had passed laws protecting creative property, and some believed that these laws simply supplemented common law rights that already protected creative authorship.[8] This meant that there was no guaranteed public domain in the United States in 1790. If copyrights were protected by the common law, then there was no simple way to know whether a work published in the United States was controlled or free. Just as in England, this lingering uncertainty would make it hard for publishers to rely upon a public domain to reprint and distribute works.

That uncertainty ended after Congress passed legislation granting copyrights. Because federal law overrides any contrary state law, federal protections for copyrighted works displaced any state law protections. Just as in England the Statute of Anne eventually meant that the copyrights for all English works expired, a federal statute meant that any state copyrights expired as well.

In 1790, Congress enacted the first copyright law. It created a federal copyright and secured that copyright for fourteen years. If the author was alive at the end of that fourteen years, then he could opt to renew the copyright for another fourteen years. If he did not renew the copyright, his work passed into the public domain.

While there were many works created in the United States in the first ten years of the Republic, only 5 percent of the works were actually registered under the federal copyright regime. Of all the work created in the United States both before 1790 and from 1790 through 1800, 95 percent immediately passed into the public domain; the balance would pass into the pubic domain within twenty-eight years at most, and more likely within fourteen years.[9]

This system of renewal was a crucial part of the American system of copyright. It assured that the maximum terms of copyright would be granted only for works where they were wanted. After the initial term of fourteen years, if it wasn't worth it to an author to renew his copyright, then it wasn't worth it to society to insist on the copyright, either.

Fourteen years may not seem long to us, but for the vast majority of copyright owners at that time, it was long enough: Only a small minority of them renewed their copyright after fourteen years; the balance allowed their work to pass into the public domain.[10]

Even today, this structure would make sense. Most creative work has an actual commercial life of just a couple of years. Most books fall out of print after one year.[11] When that happens, the used books are traded free of copyright regulation. Thus the books are no longer *effectively* controlled by copyright. The only practical commercial use of the books at that time is to sell the books as used books; that use—because it does not involve publication—is effectively free.

In the first hundred years of the Republic, the term of copyright was changed once. In 1831, the term was increased from a maximum of 28 years to a maximum of 42 by increasing the initial term of copyright from 14 years to 28 years. In the next fifty years of the Republic, the term increased once again. In 1909, Congress extended the renewal term of 14 years to 28 years, setting a maximum term of 56 years.

Then, beginning in 1962, Congress started a practice that has defined copyright law since. Eleven times in the last forty years, Congress has extended the terms of existing copyrights; twice in those forty years, Congress extended the term of future copyrights. Initially, the extensions of existing copyrights were short, a mere one to two years. In 1976, Congress extended all existing copyrights by nineteen years. And in 1998, in the Sonny Bono Copyright Term Extension Act, Congress extended the term of existing and future copyrights by twenty years.

The effect of these extensions is simply to toll, or delay, the passing of works into the public domain. This latest extension means that the public domain will have been tolled for thirty-nine out of fifty-five years, or 70 percent of the time since 1962. Thus, in the twenty years after the Sonny Bono Act, while one million patents will pass into the public domain, zero copyrights will pass into the public domain by virtue of the expiration of a copyright term.

The effect of these extensions has been exacerbated by another, little-noticed change in the copyright law. Remember I said that the framers established a two-part copyright regime, requiring a copyright owner to renew his copyright after an initial term. The requirement of renewal meant that works that no longer needed copyright protection would pass more quickly into the public domain. The works remaining under protection would be those that had some continuing commercial value.

The United States abandoned this sensible system in 1976. For all works created after 1978, there was only one copyright term—the maximum term. For "natural" authors, that term was life plus fifty years. For corporations, the term was seventy-five years. Then, in 1992, Congress abandoned the renewal requirement for all works created before 1978. All works still under copyright would be accorded the maximum term then available. After the Sonny Bono Act, that term was ninety-five years.

This change meant that American law no longer had an automatic way to assure that works that were no longer exploited passed into the public domain. And indeed, after these changes, it is unclear whether it is even possible to put works into the public domain. The public domain is orphaned by these changes in copyright law. Despite the requirement that terms be "limited," we have no evidence that anything will limit them.

The effect of these changes on the average duration of copyright is dramatic. In 1973, more than 85 percent of copyright owners failed to renew their copyright. That meant that the average term of copyright in 1973 was just 32.2 years. Because of the elimination of the renewal requirement, the average term of copyright is now the maximum term. In thirty years, then, the average term has tripled, from 32.2 years to 95 years.[12]

Law: Scope

The "scope" of a copyright is the range of rights granted by the law. The scope of American copyright has changed dramatically. Those changes are not necessarily bad. But we should understand the extent of the changes if we're to keep this debate in context.

In 1790, that scope was very narrow. Copyright covered only "maps, charts, and books." That means it didn't cover, for example, music or architecture. More significantly, the right granted by a copyright gave the author the exclusive right to "publish" copyrighted works. That means someone else violated the copyright only if he republished the work without the copyright owner's permission. Finally, the right granted by a copyright was an exclusive right to that particular book. The right did not extend to what lawyers call "derivative works." It would not, therefore, interfere with the right of someone other than the author to translate a copyrighted book, or to adapt the story to a different form (such as a drama based on a published book).

This, too, has changed dramatically. While the contours of copyright today are extremely hard to describe simply, in general terms, the right covers practically any creative work that is reduced to a tangible form. It covers music as well as architecture, drama as well as computer programs. It gives the copyright owner of that creative work not only the exclusive right to "publish" the work, but also the exclusive right of control over any "copies" of that work. And most significant for our purposes here, the right gives the copyright owner control over not only his or her particular work, but also any "derivative work" that might grow out of the original work. In this way, the right covers more creative work, protects the creative work more broadly, and protects works that are based in a significant way on the initial creative work.

At the same time that the scope of copyright has expanded, procedural limitations on the right have been relaxed. I've already described the complete removal of the renewal requirement in 1992. In addition to the renewal requirement, for most of the history of American copyright law, there was a requirement that a work be registered before it could receive the protection of a copyright. There was also a requirement that any copyrighted work be marked either with that famous © or the word *copyright*. And for most of the history of American copyright law, there was a requirement that works be deposited with the government before a copyright could be secured.

The reason for the registration requirement was the sensible understanding that for most works, no copyright was required. Again, in the first ten years of the Republic, 95 percent of works eligible for copyright were never copyrighted. Thus, the rule reflected the norm: Most works apparently didn't need copyright, so registration narrowed the regulation of the law to the few that did. The same reasoning justified the requirement that a work be marked as copyrighted—that way it was easy to know whether a copyright was being claimed. The requirement that works be deposited was to assure that after the copyright expired, there would be a copy of the work somewhere so that it could be copied by others without locating the original author.

All of these "formalities" were abolished in the American system when we decided to follow European copyright law. There is no requirement that you register a work to get a copyright; the copyright now is automatic; the copyright exists whether or not you mark your work with a ©; and the copyright exists whether or not you actually make a copy available for others to copy.

Consider a practical example to understand the scope of these differences.

If, in 1790, you wrote a book and you were one of the 5 percent who actually copyrighted that book, then the copyright law protected you against another publisher's taking your book and republishing it without your permission. The aim of the act was to regulate publishers so as to prevent that kind of unfair competition. In 1790, there were 174 publishers in the United States.[13] The Copyright Act was thus a tiny regulation of a tiny proportion of a tiny part of the creative market in the United States—publishers.

The act left other creators totally unregulated. If I copied your poem by hand, over and over again, as a way to learn it by heart, my act was totally unregulated by the 1790 act. If I took your novel and made a play based upon it, or if I translated it or abridged it, none of those activities were regulated by the original copyright act. These creative activities remained free, while the activities of publishers were restrained.

Today the story is very different: If you write a book, your book is automatically protected. Indeed, not just your book. Every e-mail, every note to your spouse, every doodle, *every* creative act that's reduced to a tangible form—all of this is automatically copyrighted. There is no need to register or mark your work. The protection follows the creation, not the steps you take to protect it.

That protection gives you the right (subject to a narrow range of fair use exceptions) to control how others copy the work, whether they copy it to republish it or to share an excerpt.

That much is the obvious part. Any system of copyright would control competing publishing. But there's a second part to the copyright of today that is not at all obvious. This is the protection of "derivative rights." If you write a book, no one can make a movie out of your book without permission. No one can translate it without permission. CliffsNotes can't make an abridgment unless permission is granted. All of these derivative uses of your original work are controlled by the copyright holder. The copyright, in other words, is now not just an exclusive right to your writings, but an exclusive right to your writings and a large proportion of the writings inspired by them.

It is this derivative right that would seem most bizarre to our framers, though it has become second nature to us. Initially, this expansion was created to deal with obvious evasions of a narrower copyright. If I write a book, can you change one word and then claim a copyright in a new and different book? Obviously that would make a joke of the copyright, so the law was properly expanded to include those slight modifications as well as the verbatim original work.

In preventing that joke, the law created an astonishing power within a free culture—at least, it's astonishing when you understand that the law applies not just to the commercial publisher but to anyone with a computer. I understand the wrong in duplicating and selling someone else's work. But whatever *that* wrong is, transforming someone else's work is a different wrong. Some view transformation as no wrong at all—they believe that our law, as the framers penned it, should not protect derivative rights at all.[14] Whether or not you go that far, it seems plain that whatever wrong is involved is fundamentally different from the wrong of direct piracy.

Yet copyright law treats these two different wrongs in the same way. I can go to court and get an injunction against your pirating my book. I can go to court and get an injunction against your transformative use of my book.[15] These two different uses of my creative work are treated the same.

This again may seem right to you. If I wrote a book, then why should you be able to write a movie that takes my story and makes money from it without paying me or crediting me? Or if Disney creates a creature called "Mickey Mouse," why should you be able to make Mickey Mouse toys and be the one to trade on the value that Disney originally created?

These are good arguments, and, in general, my point is not that the derivative right is unjustified. My aim just now is much narrower: simply to make clear that this expansion is a significant change from the rights originally granted.

Law and Architecture: Reach

Whereas originally the law regulated only publishers, the change in copyright's scope means that the law today regulates publishers, users, and authors. It regulates them because all three are capable of making copies, and the core of the regulation of copyright law is copies.[16]

"Copies." That certainly sounds like the obvious thing for *copy*right law to regulate. But as with Jack Valenti's argument at the start of this chapter, that "creative property" deserves the "same rights" as all other property, it is the *obvious* that we need to be most careful about. For while it may be obvious that in the world before the Internet, copies were the obvious trigger for copyright law, upon reflection, it should be obvious that in the world with the Internet, copies should *not* be the trigger for copyright law. More precisely, they should not *always* be the trigger for copyright law.

This is perhaps the central claim of this book, so let me take this very slowly so that the point is not easily missed. My claim is that the Internet should at least force us to rethink the conditions under which the law of copyright automatically applies,[17] because it is clear that the current reach of copyright was never contemplated, much less chosen, by the legislators who enacted copyright law.

We can see this point abstractly by beginning with this largely empty circle.

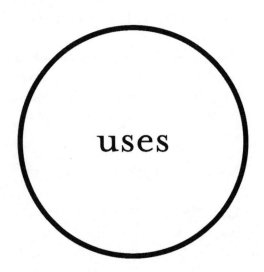

uses

Think about a book in real space, and imagine this circle to represent all its potential *uses*. Most of these uses are unregulated by copyright law, because the uses don't create a copy. If you read a book, that act is not regulated by copyright law. If you give someone the book, that act is not regulated by copyright law. If you resell a book, that act is not regulated (copyright law expressly states that after the first sale of a book, the copyright owner can impose no further conditions on the disposition of the book). If you sleep on the book or use it to hold up a lamp or let your puppy chew it up, those acts are not regulated by copyright law, because those acts do not make a copy.

Obviously, however, some uses of a copyrighted book are regulated by copyright law. Republishing the book, for example, makes a copy. It is therefore regulated by copyright law. Indeed, this particular use stands at the core of this circle of possible uses of a copyrighted work. It is the paradigmatic use properly regulated by copyright regulation (see first diagram on next page).

Finally, there is a tiny sliver of otherwise regulated copying uses that remain unregulated because the law considers these "fair uses."

These are uses that themselves involve copying, but which the law treats as unregulated because public policy demands that they remain unregulated. You are free to quote from this book, even in a review that is quite negative, without my permission, even though that quoting makes a copy. That copy would ordinarily give the copyright owner the exclusive right to say whether the copy is allowed or not, but the law denies the owner any exclusive right over such "fair uses" for public policy (and possibly First Amendment) reasons.

In real space, then, the possible uses of a book are divided into three sorts: (1) unregulated uses, (2) regulated uses, and (3) regulated uses that are nonetheless deemed "fair" regardless of the copyright owner's views.

Enter the Internet—a distributed, digital network where every use of a copyrighted work produces a copy.[18] And because of this single, arbitrary feature of the design of a digital network, the scope of category 1 changes dramatically. Uses that before were presumptively unregulated are now presumptively regulated. No longer is there a set of presumptively unregulated uses that define a freedom associated with a copyrighted work. Instead, each use is now subject to the copyright, because each use also makes a copy—category 1 gets sucked into category 2. And those who would defend the unregulated uses of copyrighted work must look exclusively to category 3, fair uses, to bear the burden of this shift.

So let's be very specific to make this general point clear. Before the Internet, if you purchased a book and read it ten times, there would be no plausible *copyright*-related argument that the copyright owner could make to control that use of her book. Copyright law would have nothing to say about whether you read the book once, ten times, or every night before you went to bed. None of those instances of use—reading—could be regulated by copyright law because none of those uses produced a copy.

But the same book as an e-book is effectively governed by a different set of rules. Now if the copyright owner says you may read the book only once or only once a month, then *copyright law* would aid the copyright owner in exercising this degree of control, because of the accidental feature of copyright law that triggers its application upon there being a copy. Now if you read the book ten times and the license says you may read it only five times, then whenever you read the book (or any portion of it) beyond the fifth time, you are making a copy of the book contrary to the copyright owner's wish.

There are some people who think this makes perfect sense. My aim just now is not to argue about whether it makes sense or not. My aim is only to make clear the change. Once you see this point, a few other points also become clear:

First, making category 1 disappear is not anything any policy maker ever intended. Congress did not think through the collapse of the presumptively unregulated uses of copyrighted works. There is no evidence at all that policy makers had this idea in mind when they allowed our policy here to shift. Unregulated uses were an important part of free culture before the Internet.

Second, this shift is especially troubling in the context of transformative uses of creative content. Again, we can all understand the wrong in commercial piracy. But the law now purports to regulate *any* transformation you make of creative work using a machine. "Copy and paste" and "cut and paste" become crimes. Tinkering with a story and releasing it to others exposes the tinkerer to at least a requirement of justification. However troubling the expansion with respect to copying a particular work, it is extraordinarily troubling with respect to transformative uses of creative work.

Third, this shift from category 1 to category 2 puts an extraordinary burden on category 3 ("fair use") that fair use never before had to bear. If a copyright owner now tried to control how many times I could read a book on-line, the natural response would be to argue that this is a violation of my fair use rights. But there has never been any litigation about whether I have a fair use right to read, because before the Internet, reading did not trigger the application of copyright law and hence the need for a fair use defense. The right to read was effectively protected before because reading was not regulated.

This point about fair use is totally ignored, even by advocates for free culture. We have been cornered into arguing that our rights depend upon fair use—never even addressing the earlier question about the expansion in effective regulation. A thin protection grounded in fair use makes sense when the vast majority of uses are *unregulated.* But when everything becomes presumptively regulated, then the protections of fair use are not enough.

The case of Video Pipeline is a good example. Video Pipeline was in the business of making "trailer" advertisements for movies available to video stores. The video stores displayed the trailers as a way to sell videos. Video Pipeline got the trailers from the film distributors, put the trailers on tape, and sold the tapes to the retail stores.

The company did this for about fifteen years. Then, in 1997, it began to think about the Internet as another way to distribute these previews. The idea was to expand their "selling by sampling" technique by giving on-line stores the same ability to enable "browsing." Just as in a bookstore you can read a few pages of a book before you buy the book, so, too, you would be able to sample a bit from the movie on-line before you bought it.

In 1998, Video Pipeline informed Disney and other film distributors that it intended to distribute the trailers through the Internet (rather than sending the tapes) to distributors of their videos. Two years later, Disney told Video Pipeline to stop. The owner of Video Pipeline asked Disney to talk about the matter—he had built a business on distributing this content as a way to help sell Disney films; he had customers who depended upon his delivering this content. Disney would agree to talk only if Video Pipeline stopped the distribution immediately. Video Pipeline thought it was within their "fair use" rights to distribute the clips as they had. So they filed a lawsuit to ask the court to declare that these rights were in fact their rights.

Disney countersued—for $100 million in damages. Those damages were predicated upon a claim that Video Pipeline had "willfully infringed" on Disney's copyright. When a court makes a finding of willful infringement, it can award damages not on the basis of the actual harm to the copyright owner, but on the basis of an amount set in the statute. Because Video Pipeline had distributed seven hundred clips of Disney movies to enable video stores to sell copies of those movies, Disney was now suing Video Pipeline for $100 million.

Disney has the right to control its property, of course. But the video stores that were selling Disney's films also had some sort of right to be able to sell the films that they had bought from Disney. Disney's claim in court was that the stores were allowed to sell the films and they were permitted to list the titles of the films they were selling, but they were not allowed to show clips of the films as a way of selling them without Disney's permission.

Now, you might think this is a close case, and I think the courts would consider it a close case. My point here is to map the change that gives Disney this power. Before the Internet, Disney couldn't really control how people got access to their content. Once a video was in the marketplace, the "first-sale doctrine" would free the seller to use the video as he wished, including showing portions of it in order to engender sales of the entire movie video. But with the Internet, it becomes possible for Disney to centralize control over access to this content. Because each use of the Internet produces a copy, use on the Internet becomes subject to the copyright owner's control. The technology expands the scope of effective control, because the technology builds a copy into every transaction.

No doubt, a potential is not yet an abuse, and so the potential for control is not yet the abuse of control. Barnes & Noble has the right to say you can't touch a book in their store; property law gives them that right. But the market effectively protects against that abuse. If Barnes & Noble banned browsing, then consumers would choose other bookstores. Competition protects against the extremes. And it may well be (my argument so far does not even question this) that competition would prevent any similar danger when it comes to copyright. Sure, publishers exercising the rights that authors have assigned to them might try to regulate how many times you read a book, or try to stop you from sharing the book with anyone. But in a competitive market such as the book market, the dangers of this happening are quite slight.

Again, my aim so far is simply to map the changes that this changed architecture enables. Enabling technology to enforce the control of copyright means that the control of copyright is no longer defined by balanced policy. The control of copyright is simply what private owners choose. In some contexts, at least, that fact is harmless. But in some contexts it is a recipe for disaster.

Architecture and Law: Force

The disappearance of unregulated uses would be change enough, but a second important change brought about by the Internet magnifies its significance. This second change does not affect the reach of copyright regulation; it affects how such regulation is enforced.

In the world before digital technology, it was generally the law that controlled whether and how someone was regulated by copyright law. The law, meaning a court, meaning a judge: In the end, it was a human, trained in the tradition of the law and cognizant of the balances that tradition embraced, who said whether and how the law would restrict your freedom.

There's a famous story about a battle between the Marx Brothers and Warner Brothers. The Marxes intended to make a parody of

Casablanca. Warner Brothers objected. They wrote a nasty letter to the Marxes, warning them that there would be serious legal consequences if they went forward with their plan.[19]

This led the Marx Brothers to respond in kind. They warned Warner Brothers that the Marx Brothers "were brothers long before you were."[20] The Marx Brothers therefore owned the word *brothers,* and if Warner Brothers insisted on trying to control *Casablanca,* then the Marx Brothers would insist on control over *brothers.*

An absurd and hollow threat, of course, because Warner Brothers, like the Marx Brothers, knew that no court would ever enforce such a silly claim. This extremism was irrelevant to the real freedoms anyone (including Warner Brothers) enjoyed.

On the Internet, however, there is no check on silly rules, because on the Internet, increasingly, rules are enforced not by a human but by a machine: Increasingly, the rules of copyright law, as interpreted by the copyright owner, get built into the technology that delivers copyrighted content. It is code, rather than law, that rules. And the problem with code regulations is that, unlike law, code has no shame. Code would not get the humor of the Marx Brothers. The consequence of that is not at all funny.

Consider the life of my Adobe eBook Reader.

An e-book is a book delivered in electronic form. An Adobe eBook is not a book that Adobe has published; Adobe simply produces the software that publishers use to deliver e-books. It provides the technology, and the publisher delivers the content by using the technology.

On the next page is a picture of an old version of my Adobe eBook Reader.

As you can see, I have a small collection of e-books within this e-book library. Some of these books reproduce content that is in the public domain: *Middlemarch,* for example, is in the public domain. Some of them reproduce content that is not in the public domain: My own book *The Future of Ideas* is not yet within the public domain.

Consider *Middlemarch* first. If you click on my e-book copy of

Middlemarch, you'll see a fancy cover, and then a button at the bottom called Permissions.

If you click on the Permissions button, you'll see a list of the permissions that the publisher purports to grant with this book.

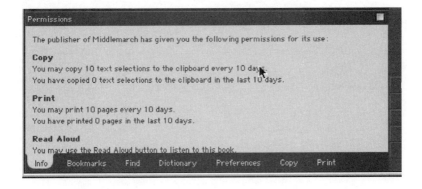

According to my eBook
Reader, I have the permission
to copy to the clipboard of the
computer ten text selections
every ten days. (So far, I've
copied no text to the clipboard.)
I also have the permission to
print ten pages from the book
every ten days. Lastly, I have
the permission to use the Read
Aloud button to hear *Middle-march* read aloud through the
computer.

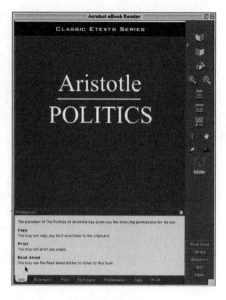

Here's the e-book for another
work in the public domain (in-cluding the translation): Aristo-tle's *Politics*.

According to its permissions, no printing or copying is permitted
at all. But fortunately, you can use the Read Aloud button to hear
the book.

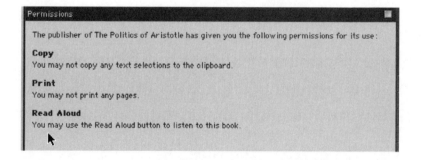

Finally (and most embarrassingly), here are the permissions for the
original e-book version of my last book, *The Future of Ideas*:

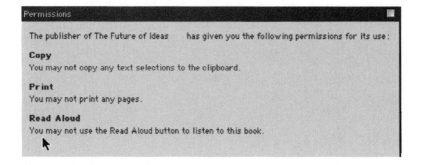

No copying, no printing, and don't you dare try to listen to this book!

Now, the Adobe eBook Reader calls these controls "permissions"— as if the publisher has the power to control how you use these works. For works under copyright, the copyright owner certainly does have the power—up to the limits of the copyright law. But for work not under copyright, there is no such copyright power.[21] When my e-book of *Middlemarch* says I have the permission to copy only ten text selections into the memory every ten days, what that really means is that the eBook Reader has enabled the publisher to control how I use the book on my computer, far beyond the control that the law would enable.

The control comes instead from the code—from the technology within which the e-book "lives." Though the e-book says that these are permissions, they are not the sort of "permissions" that most of us deal with. When a teenager gets "permission" to stay out till midnight, she knows (unless she's Cinderella) that she can stay out till 2 A.M., but will suffer a punishment if she's caught. But when the Adobe eBook Reader says I have the permission to make ten copies of the text into the computer's memory, that means that after I've made ten copies, the computer will not make any more. The same with the printing restrictions: After ten pages, the eBook Reader will not print any more pages. It's the same with the silly restriction that says that you can't use the Read Aloud button to read my book aloud—it's not that the company will sue you if you do; instead, if you push the Read Aloud button with my book, the machine simply won't read aloud.

These are *controls,* not permissions. Imagine a world where the Marx Brothers sold word processing software that, when you tried to type "Warner Brothers," erased "Brothers" from the sentence.

This is the future of copyright law: not so much copyright *law* as copyright *code.* The controls over access to content will not be controls that are ratified by courts; the controls over access to content will be controls that are coded by programmers. And whereas the controls that are built into the law are always to be checked by a judge, the controls that are built into the technology have no similar built-in check.

How significant is this? Isn't it always possible to get around the controls built into the technology? Software used to be sold with technologies that limited the ability of users to copy the software, but those were trivial protections to defeat. Why won't it be trivial to defeat these protections as well?

We've only scratched the surface of this story. Return to the Adobe eBook Reader.

Early in the life of the Adobe eBook Reader, Adobe suffered a public relations nightmare. Among the books that you could download for free on the Adobe site was a copy of *Alice's Adventures in Wonderland.* This wonderful book is in the public domain. Yet when you clicked on Permissions for that book, you got the following report:

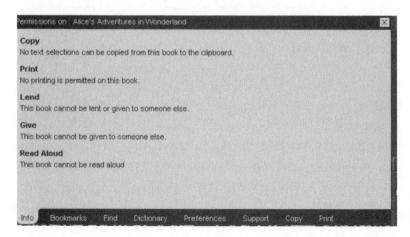

Here was a public domain children's book that you were not allowed to copy, not allowed to lend, not allowed to give, and, as the "permissions" indicated, not allowed to "read aloud"!

The public relations nightmare attached to that final permission. For the text did not say that you were not permitted to use the Read Aloud button; it said you did not have the permission to read the book aloud. That led some people to think that Adobe was restricting the right of parents, for example, to read the book to their children, which seemed, to say the least, absurd.

Adobe responded quickly that it was absurd to think that it was trying to restrict the right to read a book aloud. Obviously it was only restricting the ability to use the Read Aloud button to have the book read aloud. But the question Adobe never did answer is this: Would Adobe thus agree that a consumer was free to use software to hack around the restrictions built into the eBook Reader? If some company (call it Elcomsoft) developed a program to disable the technological protection built into an Adobe eBook so that a blind person, say, could use a computer to read the book aloud, would Adobe agree that such a use of an eBook Reader was fair? Adobe didn't answer because the answer, however absurd it might seem, is no.

The point is not to blame Adobe. Indeed, Adobe is among the most innovative companies developing strategies to balance open access to content with incentives for companies to innovate. But Adobe's technology enables control, and Adobe has an incentive to defend this control. That incentive is understandable, yet what it creates is often crazy.

To see the point in a particularly absurd context, consider a favorite story of mine that makes the same point.

Consider the robotic dog made by Sony named "Aibo." The Aibo learns tricks, cuddles, and follows you around. It eats only electricity and that doesn't leave that much of a mess (at least in your house).

The Aibo is expensive and popular. Fans from around the world have set up clubs to trade stories. One fan in particular set up a Web site to enable information about the Aibo dog to be shared. This fan set up aibopet.com (and aibohack.com, but that resolves to the same site), and on that site he provided information about how to teach an Aibo to do tricks in addition to the ones Sony had taught it.

"Teach" here has a special meaning. Aibos are just cute computers. You teach a computer how to do something by programming it differently. So to say that aibopet.com was giving information about how to teach the dog to do new tricks is just to say that aibopet.com was giving information to users of the Aibo pet about how to hack their computer "dog" to make it do new tricks (thus, aibohack.com).

If you're not a programmer or don't know many programmers, the word *hack* has a particularly unfriendly connotation. Nonprogrammers hack bushes or weeds. Nonprogrammers in horror movies do even worse. But to programmers, or coders, as I call them, *hack* is a much more positive term. *Hack* just means code that enables the program to do something it wasn't originally intended or enabled to do. If you buy a new printer for an old computer, you might find the old computer doesn't run, or "drive," the printer. If you discovered that, you'd later be happy to discover a hack on the Net by someone who has written a driver to enable the computer to drive the printer you just bought.

Some hacks are easy. Some are unbelievably hard. Hackers as a community like to challenge themselves and others with increasingly difficult tasks. There's a certain respect that goes with the talent to hack well. There's a well-deserved respect that goes with the talent to hack ethically.

The Aibo fan was displaying a bit of both when he hacked the program and offered to the world a bit of code that would enable the Aibo to dance jazz. The dog wasn't programmed to dance jazz. It was a clever bit of tinkering that turned the dog into a more talented creature than Sony had built.

I've told this story in many contexts, both inside and outside the United States. Once I was asked by a puzzled member of the audience, is it permissible for a dog to dance jazz in the United States? We forget that stories about the backcountry still flow across much of the world. So let's just be clear before we continue: It's not a crime any-where (anymore) to dance jazz. Nor is it a crime to teach your dog to dance jazz. Nor should it be a crime (though we don't have a lot to go on here) to teach your robot dog to dance jazz. Dancing jazz is a completely legal activity. One imagines that the owner of aibopet.com thought, *What possible problem could there be with teaching a robot dog to dance?*

Let's put the dog to sleep for a minute, and turn to a pony show—not literally a pony show, but rather a paper that a Princeton academic named Ed Felten prepared for a conference. This Princeton academic is well known and respected. He was hired by the government in the Microsoft case to test Microsoft's claims about what could and could not be done with its own code. In that trial, he demonstrated both his brilliance and his coolness. Under heavy badgering by Microsoft lawyers, Ed Felten stood his ground. He was not about to be bullied into being silent about something he knew very well.

But Felten's bravery was really tested in April 2001.[22] He and a group of colleagues were working on a paper to be submitted at conference. The paper was intended to describe the weakness in an encryption system being developed by the Secure Digital Music Initiative as a technique to control the distribution of music.

The SDMI coalition had as its goal a technology to enable content owners to exercise much better control over their content than the Internet, as it originally stood, granted them. Using encryption, SDMI hoped to develop a standard that would allow the content owner to say "this music cannot be copied," and have a computer respect that command. The technology was to be part of a "trusted system" of control that would get content owners to trust the system of the Internet much more.

When SDMI thought it was close to a standard, it set up a competition. In exchange for providing contestants with the code to an SDMI-encrypted bit of content, contestants were to try to crack it and, if they did, report the problems to the consortium.

Felten and his team figured out the encryption system quickly. He and the team saw the weakness of this system as a type: Many encryption systems would suffer the same weakness, and Felten and his team thought it worthwhile to point this out to those who study encryption.

Let's review just what Felten was doing. Again, this is the United States. We have a principle of free speech. We have this principle not just because it is the law, but also because it is a really great idea. A strongly protected tradition of free speech is likely to encourage a wide range of criticism. That criticism is likely, in turn, to improve the systems or people or ideas criticized.

What Felten and his colleagues were doing was publishing a paper describing the weakness in a technology. They were not spreading free music, or building and deploying this technology. The paper was an academic essay, unintelligible to most people. But it clearly showed the weakness in the SDMI system, and why SDMI would not, as presently constituted, succeed.

What links these two, aibopet.com and Felten, is the letters they then received. Aibopet.com received a letter from Sony about the aibopet.com hack. Though a jazz-dancing dog is perfectly legal, Sony wrote:

> Your site contains information providing the means to circumvent AIBO-ware's copy protection protocol constituting a violation of the anti-circumvention provisions of the Digital Millennium Copyright Act.

And though an academic paper describing the weakness in a system of encryption should also be perfectly legal, Felten received a letter from an RIAA lawyer that read:

> Any disclosure of information gained from participating in the Public Challenge would be outside the scope of activities permit-

ted by the Agreement and could subject you and your research team to actions under the Digital Millennium Copyright Act ("DMCA").

In both cases, this weirdly Orwellian law was invoked to control the spread of information. The Digital Millennium Copyright Act made spreading such information an offense.

The DMCA was enacted as a response to copyright owners' first fear about cyberspace. The fear was that copyright control was effectively dead; the response was to find technologies that might compensate. These new technologies would be copyright protection technologies— technologies to control the replication and distribution of copyrighted material. They were designed as *code* to modify the original *code* of the Internet, to reestablish some protection for copyright owners.

The DMCA was a bit of law intended to back up the protection of this code designed to protect copyrighted material. It was, we could say, *legal code* intended to buttress *software code* which itself was intended to support the *legal code of copyright.*

But the DMCA was not designed merely to protect copyrighted works to the extent copyright law protected them. Its protection, that is, did not end at the line that copyright law drew. The DMCA regulated devices that were designed to circumvent copyright protection measures. It was designed to ban those devices, whether or not the use of the copyrighted material made possible by that circumvention would have been a copyright violation.

Aibopet.com and Felten make the point. The Aibo hack circumvented a copyright protection system for the purpose of enabling the dog to dance jazz. That enablement no doubt involved the use of copyrighted material. But as aibopet.com's site was noncommercial, and the use did not enable subsequent copyright infringements, there's no doubt that aibopet.com's hack was fair use of Sony's copyrighted material. Yet fair use is not a defense to the DMCA. The question is not whether the use of the copyrighted material was a copyright violation. The question is whether a copyright protection system was circumvented.

The threat against Felten was more attenuated, but it followed the same line of reasoning. By publishing a paper describing how a copyright protection system could be circumvented, the RIAA lawyer suggested, Felten himself was distributing a circumvention technology. Thus, even though he was not himself infringing anyone's copyright, his academic paper was enabling others to infringe others' copyright.

The bizarreness of these arguments is captured in a cartoon drawn in 1981 by Paul Conrad. At that time, a court in California had held that the VCR could be banned because it was a copyright-infringing technology: It enabled consumers to copy films without the permission of the copyright owner. No doubt there were uses of the technology that were legal: Fred Rogers, aka "Mr. Rogers," for example, had testified in that case that he wanted people to feel free to tape *Mr. Rogers' Neighborhood.*

> Some public stations, as well as commercial stations, program the "Neighborhood" at hours when some children cannot use it. I think that it's a real service to families to be able to record such programs and show them at appropriate times. I have always felt that with the advent of all of this new technology that allows people to tape the "Neighborhood" off-the-air, and I'm speaking for the "Neighborhood" because that's what I produce, that they then become much more active in the programming of their family's television life. Very frankly, I am opposed to people being programmed by others. My whole approach in broadcasting has always been "You are an important person just the way you are. You can make healthy decisions." Maybe I'm going on too long, but I just feel that anything that allows a person to be more active in the control of his or her life, in a healthy way, is important.[23]

Even though there were uses that were legal, because there were some uses that were illegal, the court held the companies producing the VCR responsible.

This led Conrad to draw the cartoon below, which we can adopt to the DMCA.

No argument I have can top this picture, but let me try to get close.

The anticircumvention provisions of the DMCA target copyright circumvention technologies. Circumvention technologies can be used for different ends. They can be used, for example, to enable massive pirating of copyrighted material—a bad end. Or they can be used to enable the use of particular copyrighted materials in ways that would be considered fair use—a good end.

A handgun can be used to shoot a police officer or a child. Most

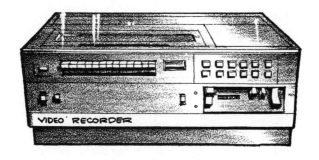

ON WHICH ITEM HAVE THE COURTS RULED THAT MANUFACTURERS AND RETAILERS BE HELD RESPONSIBLE FOR HAVING SUPPLIED THE EQUIPMENT?

would agree such a use is bad. Or a handgun can be used for target practice or to protect against an intruder. At least some would say that such a use would be good. It, too, is a technology that has both good and bad uses.

The obvious point of Conrad's cartoon is the weirdness of a world where guns are legal, despite the harm they can do, while VCRs (and circumvention technologies) are illegal. Flash: *No one ever died from copyright circumvention.* Yet the law bans circumvention technologies absolutely, despite the potential that they might do some good, but permits guns, despite the obvious and tragic harm they do.

The Aibo and RIAA examples demonstrate how copyright owners are changing the balance that copyright law grants. Using code, copyright owners restrict fair use; using the DMCA, they punish those who would attempt to evade the restrictions on fair use that they impose through code. Technology becomes a means by which fair use can be erased; the law of the DMCA backs up that erasing.

This is how *code* becomes *law.* The controls built into the technology of copy and access protection become rules the violation of which is also a violation of the law. In this way, the code extends the law—increasing its regulation, even if the subject it regulates (activities that would otherwise plainly constitute fair use) is beyond the reach of the law. Code becomes law; code extends the law; code thus extends the control that copyright owners effect—at least for those copyright holders with the lawyers who can write the nasty letters that Felten and aibopet.com received.

There is one final aspect of the interaction between architecture and law that contributes to the force of copyright's regulation. This is the ease with which infringements of the law can be detected. For contrary to the rhetoric common at the birth of cyberspace that on the Internet, no one knows you're a dog, increasingly, given changing technologies deployed on the Internet, it is easy to find the dog who committed a legal wrong. The technologies of the Internet are open to snoops as well as sharers, and the snoops are increasingly good at tracking down the identity of those who violate the rules.

For example, imagine you were part of a *Star Trek* fan club. You gathered every month to share trivia, and maybe to enact a kind of fan fiction about the show. One person would play Spock, another, Captain Kirk. The characters would begin with a plot from a real story, then simply continue it.[24]

Before the Internet, this was, in effect, a totally unregulated activity. No matter what happened inside your club room, you would never be interfered with by the copyright police. You were free in that space to do as you wished with this part of our culture. You were allowed to build on it as you wished without fear of legal control.

But if you moved your club onto the Internet, and made it generally available for others to join, the story would be very different. Bots scouring the Net for trademark and copyright infringement would quickly find your site. Your posting of fan fiction, depending upon the ownership of the series that you're depicting, could well inspire a lawyer's threat. And ignoring the lawyer's threat would be extremely costly indeed. The law of copyright is extremely efficient. The penalties are severe, and the process is quick.

This change in the effective force of the law is caused by a change in the ease with which the law can be enforced. That change too shifts the law's balance radically. It is as if your car transmitted the speed at which you traveled at every moment that you drove; that would be just one step before the state started issuing tickets based upon the data you transmitted. That is, in effect, what is happening here.

Market: Concentration

So copyright's duration has increased dramatically—tripled in the past thirty years. And copyright's scope has increased as well—from regulating only publishers to now regulating just about everyone. And copyright's reach has changed, as every action becomes a copy and hence presumptively regulated. And as technologists find better ways to control the use of content, and as copyright is increasingly enforced through technology, copyright's force changes, too. Misuse is easier to find and easier to control. This regulation of the creative process, which began as a tiny regulation governing a tiny part of the market for creative work, has become the single most important regulator of creativity there is. It is a massive expansion in the scope of the government's control over innovation and creativity; it would be totally unrecognizable to those who gave birth to copyright's control.

Still, in my view, all of these changes would not matter much if it weren't for one more change that we must also consider. This is a change that is in some sense the most familiar, though its significance and scope are not well understood. It is the one that creates precisely the reason to be concerned about all the other changes I have described.

This is the change in the concentration and integration of the media. In the past twenty years, the nature of media ownership has undergone a radical alteration, caused by changes in legal rules governing the media. Before this change happened, the different forms of media were owned by separate media companies. Now, the media is increasingly owned by only a few companies. Indeed, after the changes that the FCC announced in June 2003, most expect that within a few years, we will live in a world where just three companies control more than 85 percent of the media.

These changes are of two sorts: the scope of concentration, and its nature.

Changes in scope are the easier ones to describe. As Senator John McCain summarized the data produced in the FCC's review of media ownership, "five companies control 85 percent of our media sources."[25] The five recording labels of Universal Music Group, BMG, Sony Music Entertainment, Warner Music Group, and EMI control 84.8 percent of the U.S. music market.[26] The "five largest cable companies pipe programming to 74 percent of the cable subscribers nationwide."[27]

The story with radio is even more dramatic. Before deregulation, the nation's largest radio broadcasting conglomerate owned fewer than seventy-five stations. Today *one* company owns more than 1,200 stations. During that period of consolidation, the total number of radio owners dropped by 34 percent. Today, in most markets, the two largest broadcasters control 74 percent of that market's revenues. Overall, just four companies control 90 percent of the nation's radio advertising revenues.

Newspaper ownership is becoming more concentrated as well. Today, there are six hundred fewer daily newspapers in the United States than there were eighty years ago, and ten companies control half of the nation's circulation. There are twenty major newspaper publishers in the United States. The top ten film studios receive 99 percent of all film revenue. The ten largest cable companies account for 85 percent of all cable revenue. This is a market far from the free press the framers sought to protect. Indeed, it is a market that is quite well protected— by the market.

Concentration in size alone is one thing. The more invidious change is in the nature of that concentration. As author James Fallows put it in a recent article about Rupert Murdoch,

> Murdoch's companies now constitute a production system unmatched in its integration. They supply content—Fox movies . . . Fox TV shows . . . Fox-controlled sports broadcasts, plus newspapers and books. They sell the content to the public and to advertisers—in newspapers, on the broadcast network, on the cable channels. And they operate the physical distribution system through which the content reaches the customers. Murdoch's satellite systems now distribute News Corp. content in Europe and Asia; if Murdoch becomes DirecTV's largest single owner, that system will serve the same function in the United States.[28]

The pattern with Murdoch is the pattern of modern media. Not just large companies owning many radio stations, but a few companies owning as many outlets of media as possible. A picture describes this pattern better than a thousand words could do:

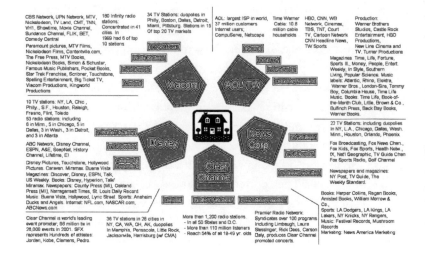

Does this concentration matter? Will it affect what is made, or what is distributed? Or is it merely a more efficient way to produce and distribute content?

My view was that concentration wouldn't matter. I thought it was nothing more than a more efficient financial structure. But now, after reading and listening to a barrage of creators try to convince me to the contrary, I am beginning to change my mind.

Here's a representative story that begins to suggest how this integration may matter.

In 1969, Norman Lear created a pilot for *All in the Family*. He took the pilot to ABC. The network didn't like it. It was too edgy, they told Lear. Make it again. Lear made a second pilot, more edgy than the first. ABC was exasperated. You're missing the point, they told Lear. We wanted less edgy, not more.

Rather than comply, Lear simply took the show elsewhere. CBS was happy to have the series; ABC could not stop Lear from walking. The copyrights that Lear held assured an independence from network control.[29]

The network did not control those copyrights because the law forbade the networks from controlling the content they syndicated. The law required a separation between the networks and the content producers; that separation would guarantee Lear freedom. And as late as 1992, because of these rules, the vast majority of prime time television—75 percent of it—was "independent" of the networks.

In 1994, the FCC abandoned the rules that required this independence. After that change, the networks quickly changed the balance. In 1985, there were twenty-five independent television production studios; in 2002, only five independent television studios remained. "In 1992, only 15 percent of new series were produced for a network by a company it controlled. Last year, the percentage of shows produced by controlled companies more than quintupled to 77 percent." "In 1992, 16 new series were produced independently of conglomerate control, last year there was one."[30] In 2002, 75 percent of prime time television was owned by the networks that ran it. "In the ten-year period between 1992 and 2002, the number of prime time television hours per week produced by network studios increased over 200%, whereas the number of prime time television hours per week produced by independent studios decreased 63%."[31]

Today, another Norman Lear with another *All in the Family* would find that he had the choice either to make the show less edgy or to be fired: The content of any show developed for a network is increasingly owned by the network.

While the number of channels has increased dramatically, the ownership of those channels has narrowed to an ever smaller and smaller few. As Barry Diller said to Bill Moyers,

Well, if you have companies that produce, that finance, that air on their channel and then distribute worldwide everything that goes through their controlled distribution system, then what you get is fewer and fewer actual voices participating in the process. [We u]sed to have dozens and dozens of thriving independent production companies producing television programs. Now you have less than a handful.[32]

This narrowing has an effect on what is produced. The product of such large and concentrated networks is increasingly homogenous. Increasingly safe. Increasingly sterile. The product of news shows from networks like this is increasingly tailored to the message the network wants to convey. This is not the communist party, though from the inside, it must feel a bit like the communist party. No one can question without risk of consequence—not necessarily banishment to Siberia, but punishment nonetheless. Independent, critical, different views are quashed. This is not the environment for a democracy.

Economics itself offers a parallel that explains why this integration affects creativity. Clay Christensen has written about the "Innovator's Dilemma": the fact that large traditional firms find it rational to ignore new, breakthrough technologies that compete with their core business. The same analysis could help explain why large, traditional media companies would find it rational to ignore new cultural trends.[33] Lumbering giants not only don't, but should not, sprint. Yet if the field is only open to the giants, there will be far too little sprinting.

I don't think we know enough about the economics of the media market to say with certainty what concentration and integration will do. The efficiencies are important, and the effect on culture is hard to measure.

But there is a quintessentially obvious example that does strongly suggest the concern.

In addition to the copyright wars, we're in the middle of the drug wars. Government policy is strongly directed against the drug cartels; criminal and civil courts are filled with the consequences of this battle.

Let me hereby disqualify myself from any possible appointment to any position in government by saying I believe this war is a profound mistake. I am not pro drugs. Indeed, I come from a family once wrecked by drugs—though the drugs that wrecked my family were all quite legal. I believe this war is a profound mistake because the collateral damage from it is so great as to make waging the war insane. When you add together the burdens on the criminal justice system, the desperation of generations of kids whose only real economic opportunities are as drug warriors, the queering of constitutional protections because of the constant surveillance this war requires, and, most profoundly, the total destruction of the legal systems of many South American nations because of the power of the local drug cartels, I find it impossible to believe that the marginal benefit in reduced drug consumption by Americans could possibly outweigh these costs.

You may not be convinced. That's fine. We live in a democracy, and it is through votes that we are to choose policy. But to do that, we depend fundamentally upon the press to help inform Americans about these issues.

Beginning in 1998, the Office of National Drug Control Policy launched a media campaign as part of the "war on drugs." The campaign produced scores of short film clips about issues related to illegal drugs. In one series (the Nick and Norm series) two men are in a bar, discussing the idea of legalizing drugs as a way to avoid some of the collateral damage from the war. One advances an argument in favor of drug legalization. The other responds in a powerful and effective way against the argument of the first. In the end, the first guy changes his mind (hey, it's television). The plug at the end is a damning attack on the pro-legalization campaign.

Fair enough. It's a good ad. Not terribly misleading. It delivers its message well. It's a fair and reasonable message.

But let's say you think it is a wrong message, and you'd like to run a countercommercial. Say you want to run a series of ads that try to demonstrate the extraordinary collateral harm that comes from the drug war. Can you do it?

Well, obviously, these ads cost lots of money. Assume you raise the money. Assume a group of concerned citizens donates all the money in the world to help you get your message out. Can you be sure your message will be heard then?

No. You cannot. Television stations have a general policy of avoiding "controversial" ads. Ads sponsored by the government are deemed uncontroversial; ads disagreeing with the government are controversial. This selectivity might be thought inconsistent with the First Amendment, but the Supreme Court has held that stations have the right to choose what they run. Thus, the major channels of commercial media will refuse one side of a crucial debate the opportunity to present its case. And the courts will defend the rights of the stations to be this biased.[34]

I'd be happy to defend the networks' rights, as well—if we lived in a media market that was truly diverse. But concentration in the media throws that condition into doubt. If a handful of companies control access to the media, and that handful of companies gets to decide which political positions it will allow to be promoted on its channels, then in an obvious and important way, concentration matters. You might like the positions the handful of companies selects. But you should not like a world in which a mere few get to decide which issues the rest of us get to know about.

Together

There is something innocent and obvious about the claim of the copyright warriors that the government should "protect my property." In the abstract, it is obviously true and, ordinarily, totally harmless. No sane sort who is not an anarchist could disagree.

But when we see how dramatically this "property" has changed—when we recognize how it might now interact with both technology and markets to mean that the effective constraint on the liberty to cultivate our culture is dramatically different—the claim begins to seem less innocent and obvious. Given (1) the power of technology to supplement the law's control, and (2) the power of concentrated markets to weaken the opportunity for dissent, if strictly enforcing the massively expanded "property" rights granted by copyright fundamentally changes the freedom within this culture to cultivate and build upon our past, then we have to ask whether this property should be redefined.

Not starkly. Or absolutely. My point is not that we should abolish copyright or go back to the eighteenth century. That would be a total mistake, disastrous for the most important creative enterprises within our culture today.

But there is a space between zero and one, Internet culture notwithstanding. And these massive shifts in the effective power of copyright regulation, tied to increased concentration of the content industry and resting in the hands of technology that will increasingly enable control over the use of culture, should drive us to consider whether another adjustment is called for. Not an adjustment that increases copyright's power. Not an adjustment that increases its term. Rather, an adjustment to restore the balance that has traditionally defined copyright's regulation—a weakening of that regulation, to strengthen creativity.

Copyright law has not been a rock of Gibraltar. It's not a set of constant commitments that, for some mysterious reason, teenagers and geeks now flout. Instead, copyright power has grown dramatically in a short period of time, as the technologies of distribution and creation have changed and as lobbyists have pushed for more control by copyright holders. Changes in the past in response to changes in technology suggest that we may well need similar changes in the future. And these changes have to be *reductions* in the scope of copyright, in response to the extraordinary increase in control that technology and the market enable.

For the single point that is lost in this war on pirates is a point that we see only after surveying the range of these changes. When you add together the effect of changing law, concentrated markets, and changing technology, together they produce an astonishing conclusion: *Never in our history have fewer had a legal right to control more of the development of our culture than now.*

Not when copyrights were perpetual, for when copyrights were perpetual, they affected only that precise creative work. Not when only publishers had the tools to publish, for the market then was much more diverse. Not when there were only three television networks, for even then, newspapers, film studios, radio stations, and publishers were independent of the networks. *Never* has copyright protected such a wide range of rights, against as broad a range of actors, for a term that was remotely as long. This form of regulation—a tiny regulation of a tiny part of the creative energy of a nation at the founding—is now a massive regulation of the overall creative process. Law plus technology plus the market now interact to turn this historically benign regulation into the most significant regulation of culture that our free society has known.[35]

This has been a long chapter. Its point can now be briefly stated.

At the start of this book, I distinguished between commercial and noncommercial culture. In the course of this chapter, I have distinguished between copying a work and transforming it. We can now combine these two distinctions and draw a clear map of the changes that copyright law has undergone.

In 1790, the law looked like this:

	PUBLISH	TRANSFORM
Commercial	©	Free
Noncommercial	Free	Free

The act of publishing a map, chart, and book was regulated by copyright law. Nothing else was. Transformations were free. And as copyright attached only with registration, and only those who intended to benefit commercially would register, copying through publishing of noncommercial work was also free.

By the end of the nineteenth century, the law had changed to this:

	PUBLISH	TRANSFORM
Commercial	©	©
Noncommercial	Free	Free

Derivative works were now regulated by copyright law—if published, which again, given the economics of publishing at the time, means if offered commercially. But noncommercial publishing and transformation were still essentially free.

In 1909 the law changed to regulate copies, not publishing, and after this change, the scope of the law was tied to technology. As the technology of copying became more prevalent, the reach of the law expanded. Thus by 1975, as photocopying machines became more common, we could say the law began to look like this:

	COPY	TRANSFORM
Commercial	©	©
Noncommercial	©/Free	Free

The law was interpreted to reach noncommercial copying through, say, copy machines, but still much of copying outside of the commercial market remained free. But the consequence of the emergence of digital technologies, especially in the context of a digital network, means that the law now looks like this:

	COPY	TRANSFORM
Commercial	©	©
Noncommercial	©	©

Every realm is governed by copyright law, whereas before most creativity was not. The law now regulates the full range of creativity—

commercial or not, transformative or not—with the same rules designed to regulate commercial publishers.

Obviously, copyright law is not the enemy. The enemy is regulation that does no good. So the question that we should be asking just now is whether extending the regulations of copyright law into each of these domains actually does any good.

I have no doubt that it does good in regulating commercial copying. But I also have no doubt that it does more harm than good when regulating (as it regulates just now) noncommercial copying and, especially, noncommercial transformation. And increasingly, for the reasons sketched especially in chapters 7 and 8, one might well wonder whether it does more harm than good for commercial transformation. More commercial transformative work would be created if derivative rights were more sharply restricted.

The issue is therefore not simply whether copyright is property. Of course copyright is a kind of "property," and of course, as with any property, the state ought to protect it. But first impressions notwithstanding, historically, this property right (as with all property rights[36]) has been crafted to balance the important need to give authors and artists incentives with the equally important need to assure access to creative work. This balance has always been struck in light of new technologies. And for almost half of our tradition, the "copyright" did not control *at all* the freedom of others to build upon or transform a creative work. American culture was born free, and for almost 180 years our country consistently protected a vibrant and rich free culture.

We achieved that free culture because our law respected important limits on the scope of the interests protected by "property." The very birth of "copyright" as a statutory right recognized those limits, by granting copyright owners protection for a limited time only (the story of chapter 6). The tradition of "fair use" is animated by a similar concern that is increasingly under strain as the costs of exercising any fair use right become unavoidably high (the story of chapter 7). Adding statutory rights where markets might stifle innovation is another familiar limit on the property right that copyright is (chapter 8). And granting archives and libraries a broad freedom to collect, claims of property notwithstanding, is a crucial part of guaranteeing the soul of a culture (chapter 9). Free cultures, like free markets, are built with property. But the nature of the property that builds a free culture is very different from the extremist vision that dominates the debate today.

Free culture is increasingly the casualty in this war on piracy. In response to a real, if not yet quantified, threat that the technologies of the Internet present to twentieth-century business models for producing and distributing culture, the law and technology are being transformed in a way that will undermine our tradition of free culture. The property right that is copyright is no longer the balanced right that it was, or was intended to be. The property right that is copyright has become unbalanced, tilted toward an extreme. The opportunity to create and transform becomes weakened in a world in which creation requires permission and creativity must check with a lawyer.

PUZZLES

CHAPTER ELEVEN: Chimera

In a well-known short story by H. G. Wells, a mountain climber named Nunez trips (literally, down an ice slope) into an unknown and isolated valley in the Peruvian Andes.[1] The valley is extraordinarily beautiful, with "sweet water, pasture, an even climate, slopes of rich brown soil with tangles of a shrub that bore an excellent fruit." But the villagers are all blind. Nunez takes this as an opportunity. "In the Country of the Blind," he tells himself, "the One-Eyed Man is King." So he resolves to live with the villagers to explore life as a king.

Things don't go quite as he planned. He tries to explain the idea of sight to the villagers. They don't understand. He tells them they are "blind." They don't have the word *blind*. They think he's just thick. Indeed, as they increasingly notice the things he can't do (hear the sound of grass being stepped on, for example), they increasingly try to control him. He, in turn, becomes increasingly frustrated. "'You don't understand,' he cried, in a voice that was meant to be great and resolute, and which broke. 'You are blind and I can see. Leave me alone!'"

The villagers don't leave him alone. Nor do they see (so to speak) the virtue of his special power. Not even the ultimate target of his affection, a young woman who to him seems "the most beautiful thing in the whole of creation," understands the beauty of sight. Nunez's description of what he sees "seemed to her the most poetical of fancies, and she listened to his description of the stars and the mountains and her own sweet white-lit beauty as though it was a guilty indulgence." "She did not believe," Wells tells us, and "she could only half understand, but she was mysteriously delighted."

When Nunez announces his desire to marry his "mysteriously delighted" love, the father and the village object. "You see, my dear," her father instructs, "he's an idiot. He has delusions. He can't do anything right." They take Nunez to the village doctor.

After a careful examination, the doctor gives his opinion. "His brain is affected," he reports.

"What affects it?" the father asks.

"Those queer things that are called the eyes . . . are diseased . . . in such a way as to affect his brain."

The doctor continues: "I think I may say with reasonable certainty that in order to cure him completely, all that we need to do is a simple and easy surgical operation—namely, to remove these irritant bodies [the eyes]."

"Thank Heaven for science!" says the father to the doctor. They inform Nunez of this condition necessary for him to be allowed his bride. (You'll have to read the original to learn what happens in the end. I believe in free culture, but never in giving away the end of a story.)

It sometimes happens that the eggs of twins fuse in the mother's womb. That fusion produces a "chimera." A chimera is a single creature with two sets of DNA. The DNA in the blood, for example, might be different from the DNA of the skin. This possibility is an underused plot for murder mysteries. "But the DNA shows with 100 percent certainty that she was not the person whose blood was at the scene. . . ."

Before I had read about chimeras, I would have said they were impossible. A single person can't have two sets of DNA. The very idea of DNA is that it is the code of an individual. Yet in fact, not only can two individuals have the same set of DNA (identical twins), but one person can have two different sets of DNA (a chimera). Our understanding of a "person" should reflect this reality.

The more I work to understand the current struggle over copyright and culture, which I've sometimes called unfairly, and sometimes not unfairly enough, "the copyright wars," the more I think we're dealing with a chimera. For example, in the battle over the question "What is p2p file sharing?" both sides have it right, and both sides have it wrong. One side says, "File sharing is just like two kids taping each others' records—the sort of thing we've been doing for the last thirty years without any question at all." That's true, at least in part. When I tell my best friend to try out a new CD that I've bought, but rather than just send the CD, I point him to my p2p server, that is, in all relevant respects, just like what every executive in every recording company no doubt did as a kid: sharing music.

But the description is also false in part. For when my p2p server is on a p2p network through which anyone can get access to my music, then sure, my friends can get access, but it stretches the meaning of "friends" beyond recognition to say "my ten thousand best friends" can get access. Whether or not sharing my music with my best friend is what "we have always been allowed to do," we have not always been allowed to share music with "our ten thousand best friends."

Likewise, when the other side says, "File sharing is just like walking into a Tower Records and taking a CD off the shelf and walking out with it," that's true, at least in part. If, after Lyle Lovett (finally) releases a new album, rather than buying it, I go to Kazaa and find a free copy to take, that is very much like stealing a copy from Tower.

But it is not quite stealing from Tower. After all, when I take a CD from Tower Records, Tower has one less CD to sell. And when I take a CD from Tower Records, I get a bit of plastic and a cover, and something to show on my shelves. (And, while we're at it, we could also note that when I take a CD from Tower Records, the maximum fine that might be imposed on me, under California law, at least, is $1,000. According to the RIAA, by contrast, if I download a ten-song CD, I'm liable for $1,500,000 in damages.)

The point is not that it is as neither side describes. The point is that it is both—both as the RIAA describes it and as Kazaa describes it. It is a chimera. And rather than simply denying what the other side asserts, we need to begin to think about how we should respond to this chimera. What rules should govern it?

We could respond by simply pretending that it is not a chimera. We could, with the RIAA, decide that every act of file sharing should be a felony. We could prosecute families for millions of dollars in damages just because file sharing occurred on a family computer. And we can get universities to monitor all computer traffic to make sure that no computer is used to commit this crime. These responses might be extreme, but each of them has either been proposed or actually implemented.[2]

Alternatively, we could respond to file sharing the way many kids act as though we've responded. We could totally legalize it. Let there be no copyright liability, either civil or criminal, for making copyrighted content available on the Net. Make file sharing like gossip: regulated, if at all, by social norms but not by law.

Either response is possible. I think either would be a mistake. Rather than embrace one of these two extremes, we should embrace something that recognizes the truth in both. And while I end this book with a sketch of a system that does just that, my aim in the next chapter is to show just how awful it would be for us to adopt the zero-tolerance extreme. I believe *either* extreme would be worse than a reasonable alternative. But I believe the zero-tolerance solution would be the worse of the two extremes.

Yet zero tolerance is increasingly our government's policy. In the middle of the chaos that the Internet has created, an extraordinary land grab is occurring. The law and technology are being shifted to give content holders a kind of control over our culture that they have never had before. And in this extremism, many an opportunity for new innovation and new creativity will be lost.

I'm not talking about the opportunities for kids to "steal" music. My focus instead is the commercial and cultural innovation that this war will also kill. We have never seen the power to innovate spread so broadly among our citizens, and we have just begun to see the innovation that this power will unleash. Yet the Internet has already seen the passing of one cycle of innovation around technologies to distribute content. The law is responsible for this passing. As the vice president for global public policy at one of these new innovators, eMusic.com, put it when criticizing the DMCA's added protection for copyrighted material,

> eMusic opposes music piracy. We are a distributor of copyrighted material, and we want to protect those rights.
>
> But building a technology fortress that locks in the clout of the major labels is by no means the only way to protect copyright interests, nor is it necessarily the best. It is simply too early to answer that question. Market forces operating naturally may very well produce a totally different industry model.
>
> This is a critical point. The choices that industry sectors make with respect to these systems will in many ways directly shape the market for digital media and the manner in which digital media are distributed. This in turn will directly influence the options that are available to consumers, both in terms of the ease with which they will be able to access digital media and the equipment that they will require to do so. Poor choices made this early in the game will retard the growth of this market, hurting everyone's interests.[3]

In April 2001, eMusic.com was purchased by Vivendi Universal, one of "the major labels." Its position on these matters has now changed.

Reversing our tradition of tolerance now will not merely quash piracy. It will sacrifice values that are important to this culture, and will kill opportunities that could be extraordinarily valuable.

CHAPTER TWELVE: Harms

To fight "piracy," to protect "property," the content industry has launched a war. Lobbying and lots of campaign contributions have now brought the government into this war. As with any war, this one will have both direct and collateral damage. As with any war of prohibition, these damages will be suffered most by our own people.

My aim so far has been to describe the consequences of this war, in particular, the consequences for "free culture." But my aim now is to extend this description of consequences into an argument. Is this war justified?

In my view, it is not. There is no good reason why this time, for the first time, the law should defend the old against the new, just when the power of the property called "intellectual property" is at its greatest in our history.

Yet "common sense" does not see it this way. Common sense is still on the side of the Causbys and the content industry. The extreme claims of control in the name of property still resonate; the uncritical rejection of "piracy" still has play.

There will be many consequences of continuing this war. I want to describe just three. All three might be said to be unintended. I am quite confident the third is unintended. I'm less sure about the first two. The first two protect modern RCAs, but there is no Howard Armstrong in the wings to fight today's monopolists of culture.

Constraining Creators

In the next ten years we will see an explosion of digital technologies. These technologies will enable almost anyone to capture and share content. Capturing and sharing content, of course, is what humans have done since the dawn of man. It is how we learn and communicate. But capturing and sharing through digital technology is different. The fidelity and power are different. You could send an e-mail telling someone about a joke you saw on Comedy Central, or you could send the clip. You could write an essay about the inconsistencies in the arguments of the politician you most love to hate, or you could make a short film that puts statement against statement. You could write a poem to express your love, or you could weave together a string—a mash-up— of songs from your favorite artists in a collage and make it available on the Net.

This digital "capturing and sharing" is in part an extension of the capturing and sharing that has always been integral to our culture, and in part it is something new. It is continuous with the Kodak, but it explodes the boundaries of Kodak-like technologies. The technology of digital "capturing and sharing" promises a world of extraordinarily diverse creativity that can be easily and broadly shared. And as that creativity is applied to democracy, it will enable a broad range of citizens to use technology to express and criticize and contribute to the culture all around.

Technology has thus given us an opportunity to do something with culture that has only ever been possible for individuals in small groups, isolated from others. Think about an old man telling a story to a collection of neighbors in a small town. Now imagine that same storytelling extended across the globe.

Yet all this is possible only if the activity is presumptively legal. In the current regime of legal regulation, it is not. Forget file sharing for a moment. Think about your favorite amazing sites on the Net. Web sites that offer plot summaries from forgotten television shows; sites that catalog cartoons from the 1960s; sites that mix images and sound to criticize politicians or businesses; sites that gather newspaper articles on remote topics of science or culture. There is a vast amount of creative work spread across the Internet. But as the law is currently crafted, this work is presumptively illegal.

That presumption will increasingly chill creativity, as the examples of extreme penalties for vague infringements continue to proliferate. It is impossible to get a clear sense of what's allowed and what's not, and at the same time, the penalties for crossing the line are astonishingly harsh. The four students who were threatened by the RIAA (Jesse Jordan of chapter 3 was just one) were threatened with a $98 billion lawsuit for building search engines that permitted songs to be copied. Yet World-Com—which defrauded investors of $11 billion, resulting in a loss to investors in market capitalization of over $200 billion—received a fine of a mere $750 million.[1] And under legislation being pushed in Congress right now, a doctor who negligently removes the wrong leg in an operation would be liable for no more than $250,000 in damages for pain and suffering.[2] Can common sense recognize the absurdity in a world where the maximum fine for downloading two songs off the Internet is more than the fine for a doctor's negligently butchering a patient?

The consequence of this legal uncertainty, tied to these extremely high penalties, is that an extraordinary amount of creativity will either never be exercised, or never be exercised in the open. We drive this creative process underground by branding the modern-day Walt Disneys "pirates." We make it impossible for businesses to rely upon a public domain, because the boundaries of the public domain are designed to be unclear. It never pays to do anything except pay for the right to create, and hence only those who can pay are allowed to create. As was the case in the Soviet Union, though for very different reasons, we will begin to see a world of underground art—not because the message is necessarily political, or because the subject is controversial, but because the very act of creating the art is legally fraught. Already, exhibits of "illegal art" tour the United States.[3] In what does their "illegality" consist? In the act of mixing the culture around us with an expression that is critical or reflective.

Part of the reason for this fear of illegality has to do with the changing law. I described that change in detail in chapter 10. But an even bigger part has to do with the increasing ease with which infractions can be tracked. As users of file-sharing systems discovered in 2002, it is a trivial matter for copyright owners to get courts to order Internet service providers to reveal who has what content. It is as if your cassette tape player transmitted a list of the songs that you played in the privacy of your own home that anyone could tune into for whatever reason they chose.

Never in our history has a painter had to worry about whether his painting infringed on someone else's work; but the modern-day painter, using the tools of Photoshop, sharing content on the Web, must worry all the time. Images are all around, but the only safe images to use in the act of creation are those purchased from Corbis or another image farm. And in purchasing, censoring happens. There is a free market in pencils; we needn't worry about its effect on creativity. But there is a highly regulated, monopolized market in cultural icons; the right to cultivate and transform them is not similarly free.

Lawyers rarely see this because lawyers are rarely empirical. As I described in chapter 7, in response to the story about documentary filmmaker Jon Else, I have been lectured again and again by lawyers who insist Else's use was fair use, and hence I am wrong to say that the law regulates such a use.

But fair use in America simply means the right to hire a lawyer to defend your right to create. And as lawyers love to forget, our system for defending rights such as fair use is astonishingly bad—in practically every context, but especially here. It costs too much, it delivers too slowly, and what it delivers often has little connection to the justice underlying the claim. The legal system may be tolerable for the very rich. For everyone else, it is an embarrassment to a tradition that prides itself on the rule of law.

Judges and lawyers can tell themselves that fair use provides adequate "breathing room" between regulation by the law and the access the law should allow. But it is a measure of how out of touch our legal system has become that anyone actually believes this. The rules that publishers impose upon writers, the rules that film distributors impose upon filmmakers, the rules that newspapers impose upon journalists— these are the real laws governing creativity. And these rules have little relationship to the "law" with which judges comfort themselves.

For in a world that threatens $150,000 for a single willful infringement of a copyright, and which demands tens of thousands of dollars to even defend against a copyright infringement claim, and which would never return to the wrongfully accused defendant anything of the costs she suffered to defend her right to speak—in that world, the astonishingly broad regulations that pass under the name "copyright" silence speech and creativity. And in that world, it takes a studied blindness for people to continue to believe they live in a culture that is free.

As Jed Horovitz, the businessman behind Video Pipeline, said to me,

We're losing [creative] opportunities right and left. Creative people are being forced not to express themselves. Thoughts are not being expressed. And while a lot of stuff may [still] be created, it still won't get distributed. Even if the stuff gets made . . . you're not going to get it distributed in the mainstream media unless you've got a little note from a lawyer saying, "This has been cleared." You're not even going to get it on PBS without that kind of permission. That's the point at which they control it.

Constraining Innovators

The story of the last section was a crunchy-lefty story—creativity quashed, artists who can't speak, yada yada yada. Maybe that doesn't get you going. Maybe you think there's enough weird art out there, and enough expression that is critical of what seems to be just about everything. And if you think that, you might think there's little in this story to worry you.

But there's an aspect of this story that is not lefty in any sense. Indeed, it is an aspect that could be written by the most extreme pro-market ideologue. And if you're one of these sorts (and a special one at that, 188 pages into a book like this), then you can see this other aspect by substituting "free market" every place I've spoken of "free culture." The point is the same, even if the interests affecting culture are more fundamental.

The charge I've been making about the regulation of culture is the same charge free marketers make about regulating markets. Everyone, of course, concedes that some regulation of markets is necessary—at a minimum, we need rules of property and contract, and courts to enforce both. Likewise, in this culture debate, everyone concedes that at least some framework of copyright is also required. But both perspectives vehemently insist that just because some regulation is good, it doesn't follow that more regulation is better. And both perspectives are constantly attuned to the ways in which regulation simply enables the powerful industries of today to protect themselves against the competitors of tomorrow.

This is the single most dramatic effect of the shift in regulatory strategy that I described in chapter 10. The consequence of this massive threat of liability tied to the murky boundaries of copyright law is that innovators who want to innovate in this space can safely innovate only if they have the sign-off from last generation's dominant industries. That lesson has been taught through a series of cases that were designed and executed to teach venture capitalists a lesson. That lesson—what former Napster CEO Hank Barry calls a "nuclear pall" that has fallen over the Valley—has been learned.

Consider one example to make the point, a story whose beginning I told in *The Future of Ideas* and which has progressed in a way that even I (pessimist extraordinaire) would never have predicted.

In 1997, Michael Roberts launched a company called MP3.com. MP3.com was keen to remake the music business. Their goal was not just to facilitate new ways to get access to content. Their goal was also to facilitate new ways to create content. Unlike the major labels, MP3.com offered creators a venue to distribute their creativity, without demanding an exclusive engagement from the creators.

To make this system work, however, MP3.com needed a reliable way to recommend music to its users. The idea behind this alternative was to leverage the revealed preferences of music listeners to recommend new artists. If you like Lyle Lovett, you're likely to enjoy Bonnie Raitt. And so on.

This idea required a simple way to gather data about user preferences. MP3.com came up with an extraordinarily clever way to gather this preference data. In January 2000, the company launched a service called my.mp3.com. Using software provided by MP3.com, a user would sign into an account and then insert into her computer a CD. The software would identify the CD, and then give the user access to that content. So, for example, if you inserted a CD by Jill Sobule, then wherever you were—at work or at home—you could get access to that music once you signed into your account. The system was therefore a kind of music-lockbox.

No doubt some could use this system to illegally copy content. But that opportunity existed with or without MP3.com. The aim of the my.mp3.com service was to give users access to their own content, and as a by-product, by seeing the content they already owned, to discover the kind of content the users liked.

To make this system function, however, MP3.com needed to copy 50,000 CDs to a server. (In principle, it could have been the user who uploaded the music, but that would have taken a great deal of time, and would have produced a product of questionable quality.) It therefore purchased 50,000 CDs from a store, and started the process of making copies of those CDs. Again, it would not serve the content from those copies to anyone except those who authenticated that they had a copy of the CD they wanted to access. So while this was 50,000 copies, it was 50,000 copies directed at giving customers something they had already bought.

Nine days after MP3.com launched its service, the five major labels, headed by the RIAA, brought a lawsuit against MP3.com. MP3.com settled with four of the five. Nine months later, a federal judge found MP3.com to have been guilty of willful infringement with respect to the fifth. Applying the law as it is, the judge imposed a fine against MP3.com of $118 million. MP3.com then settled with the remaining plaintiff, Vivendi Universal, paying over $54 million. Vivendi purchased MP3.com just about a year later.

That part of the story I have told before. Now consider its conclusion.

After Vivendi purchased MP3.com, Vivendi turned around and filed a malpractice lawsuit against the lawyers who had advised it that they had a good faith claim that the service they wanted to offer would be considered legal under copyright law. This lawsuit alleged that it should have been obvious that the courts would find this behavior illegal; therefore, this lawsuit sought to punish any lawyer who had dared to suggest that the law was less restrictive than the labels demanded.

The clear purpose of this lawsuit (which was settled for an unspecified amount shortly after the story was no longer covered in the press) was to send an unequivocal message to lawyers advising clients in this space: It is not just your clients who might suffer if the content industry directs its guns against them. It is also you. So those of you who believe the law should be less restrictive should realize that such a view of the law will cost you and your firm dearly.

This strategy is not just limited to the lawyers. In April 2003, Universal and EMI brought a lawsuit against Hummer Winblad, the venture capital firm (VC) that had funded Napster at a certain stage of its development, its cofounder (John Hummer), and general partner (Hank Barry).[4] The claim here, as well, was that the VC should have recognized the right of the content industry to control how the industry should develop. They should be held personally liable for funding a company whose business turned out to be beyond the law. Here again, the aim of the lawsuit is transparent: Any VC now recognizes that if you fund a company whose business is not approved of by the dinosaurs, you are at risk not just in the marketplace, but in the courtroom as well. Your investment buys you not only a company, it also buys you a lawsuit.

So extreme has the environment become that even car manufacturers are afraid of technologies that touch content. In an article in *Business 2.0*, Rafe Needleman describes a discussion with BMW:

> I asked why, with all the storage capacity and computer power in the car, there was no way to play MP3 files. I was told that BMW engineers in Germany had rigged a new vehicle to play MP3s via the car's built-in sound system, but that the company's marketing and legal departments weren't comfortable with pushing this forward for release stateside. Even today, no new cars are sold in the United States with bona fide MP3 players. . . . [5]

This is the world of the mafia—filled with "your money or your life" offers, governed in the end not by courts but by the threats that the law empowers copyright holders to exercise. It is a system that will obviously and necessarily stifle new innovation. It is hard enough to start a company. It is impossibly hard if that company is constantly threatened by litigation.

The point is not that businesses should have a right to start illegal enterprises. The point is the definition of "illegal." The law is a mess of uncertainty. We have no good way to know how it should apply to new technologies. Yet by reversing our tradition of judicial deference, and by embracing the astonishingly high penalties that copyright law imposes, that uncertainty now yields a reality which is far more conservative than is right. If the law imposed the death penalty for parking tickets, we'd not only have fewer parking tickets, we'd also have much less driving. The same principle applies to innovation. If innovation is constantly checked by this uncertain and unlimited liability, we will have much less vibrant innovation and much less creativity.

The point is directly parallel to the crunchy-lefty point about fair use. Whatever the "real" law is, realism about the effect of law in both contexts is the same. This wildly punitive system of regulation will systematically stifle creativity and innovation. It will protect some industries and some creators, but it will harm industry and creativity generally. Free market and free culture depend upon vibrant competition. Yet the effect of the law today is to stifle just this kind of competition. The effect is to produce an overregulated culture, just as the effect of too much control in the market is to produce an overregulated-regulated market.

The building of a permission culture, rather than a free culture, is the first important way in which the changes I have described will burden innovation. A permission culture means a lawyer's culture—a culture in which the ability to create requires a call to your lawyer. Again, I am not antilawyer, at least when they're kept in their proper place. I am certainly not antilaw. But our profession has lost the sense of its limits. And leaders in our profession have lost an appreciation of the high costs that our profession imposes upon others. The inefficiency of the law is an embarrassment to our tradition. And while I believe our profession should therefore do everything it can to make the law more efficient, it should at least do everything it can to limit the reach of the law where the law is not doing any good. The transaction costs buried within a permission culture are enough to bury a wide range of creativity. Someone needs to do a lot of justifying to justify that result.

The uncertainty of the law is one burden on innovation. There is a second burden that operates more directly. This is the effort by many in the content industry to use the law to directly regulate the technology of the Internet so that it better protects their content. The motivation for this response is obvious. The Internet enables the efficient spread of content. That efficiency is a feature of the Internet's design. But from the perspective of the content industry, this feature is a "bug." The efficient spread of content means that content distributors have a harder time controlling the distribution of content. One obvious response to this efficiency is thus to make the Internet less efficient. If the Internet enables "piracy," then, this response says, we should break the kneecaps of the Internet.

The examples of this form of legislation are many. At the urging of the content industry, some in Congress have threatened legislation that would require computers to determine whether the content they access is protected or not, and to disable the spread of protected content.[6] Congress has already launched proceedings to explore a mandatory "broadcast flag" that would be required on any device capable of transmitting digital video (i.e., a computer), and that would disable the copying of any content that is marked with a broadcast flag. Other members of Congress have proposed immunizing content providers from liability for technology they might deploy that would hunt down copyright violators and disable their machines.[7]

In one sense, these solutions seem sensible. If the problem is the code, why not regulate the code to remove the problem. But any regulation of technical infrastructure will always be tuned to the particular technology of the day. It will impose significant burdens and costs on the technology, but will likely be eclipsed by advances around exactly those requirements.

In March 2002, a broad coalition of technology companies, led by Intel, tried to get Congress to see the harm that such legislation would impose.[8] Their argument was obviously not that copyright should not be protected. Instead, they argued, any protection should not do more harm than good.

There is one more obvious way in which this war has harmed innovation—again, a story that will be quite familiar to the free market crowd.

Copyright may be property, but like all property, it is also a form of regulation. It is a regulation that benefits some and harms others. When done right, it benefits creators and harms leeches. When done wrong, it is regulation the powerful use to defeat competitors.

As I described in chapter 10, despite this feature of copyright as regulation, and subject to important qualifications outlined by Jessica Litman in her book *Digital Copyright*,[9] overall this history of copyright is not bad. As chapter 10 details, when new technologies have come along, Congress has struck a balance to assure that the new is protected from the old. Compulsory, or statutory, licenses have been one part of that strategy. Free use (as in the case of the VCR) has been another.

But that pattern of deference to new technologies has now changed with the rise of the Internet. Rather than striking a balance between the claims of a new technology and the legitimate rights of content creators, both the courts and Congress have imposed legal restrictions that will have the effect of smothering the new to benefit the old.

The response by the courts has been fairly universal.[10] It has been mirrored in the responses threatened and actually implemented by Congress. I won't catalog all of those responses here.[11] But there is one example that captures the flavor of them all. This is the story of the demise of Internet radio.

As I described in chapter 4, when a radio station plays a song, the recording artist doesn't get paid for that "radio performance" unless he or she is also the composer. So, for example if Marilyn Monroe had recorded a version of "Happy Birthday"—to memorialize her famous performance before President Kennedy at Madison Square Garden—then whenever that recording was played on the radio, the current copyright owners of "Happy Birthday" would get some money, whereas Marilyn Monroe would not.

The reasoning behind this balance struck by Congress makes some sense. The justification was that radio was a kind of advertising. The recording artist thus benefited because by playing her music, the radio station was making it more likely that her records would be purchased. Thus, the recording artist got something, even if only indirectly. Probably this reasoning had less to do with the result than with the power of radio stations: Their lobbyists were quite good at stopping any efforts to get Congress to require compensation to the recording artists.

Enter Internet radio. Like regular radio, Internet radio is a technology to stream content from a broadcaster to a listener. The broadcast travels across the Internet, not across the ether of radio spectrum. Thus, I can "tune in" to an Internet radio station in Berlin while sitting in San Francisco, even though there's no way for me to tune in to a regular radio station much beyond the San Francisco metropolitan area.

This feature of the architecture of Internet radio means that there are potentially an unlimited number of radio stations that a user could tune in to using her computer, whereas under the existing architecture for broadcast radio, there is an obvious limit to the number of broadcasters and clear broadcast frequencies. Internet radio could therefore be more competitive than regular radio; it could provide a wider range of selections. And because the potential audience for Internet radio is the whole world, niche stations could easily develop and market their content to a relatively large number of users worldwide. According to some estimates, more than eighty million users worldwide have tuned in to this new form of radio.

Internet radio is thus to radio what FM was to AM. It is an improvement potentially vastly more significant than the FM improvement over AM, since not only is the technology better, so, too, is the competition. Indeed, there is a direct parallel between the fight to establish FM radio and the fight to protect Internet radio. As one author describes Howard Armstrong's struggle to enable FM radio,

> An almost unlimited number of FM stations was possible in the shortwaves, thus ending the unnatural restrictions imposed on radio in the crowded longwaves. If FM were freely developed, the number of stations would be limited only by economics and competition rather than by technical restrictions. . . . Armstrong likened the situation that had grown up in radio to that following the invention of the printing press, when governments and ruling interests attempted to control this new instrument of mass communications by imposing restrictive licenses on it. This tyranny was broken only when it became possible for men freely to acquire printing presses and freely to run them. FM in this sense was as great an invention as the printing presses, for it gave radio the opportunity to strike off its shackles.[12]

This potential for FM radio was never realized—not because Armstrong was wrong about the technology, but because he underestimated the power of "vested interests, habits, customs and legislation"[13] to retard the growth of this competing technology.

Now the very same claim could be made about Internet radio. For again, there is no technical limitation that could restrict the number of Internet radio stations. The only restrictions on Internet radio are those imposed by the law. Copyright law is one such law. So the first question we should ask is, what copyright rules would govern Internet radio?

But here the power of the lobbyists is reversed. Internet radio is a new industry. The recording artists, on the other hand, have a very powerful lobby, the RIAA. Thus when Congress considered the phenomenon of Internet radio in 1995, the lobbyists had primed Congress to adopt a different rule for Internet radio than the rule that applies to terrestrial radio. While terrestrial radio does not have to pay our hypothetical Marilyn Monroe when it plays her hypothetical recording of "Happy Birthday" on the air, *Internet radio does.* Not only is the law not neutral toward Internet radio—the law actually burdens Internet radio more than it burdens terrestrial radio.

This financial burden is not slight. As Harvard law professor William Fisher estimates, if an Internet radio station distributed ad-free popular music to (on average) ten thousand listeners, twenty-four hours a day, the total artist fees that radio station would owe would be over $1 million a year.[14] A regular radio station broadcasting the same content would pay no equivalent fee.

The burden is not financial only. Under the original rules that were proposed, an Internet radio station (but not a terrestrial radio station) would have to collect the following data from *every listening transaction:*

1. name of the service;
2. channel of the program (AM/FM stations use station ID);
3. type of program (archived/looped/live);
4. date of transmission;
5. time of transmission;
6. time zone of origination of transmission;
7. numeric designation of the place of the sound recording within the program;
8. duration of transmission (to nearest second);
9. sound recording title;
10. ISRC code of the recording;
11. release year of the album per copyright notice and in the case of compilation albums, the release year of the album and copyright date of the track;
12. featured recording artist;

13. retail album title;
14. recording label;
15. UPC code of the retail album;
16. catalog number;
17. copyright owner information;
18. musical genre of the channel or program (station format);
19. name of the service or entity;
20. channel or program;
21. date and time that the user logged in (in the user's time zone);
22. date and time that the user logged out (in the user's time zone);
23. time zone where the signal was received (user);
24. Unique User identifier;
25. the country in which the user received the transmissions.

The Librarian of Congress eventually suspended these reporting requirements, pending further study. And he also changed the original rates set by the arbitration panel charged with setting rates. But the basic difference between Internet radio and terrestrial radio remains: Internet radio has to pay a *type of copyright fee* that terrestrial radio does not.

Why? What justifies this difference? Was there any study of the economic consequences from Internet radio that would justify these differences? Was the motive to protect artists against piracy?

In a rare bit of candor, one RIAA expert admitted what seemed obvious to everyone at the time. As Alex Alben, vice president for Public Policy at Real Networks, told me,

The RIAA, which was representing the record labels, presented some testimony about what they thought a willing buyer would pay to a willing seller, and it was much higher. It was ten times higher than what radio stations pay to perform the same songs for the same period of time. And so the attorneys representing the webcasters asked the RIAA, . . . "How do you come up with a rate that's so much higher? Why is it worth more than radio? Because here we have hundreds of thousands of webcasters who want to pay, and that should establish the market rate, and if you set the rate so high, you're going to drive the small webcasters out of business. . . ."

And the RIAA experts said, "Well, we don't really model this as an industry with thousands of webcasters, *we think it should be an industry with, you know, five or seven big players who can pay a high rate and it's a stable, predictable market.*" (Emphasis added.)

Translation: The aim is to use the law to eliminate competition, so that this platform of potentially immense competition, which would cause the diversity and range of content available to explode, would not cause pain to the dinosaurs of old. There is no one, on either the right or the left, who should endorse this use of the law. And yet there is practically no one, on either the right or the left, who is doing anything effective to prevent it.

Corrupting Citizens

Overregulation stifles creativity. It smothers innovation. It gives dinosaurs a veto over the future. It wastes the extraordinary opportunity for a democratic creativity that digital technology enables.

In addition to these important harms, there is one more that was important to our forebears, but seems forgotten today. Overregulation corrupts citizens and weakens the rule of law.

The war that is being waged today is a war of prohibition. As with every war of prohibition, it is targeted against the behavior of a very large number of citizens. According to *The New York Times,* 43 million Americans downloaded music in May 2002.[15] According to the RIAA, the behavior of those 43 million Americans is a felony. We thus have a set of rules that transform 20 percent of America into criminals. As the

RIAA launches lawsuits against not only the Napsters and Kazaas of the world, but against students building search engines, and increasingly against ordinary users downloading content, the technologies for sharing will advance to further protect and hide illegal use. It is an arms race or a civil war, with the extremes of one side inviting a more extreme response by the other.

The content industry's tactics exploit the failings of the American legal system. When the RIAA brought suit against Jesse Jordan, it knew that in Jordan it had found a scapegoat, not a defendant. The threat of having to pay either all the money in the world in damages ($15,000,000) or almost all the money in the world to defend against paying all the money in the world in damages ($250,000 in legal fees) led Jordan to choose to pay all the money he had in the world ($12,000) to make the suit go away. The same strategy animates the RIAA's suits against individual users. In September 2003, the RIAA sued 261 individuals—including a twelve-year-old girl living in public housing and a seventy-year-old man who had no idea what file sharing was.[16] As these scapegoats discovered, it will always cost more to defend against these suits than it would cost to simply settle. (The twelve year old, for example, like Jesse Jordan, paid her life savings of $2,000 to settle the case.) Our law is an awful system for defending rights. It is an embarrassment to our tradition. And the consequence of our law as it is, is that those with the power can use the law to quash any rights they oppose.

Wars of prohibition are nothing new in America. This one is just something more extreme than anything we've seen before. We experimented with alcohol prohibition, at a time when the per capita consumption of alcohol was 1.5 gallons per capita per year. The war against drinking initially reduced that consumption to just 30 percent of its preprohibition levels, but by the end of prohibition, consumption was up to 70 percent of the preprohibition level. Americans were drinking just about as much, but now, a vast number were criminals.[17] We have launched a war on drugs aimed at reducing the consumption of regulated narcotics that 7 percent (or 16 million) Americans now use.[18] That is a drop from the high (so to speak) in 1979 of 14 percent of the population. We regulate automobiles to the point where the vast majority of Americans violate the law every day. We run such a complex tax system that a majority of cash businesses regularly cheat.[19] We pride ourselves on our "free society," but an endless array of ordinary behavior is regulated within our society. And as a result, a huge proportion of Americans regularly violate at least some law.

This state of affairs is not without consequence. It is a particularly salient issue for teachers like me, whose job it is to teach law students about the importance of "ethics." As my colleague Charlie Nesson told a class at Stanford, each year law schools admit thousands of students who have illegally downloaded music, illegally consumed alcohol and sometimes drugs, illegally worked without paying taxes, illegally driven cars. These are kids for whom behaving illegally is increasingly the norm. And then we, as law professors, are supposed to teach them how to behave ethically—how to say no to bribes, or keep client funds separate, or honor a demand to disclose a document that will mean that your case is over. Generations of Americans—more significantly in some parts of America than in others, but still, everywhere in America today—can't live their lives both normally and legally, since "normally" entails a certain degree of illegality.

The response to this general illegality is either to enforce the law more severely or to change the law. We, as a society, have to learn how to make that choice more rationally. Whether a law makes sense depends, in part, at least, upon whether the costs of the law, both intended and collateral, outweigh the benefits. If the costs, intended and collateral, do outweigh the benefits, then the law ought to be changed. Alternatively, if the costs of the existing system are much greater than the costs of an alternative, then we have a good reason to consider the alternative.

My point is not the idiotic one: Just because people violate a law, we should therefore repeal it. Obviously, we could reduce murder statistics dramatically by legalizing murder on Wednesdays and Fridays. But that wouldn't make any sense, since murder is wrong every day of the week. A society is right to ban murder always and everywhere.

My point is instead one that democracies understood for generations, but that we recently have learned to forget. The rule of law depends upon people obeying the law. The more often, and more repeatedly, we as citizens experience violating the law, the less we respect the law. Obviously, in most cases, the important issue is the law, not respect for the law. I don't care whether the rapist respects the law or not; I want to catch and incarcerate the rapist. But I do care whether my students respect the law. And I do care if the rules of law sow increasing disrespect because of the extreme of regulation they impose. Twenty million Americans have come of age since the Internet introduced this different idea of "sharing." We need to be able to call these twenty million Americans "citizens," not "felons."

When at least forty-three million citizens download content from the Internet, and when they use tools to combine that content in ways unauthorized by copyright holders, the first question we should be asking is not how best to involve the FBI. The first question should be whether this particular prohibition is really necessary in order to achieve the proper ends that copyright law serves. Is there another way to assure that artists get paid without transforming forty-three million Americans into felons? Does it make sense if there are other ways to assure that artists get paid without transforming America into a nation of felons?

This abstract point can be made more clear with a particular example.

We all own CDs. Many of us still own phonograph records. These pieces of plastic encode music that in a certain sense we have bought. The law protects our right to buy and sell that plastic: It is not a copyright infringement for me to sell all my classical records at a used record store and buy jazz records to replace them. That "use" of the recordings is free.

But as the MP3 craze has demonstrated, there is another use of phonograph records that is effectively free. Because these recordings were made without copy-protection technologies, I am "free" to copy, or "rip," music from my records onto a computer hard disk. Indeed, Apple Corporation went so far as to suggest that "freedom" was a right: In a series of commercials, Apple endorsed the "Rip, Mix, Burn" capacities of digital technologies.

This "use" of my records is certainly valuable. I have begun a large process at home of ripping all of my and my wife's CDs, and storing them in one archive. Then, using Apple's iTunes, or a wonderful program called Andromeda, we can build different play lists of our music: Bach, Baroque, Love Songs, Love Songs of Significant Others—the potential is endless. And by reducing the costs of mixing play lists, these technologies help build a creativity with play lists that is itself independently valuable. Compilations of songs are creative and meaningful in their own right.

This use is enabled by unprotected media—either CDs or records. But unprotected media also enable file sharing. File sharing threatens (or so the content industry believes) the ability of creators to earn a fair return from their creativity. And thus, many are beginning to experiment with technologies to eliminate unprotected media. These technologies, for example, would enable CDs that could not be ripped. Or they might enable spy programs to identify ripped content on people's machines.

If these technologies took off, then the building of large archives of your own music would become quite difficult. You might hang in hacker circles, and get technology to disable the technologies that protect the content. Trading in those technologies is illegal, but maybe that doesn't bother you much. In any case, for the vast majority of people, these protection technologies would effectively destroy the archiving use of CDs. The technology, in other words, would force us all back to the world where we either listened to music by manipulating pieces of plastic or were part of a massively complex "digital rights management" system.

If the only way to assure that artists get paid were the elimination of the ability to freely move content, then these technologies to interfere with the freedom to move content would be justifiable. But what if there were another way to assure that artists are paid, without locking down any content? What if, in other words, a different system could assure compensation to artists while also preserving the freedom to move content easily?

My point just now is not to prove that there is such a system. I offer a version of such a system in the last chapter of this book. For now, the only point is the relatively uncontroversial one: If a different system achieved the same legitimate objectives that the existing copyright system achieved, but left consumers and creators much more free, then we'd have a very good reason to pursue this alternative—namely, freedom. The choice, in other words, would not be between property and piracy; the choice would be between different property systems and the freedoms each allowed.

I believe there is a way to assure that artists are paid without turning forty-three million Americans into felons. But the salient feature of this alternative is that it would lead to a very different market for producing and distributing creativity. The dominant few, who today control the vast majority of the distribution of content in the world, would no longer exercise this extreme of control. Rather, they would go the way of the horse-drawn buggy.

Except that this generation's buggy manufacturers have already saddled Congress, and are riding the law to protect themselves against this new form of competition. For them the choice is between forty-three million Americans as criminals and their own survival.

It is understandable why they choose as they do. It is not understandable why we as a democracy continue to choose as we do. Jack

Valenti is charming; but not so charming as to justify giving up a tradition as deep and important as our tradition of free culture.

There's one more aspect to this corruption that is particularly important to civil liberties, and follows directly from any war of prohibition. As Electronic Frontier Foundation attorney Fred von Lohmann describes, this is the "collateral damage" that "arises whenever you turn a very large percentage of the population into criminals." This is the collateral damage to civil liberties generally.

"If you can treat someone as a putative lawbreaker," von Lohmann explains,

> then all of a sudden a lot of basic civil liberty protections evaporate to one degree or another. . . . If you're a copyright infringer, how can you hope to have any privacy rights? If you're a copyright infringer, how can you hope to be secure against seizures of your computer? How can you hope to continue to receive Internet access? . . . Our sensibilities change as soon as we think, "Oh, well, but that person's a criminal, a lawbreaker." Well, what this campaign against file sharing has done is turn a remarkable percentage of the American Internet-using population into "lawbreakers."

And the consequence of this transformation of the American public into criminals is that it becomes trivial, as a matter of due process, to effectively erase much of the privacy most would presume.

Users of the Internet began to see this generally in 2003 as the RIAA launched its campaign to force Internet service providers to turn over the names of customers who the RIAA believed were violating copyright law. Verizon fought that demand and lost. With a simple request to a judge, and without any notice to the customer at all, the identity of an Internet user is revealed.

The RIAA then expanded this campaign, by announcing a general strategy to sue individual users of the Internet who are alleged to have downloaded copyrighted music from file-sharing systems. But as we've seen, the potential damages from these suits are astronomical: If a family's computer is used to download a single CD's worth of music, the family could be liable for $2 million in damages. That didn't stop the RIAA from suing a number of these families, just as they had sued Jesse Jordan.[20]

Even this understates the espionage that is being waged by the RIAA. A report from CNN late last summer described a strategy the RIAA had adopted to track Napster users.[21] Using a sophisticated hashing algorithm, the RIAA took what is in effect a fingerprint of every song in the Napster catalog. Any copy of one of those MP3s will have the same "fingerprint."

So imagine the following not-implausible scenario: Imagine a friend gives a CD to your daughter—a collection of songs just like the cassettes you used to make as a kid. You don't know, and neither does your daughter, where these songs came from. But she copies these songs onto her computer. She then takes her computer to college and connects it to a college network, and if the college network is "cooperating" with the RIAA's espionage, and she hasn't properly protected her content from the network (do you know how to do that yourself?), then the RIAA will be able to identify your daughter as a "criminal." And under the rules that universities are beginning to deploy,[22] your daughter can lose the right to use the university's computer network. She can, in some cases, be expelled.

Now, of course, she'll have the right to defend herself. You can hire a lawyer for her (at $300 per hour, if you're lucky), and she can plead that she didn't know anything about the source of the songs or that they came from Napster. And it may well be that the university believes her. But the university might not believe her. It might treat this "contraband" as presumptive of guilt. And as any number of college students have already learned, our presumptions about innocence disappear in the middle of wars of prohibition. This war is no different.

Says von Lohmann,

> So when we're talking about numbers like forty to sixty million Americans that are essentially copyright infringers, you create a situation where the civil liberties of those people are very much in peril in a general matter. [I don't] think [there is any] analog where you could randomly choose any person off the street and be confident that they were committing an unlawful act that could put them on the hook for potential felony liability or hundreds of millions of dollars of civil liability. Certainly we all speed, but speeding isn't the kind of an act for which we routinely forfeit civil liberties. Some people use drugs, and I think that's the closest analog, [but] many have noted that the war against drugs has eroded all of our civil liberties because it's treated so many Americans as criminals. Well, I think it's fair to say that file sharing is an order of magnitude larger number of Americans than drug use. . . . If forty to sixty million Americans have become lawbreakers, then we're really on a slippery slope to lose a lot of civil liberties for all forty to sixty million of them.

When forty to sixty million Americans are considered "criminals" under the law, and when the law could achieve the same objective— securing rights to authors—without these millions being considered "criminals," who is the villain? Americans or the law? Which is American, a constant war on our own people or a concerted effort through our democracy to change our law?

BALANCES

So here's the picture: You're standing at the side of the road. Your car is on fire. You are angry and upset because in part you helped start the fire. Now you don't know how to put it out. Next to you is a bucket, filled with gasoline. Obviously, gasoline won't put the fire out.

As you ponder the mess, someone else comes along. In a panic, she grabs the bucket. Before you have a chance to tell her to stop—or before she understands just why she should stop—the bucket is in the air. The gasoline is about to hit the blazing car. And the fire that gasoline will ignite is about to ignite everything around.

A war about copyright rages all around—and we're all focusing on the wrong thing. No doubt, current technologies threaten existing businesses. No doubt they may threaten artists. But technologies change. The industry and technologists have plenty of ways to use technology to protect themselves against the current threats of the Internet. This is a fire that if let alone would burn itself out.

Yet policy makers are not willing to leave this fire to itself. Primed with plenty of lobbyists' money, they are keen to intervene to eliminate the problem they perceive. But the problem they perceive is not the real threat this culture faces. For while we watch this small fire in the corner, there is a massive change in the way culture is made that is happening all around.

Somehow we have to find a way to turn attention to this more important and fundamental issue. Somehow we have to find a way to avoid pouring gasoline onto this fire.

We have not found that way yet. Instead, we seem trapped in a simpler, binary view. However much many people push to frame this debate more broadly, it is the simple, binary view that remains. We rubberneck to look at the fire when we should be keeping our eyes on the road.

This challenge has been my life these last few years. It has also been my failure. In the two chapters that follow, I describe one small brace of efforts, so far failed, to find a way to refocus this debate. We must understand these failures if we're to understand what success will require.

CHAPTER THIRTEEN: Eldred

In 1995, a father was frustrated that his daughters didn't seem to like Hawthorne. No doubt there was more than one such father, but at least one did something about it. Eric Eldred, a retired computer programmer living in New Hampshire, decided to put Hawthorne on the Web. An electronic version, Eldred thought, with links to pictures and explanatory text, would make this nineteenth-century author's work come alive.

It didn't work—at least for his daughters. They didn't find Hawthorne any more interesting than before. But Eldred's experiment gave birth to a hobby, and his hobby begat a cause: Eldred would build a library of public domain works by scanning these works and making them available for free.

Eldred's library was not simply a copy of certain public domain works, though even a copy would have been of great value to people across the world who can't get access to printed versions of these works. Instead, Eldred was producing derivative works from these public domain works. Just as Disney turned Grimm into stories more accessible to the twentieth century, Eldred transformed Hawthorne, and many others, into a form more accessible—technically accessible—today.

Eldred's freedom to do this with Hawthorne's work grew from the same source as Disney's. Hawthorne's *Scarlet Letter* had passed into the public domain in 1907. It was free for anyone to take without the permission of the Hawthorne estate or anyone else. Some, such as Dover Press and Penguin Classics, take works from the public domain and produce printed editions, which they sell in bookstores across the country. Others, such as Disney, take these stories and turn them into animated cartoons, sometimes successfully (*Cinderella*), sometimes not (*The Hunchback of Notre Dame, Treasure Planet*). These are all commercial publications of public domain works.

The Internet created the possibility of noncommercial publications of public domain works. Eldred's is just one example. There are literally thousands of others. Hundreds of thousands from across the world have discovered this platform of expression and now use it to share works that are, by law, free for the taking. This has produced what we might call the "noncommercial publishing industry," which before the Internet was limited to people with large egos or with political or social causes. But with the Internet, it includes a wide range of individuals and groups dedicated to spreading culture generally.[1]

As I said, Eldred lives in New Hampshire. In 1998, Robert Frost's collection of poems *New Hampshire* was slated to pass into the public domain. Eldred wanted to post that collection in his free public library. But Congress got in the way. As I described in chapter 10, in 1998, for the eleventh time in forty years, Congress extended the terms of existing copyrights—this time by twenty years. Eldred would not be free to add any works more recent than 1923 to his collection until 2019. Indeed, no copyrighted work would pass into the public domain until that year (and not even then, if Congress extends the term again). By contrast, in the same period, more than 1 million patents will pass into the public domain.

This was the Sonny Bono Copyright Term Extension Act (CTEA), enacted in memory of the congressman and former musician Sonny Bono, who, his widow, Mary Bono, says, believed that "copyrights should be forever."[2]

Eldred decided to fight this law. He first resolved to fight it through civil disobedience. In a series of interviews, Eldred announced that he would publish as planned, CTEA notwithstanding. But because of a second law passed in 1998, the NET (No Electronic Theft) Act, his act of publishing would make Eldred a felon—whether or not anyone complained. This was a dangerous strategy for a disabled programmer to undertake.

It was here that I became involved in Eldred's battle. I was a constitutional scholar whose first passion was constitutional interpretation. And though constitutional law courses never focus upon the Progress Clause of the Constitution, it had always struck me as importantly different. As you know, the Constitution says,

Congress has the power to promote the Progress of Science . . . by securing for limited Times to Authors . . . exclusive Right to their . . . Writings. . . .

As I've described, this clause is unique within the power-granting clause of Article I, section 8 of our Constitution. Every other clause granting power to Congress simply says Congress has the power to do something—for example, to regulate "commerce among the several states" or "declare War." But here, the "something" is something quite specific—to "promote . . . Progress"—through means that are also specific—by "securing" "exclusive Rights" (i.e., copyrights) "for limited Times."

In the past forty years, Congress has gotten into the practice of extending existing terms of copyright protection. What puzzled me about this was, if Congress has the power to extend existing terms, then the Constitution's requirement that terms be "limited" will have no practical effect. If every time a copyright is about to expire, Congress has the power to extend its term, then Congress can achieve what the Constitution plainly forbids—perpetual terms "on the installment plan," as Professor Peter Jaszi so nicely put it.

As an academic, my first response was to hit the books. I remember sitting late at the office, scouring on-line databases for any serious consideration of the question. No one had ever challenged Congress's practice of extending existing terms. That failure may in part be why Congress seemed so untroubled in its habit. That, and the fact that the practice had become so lucrative for Congress. Congress knows that copyright owners will be willing to pay a great deal of money to see their copyright terms extended. And so Congress is quite happy to keep this gravy train going.

For this is the core of the corruption in our present system of government. "Corruption" not in the sense that representatives are bribed. Rather, "corruption" in the sense that the system induces the beneficiaries of Congress's acts to raise and give money to Congress to induce it to act. There's only so much time; there's only so much Congress can do. Why not limit its actions to those things it must do—and those things that pay? Extending copyright terms pays.

If that's not obvious to you, consider the following: Say you're one of the very few lucky copyright owners whose copyright continues to make money one hundred years after it was created. The Estate of Robert Frost is a good example. Frost died in 1963. His poetry continues to be extraordinarily valuable. Thus the Robert Frost estate benefits greatly from any extension of copyright, since no publisher would pay the estate any money if the poems Frost wrote could be published by anyone for free.

So imagine the Robert Frost estate is earning $100,000 a year from three of Frost's poems. And imagine the copyright for those poems is about to expire. You sit on the board of the Robert Frost estate. Your financial adviser comes to your board meeting with a very grim report:

"Next year," the adviser announces, "our copyrights in works A, B, and C will expire. That means that after next year, we will no longer be receiving the annual royalty check of $100,000 from the publishers of those works.

"There's a proposal in Congress, however," she continues, "that could change this. A few congressmen are floating a bill to extend the terms of copyright by twenty years. That bill would be extraordinarily valuable to us. So we should hope this bill passes."

"Hope?" a fellow board member says. "Can't we be doing something about it?"

"Well, obviously, yes," the adviser responds. "We could contribute to the campaigns of a number of representatives to try to assure that they support the bill."

You hate politics. You hate contributing to campaigns. So you want to know whether this disgusting practice is worth it. "How much would we get if this extension were passed?" you ask the adviser. "How much is it worth?"

"Well," the adviser says, "if you're confident that you will continue to get at least $100,000 a year from these copyrights, and you use the 'discount rate' that we use to evaluate estate investments (6 percent), then this law would be worth $1,146,000 to the estate."

You're a bit shocked by the number, but you quickly come to the correct conclusion:

"So you're saying it would be worth it for us to pay more than $1,000,000 in campaign contributions if we were confident those contributions would assure that the bill was passed?"

"Absolutely," the adviser responds. "It is worth it to you to contribute up to the 'present value' of the income you expect from these copyrights. Which for us means over $1,000,000."

You quickly get the point—you as the member of the board and, I trust, you the reader. Each time copyrights are about to expire, every beneficiary in the position of the Robert Frost estate faces the same choice: If they can contribute to get a law passed to extend copyrights, they will benefit greatly from that extension. And so each time copyrights are about to expire, there is a massive amount of lobbying to get the copyright term extended.

Thus a congressional perpetual motion machine: So long as legislation can be bought (albeit indirectly), there will be all the incentive in the world to buy further extensions of copyright.

In the lobbying that led to the passage of the Sonny Bono Copyright Term Extension Act, this "theory" about incentives was proved real. Ten of the thirteen original sponsors of the act in the House received the maximum contribution from Disney's political action committee; in the Senate, eight of the twelve sponsors received contributions.[3] The RIAA and the MPAA are estimated to have spent over $1.5 million lobbying in the 1998 election cycle. They paid out more than $200,000 in campaign contributions.[4] Disney is estimated to have contributed more than $800,000 to reelection campaigns in the 1998 cycle.[5]

Constitutional law is not oblivious to the obvious. Or at least, it need not be. So when I was considering Eldred's complaint, this reality about the never-ending incentives to increase the copyright term was central to my thinking. In my view, a pragmatic court committed to interpreting and applying the Constitution of our framers would see that if Congress has the power to extend existing terms, then there would be no effective constitutional requirement that terms be "limited." If they could extend it once, they would extend it again and again and again.

It was also my judgment that *this* Supreme Court would not allow Congress to extend existing terms. As anyone close to the Supreme Court's work knows, this Court has increasingly restricted the power of Congress when it has viewed Congress's actions as exceeding the power granted to it by the Constitution. Among constitutional scholars, the most famous example of this trend was the Supreme Court's decision in 1995 to strike down a law that banned the possession of guns near schools.

Since 1937, the Supreme Court had interpreted Congress's granted powers very broadly; so, while the Constitution grants Congress the power to regulate only "commerce among the several states" (aka "interstate commerce"), the Supreme Court had interpreted that power to include the power to regulate any activity that merely affected interstate commerce.

As the economy grew, this standard increasingly meant that there was no limit to Congress's power to regulate, since just about every activity, when considered on a national scale, affects interstate commerce. A Constitution designed to limit Congress's power was instead interpreted to impose no limit.

The Supreme Court, under Chief Justice Rehnquist's command, changed that in *United States v. Lopez.* The government had argued that possessing guns near schools affected interstate commerce. Guns near schools increase crime, crime lowers property values, and so on. In the oral argument, the Chief Justice asked the government whether there was any activity that would not affect interstate commerce under the reasoning the government advanced. The government said there was not; if Congress says an activity affects interstate commerce, then that activity affects interstate commerce. The Supreme Court, the government said, was not in the position to second-guess Congress.

"We pause to consider the implications of the government's arguments," the Chief Justice wrote.[6] If anything Congress says is interstate commerce must therefore be considered interstate commerce, then there would be no limit to Congress's power. The decision in *Lopez* was reaffirmed five years later in *United States v. Morrison.*[7]

If a principle were at work here, then it should apply to the Progress Clause as much as the Commerce Clause.[8] And if it is applied to the Progress Clause, the principle should yield the conclusion that Congress can't extend an existing term. If Congress could extend an existing term, then there would be no "stopping point" to Congress's power over terms, though the Constitution expressly states that there is such a limit. Thus, the same principle applied to the power to grant copyrights should entail that Congress is not allowed to extend the term of existing copyrights.

If, that is, the principle announced in *Lopez* stood for a principle. Many believed the decision in *Lopez* stood for politics—a conservative Supreme Court, which believed in states' rights, using its power over Congress to advance its own personal political preferences. But I rejected that view of the Supreme Court's decision. Indeed, shortly after the decision, I wrote an article demonstrating the "fidelity" in such an interpretation of the Constitution. The idea that the Supreme Court decides cases based upon its politics struck me as extraordinarily boring. I was not going to devote my life to teaching constitutional law if these nine Justices were going to be petty politicians.

Now let's pause for a moment to make sure we understand what the argument in *Eldred* was not about. By insisting on the Constitution's limits to copyright, obviously Eldred was not endorsing piracy. Indeed, in an obvious sense, he was fighting a kind of piracy—piracy of the public domain. When Robert Frost wrote his work and when Walt Disney created Mickey Mouse, the maximum copyright term was just fifty-six years. Because of interim changes, Frost and Disney had already enjoyed a seventy-five-year monopoly for their work. They had gotten the benefit of the bargain that the Constitution envisions: In exchange for a monopoly protected for fifty-six years, they created new work. But now these entities were using their power—expressed through the power of lobbyists' money—to get another twenty-year dollop of monopoly. That twenty-year dollop would be taken from the public domain. Eric Eldred was fighting a piracy that affects us all.

Some people view the public domain with contempt. In their brief before the Supreme Court, the Nashville Songwriters Association wrote that the public domain is nothing more than "legal piracy."[9] But it is not piracy when the law allows it; and in our constitutional system, our law requires it. Some may not like the Constitution's requirements, but that doesn't make the Constitution a pirate's charter.

As we've seen, our constitutional system requires limits on copyright as a way to assure that copyright holders do not too heavily influence the development and distribution of our culture. Yet, as Eric Eldred discovered, we have set up a system that assures that copyright terms will be repeatedly extended, and extended, and extended. We have created the perfect storm for the public domain. Copyrights have not expired, and will not expire, so long as Congress is free to be bought to extend them again.

It is valuable copyrights that are responsible for terms being extended. Mickey Mouse and "Rhapsody in Blue." These works are too valuable for copyright owners to ignore. But the real harm to our society from copyright extensions is not that Mickey Mouse remains Disney's. Forget Mickey Mouse. Forget Robert Frost. Forget all the works from the 1920s and 1930s that have continuing commercial value. The real harm of term extension comes not from these famous works. The real harm is to the works that are not famous, not commercially exploited, and no longer available as a result.

If you look at the work created in the first twenty years (1923 to 1942) affected by the Sonny Bono Copyright Term Extension Act, 2 percent of that work has any continuing commercial value. It was the copyright holders for that 2 percent who pushed the CTEA through. But the law and its effect were not limited to that 2 percent. The law extended the terms of copyright generally.[10]

Think practically about the consequence of this extension—practically, as a businessperson, and not as a lawyer eager for more legal work. In 1930, 10,047 books were published. In 2000, 174 of those books were still in print. Let's say you were Brewster Kahle, and you wanted to make available to the world in your iArchive project the remaining 9,873. What would you have to do?

Well, first, you'd have to determine which of the 9,873 books were still under copyright. That requires going to a library (these data are not on-line) and paging through tomes of books, cross-checking the titles and authors of the 9,873 books with the copyright registration and renewal records for works published in 1930. That will produce a list of books still under copyright.

Then for the books still under copyright, you would need to locate the current copyright owners. How would you do that?

Most people think that there must be a list of these copyright owners somewhere. Practical people think this way. How could there be thousands and thousands of government monopolies without there being at least a list?

But there is no list. There may be a name from 1930, and then in 1959, of the person who registered the copyright. But just think practically about how impossibly difficult it would be to track down thousands of such records—especially since the person who registered is not necessarily the current owner. And we're just talking about 1930!

"But there isn't a list of who owns property generally," the apologists for the system respond. "Why should there be a list of copyright owners?"

Well, actually, if you think about it, there *are* plenty of lists of who owns what property. Think about deeds on houses, or titles to cars. And where there isn't a list, the code of real space is pretty good at suggesting who the owner of a bit of property is. (A swing set in your backyard is probably yours.) So formally or informally, we have a pretty good way to know who owns what tangible property.

So: You walk down a street and see a house. You can know who owns the house by looking it up in the courthouse registry. If you see a car, there is ordinarily a license plate that will link the owner to the car. If you see a bunch of children's toys sitting on the front lawn of a house, it's fairly easy to determine who owns the toys. And if you happen to see a baseball lying in a gutter on the side of the road, look around for a second for some kids playing ball. If you don't see any kids, then okay: Here's a bit of property whose owner we can't easily determine. It is the exception that proves the rule: that we ordinarily know quite well who owns what property.

Compare this story to intangible property. You go into a library. The library owns the books. But who owns the copyrights? As I've already described, there's no list of copyright owners. There are authors' names, of course, but their copyrights could have been assigned, or passed down in an estate like Grandma's old jewelry. To know who owns what, you would have to hire a private detective. The bottom line: The owner cannot easily be located. And in a regime like ours, in which it is a felony to use such property without the property owner's permission, the property isn't going to be used.

The consequence with respect to old books is that they won't be digitized, and hence will simply rot away on shelves. But the consequence for other creative works is much more dire.

Consider the story of Michael Agee, chairman of Hal Roach Studios, which owns the copyrights for the Laurel and Hardy films. Agee is a direct beneficiary of the Bono Act. The Laurel and Hardy films were made between 1921 and 1951. Only one of these films, *The Lucky Dog*, is currently out of copyright. But for the CTEA, films made after 1923 would have begun entering the public domain. Because Agee controls the exclusive rights for these popular films, he makes a great deal of money. According to one estimate, "Roach has sold about 60,000 videocassettes and 50,000 DVDs of the duo's silent films."[11]

Yet Agee opposed the CTEA. His reasons demonstrate a rare virtue in this culture: selflessness. He argued in a brief before the Supreme Court that the Sonny Bono Copyright Term Extension Act will, if left standing, destroy a whole generation of American film.

His argument is straightforward. A tiny fraction of this work has any continuing commercial value. The rest—to the extent it survives at all—sits in vaults gathering dust. It may be that some of this work not now commercially valuable will be deemed to be valuable by the owners of the vaults. For this to occur, however, the commercial benefit from the work must exceed the costs of making the work available for distribution.

We can't know the benefits, but we do know a lot about the costs. For most of the history of film, the costs of restoring film were very high; digital technology has lowered these costs substantially. While it cost more than $10,000 to restore a ninety-minute black-and-white film in 1993, it can now cost as little as $100 to digitize one hour of 8 mm film.[12]

Restoration technology is not the only cost, nor the most important. Lawyers, too, are a cost, and increasingly, a very important one. In addition to preserving the film, a distributor needs to secure the rights. And to secure the rights for a film that is under copyright, you need to locate the copyright owner.

Or more accurately, *owners*. As we've seen, there isn't only a single copyright associated with a film; there are many. There isn't a single person whom you can contact about those copyrights; there are as many as can hold the rights, which turns out to be an extremely large number. Thus the costs of clearing the rights to these films is exceptionally high.

"But can't you just restore the film, distribute it, and then pay the copyright owner when she shows up?" Sure, if you want to commit a felony. And even if you're not worried about committing a felony, when she does show up, she'll have the right to sue you for all the profits you have made. So, if you're successful, you can be fairly confident you'll be getting a call from someone's lawyer. And if you're not successful, you won't make enough to cover the costs of your own lawyer. Either way, you have to talk to a lawyer. And as is too often the case, saying you have to talk to a lawyer is the same as saying you won't make any money.

For some films, the benefit of releasing the film may well exceed these costs. But for the vast majority of them, there is no way the benefit would outweigh the legal costs. Thus, for the vast majority of old films, Agee argued, the film will not be restored and distributed until the copyright expires.

But by the time the copyright for these films expires, the film will have expired. These films were produced on nitrate-based stock, and nitrate stock dissolves over time. They will be gone, and the metal canisters in which they are now stored will be filled with nothing more than dust.

Of all the creative work produced by humans anywhere, a tiny fraction has continuing commercial value. For that tiny fraction, the copyright is a crucially important legal device. For that tiny fraction, the copyright creates incentives to produce and distribute the creative work. For that tiny fraction, the copyright acts as an "engine of free expression."

But even for that tiny fraction, the actual time during which the creative work has a commercial life is extremely short. As I've indicated, most books go out of print within one year. The same is true of music and film. Commercial culture is sharklike. It must keep moving. And when a creative work falls out of favor with the commercial distributors, the commercial life ends.

Yet that doesn't mean the life of the creative work ends. We don't keep libraries of books in order to compete with Barnes & Noble, and we don't have archives of films because we expect people to choose between spending Friday night watching new movies and spending Friday night watching a 1930 news documentary. The noncommercial life of culture is important and valuable—for entertainment but also, and more importantly, for knowledge. To understand who we are, and where we came from, and how we have made the mistakes that we have, we need to have access to this history.

Copyrights in this context do not drive an engine of free expression.

In this context, there is no need for an exclusive right. Copyrights in this context do no good.

Yet, for most of our history, they also did little harm. For most of our history, when a work ended its commercial life, there was no *copyright-related use* that would be inhibited by an exclusive right. When a book went out of print, you could not buy it from a publisher. But you could still buy it from a used book store, and when a used book store sells it, in America, at least, there is no need to pay the copyright owner anything. Thus, the ordinary use of a book after its commercial life ended was a use that was independent of copyright law.

The same was effectively true of film. Because the costs of restoring a film—the real economic costs, not the lawyer costs—were so high, it was never at all feasible to preserve or restore film. Like the remains of a great dinner, when it's over, it's over. Once a film passed out of its commercial life, it may have been archived for a bit, but that was the end of its life so long as the market didn't have more to offer.

In other words, though copyright has been relatively short for most of our history, long copyrights wouldn't have mattered for the works that lost their commercial value. Long copyrights for these works would not have interfered with anything.

But this situation has now changed.

One crucially important consequence of the emergence of digital technologies is to enable the archive that Brewster Kahle dreams of. Digital technologies now make it possible to preserve and give access to all sorts of knowledge. Once a book goes out of print, we can now imagine digitizing it and making it available to everyone, forever. Once a film goes out of distribution, we could digitize it and make it available to everyone, forever. Digital technologies give new life to copyrighted material after it passes out of its commercial life. It is now possible to preserve and assure universal access to this knowledge and culture, whereas before it was not.

And now copyright law does get in the way. Every step of producing this digital archive of our culture infringes on the exclusive right of copyright. To digitize a book is to copy it. To do that requires permission of the copyright owner. The same with music, film, or any other aspect of our culture protected by copyright. The effort to make these things available to history, or to researchers, or to those who just want to explore, is now inhibited by a set of rules that were written for a radically different context.

Here is the core of the harm that comes from extending terms: Now that technology enables us to rebuild the library of Alexandria, the law gets in the way. And it doesn't get in the way for any useful *copyright* purpose, for the purpose of copyright is to enable the commercial market that spreads culture. No, we are talking about culture after it has lived its commercial life. In this context, copyright is serving no purpose *at all* related to the spread of knowledge. In this context, copyright is not an engine of free expression. Copyright is a brake.

You may well ask, "But if digital technologies lower the costs for Brewster Kahle, then they will lower the costs for Random House, too. So won't Random House do as well as Brewster Kahle in spreading culture widely?"

Maybe. Someday. But there is absolutely no evidence to suggest that publishers would be as complete as libraries. If Barnes & Noble offered to lend books from its stores for a low price, would that eliminate the need for libraries? Only if you think that the only role of a library is to serve what "the market" would demand. But if you think the role of a library is bigger than this—if you think its role is to archive culture, whether there's a demand for any particular bit of that culture or not—then we can't count on the commercial market to do our library work for us.

I would be the first to agree that it should do as much as it can: We should rely upon the market as much as possible to spread and enable culture. My message is absolutely not antimarket. But where we see the market is not doing the job, then we should allow nonmarket forces the freedom to fill the gaps. As one researcher calculated for American culture, 94 percent of the films, books, and music produced between 1923 and 1946 is not commercially available. However much you love the commercial market, if access is a value, then 6 percent is a failure to provide that value.[13]

In January 1999, we filed a lawsuit on Eric Eldred's behalf in federal district court in Washington, D.C., asking the court to declare the Sonny Bono Copyright Term Extension Act unconstitutional. The two central claims that we made were (1) that extending existing terms violated the Constitution's "limited Times" requirement, and (2) that extending terms by another twenty years violated the First Amendment.

The district court dismissed our claims without even hearing an argument. A panel of the Court of Appeals for the D.C. Circuit also dismissed our claims, though after hearing an extensive argument. But that decision at least had a dissent, by one of the most conservative judges on that court. That dissent gave our claims life.

Judge David Sentelle said the CTEA violated the requirement that copyrights be for "limited Times" only. His argument was as elegant as it was simple: If Congress can extend existing terms, then there is no "stopping point" to Congress's power under the Copyright Clause. The power to extend existing terms means Congress is not required to grant terms that are "limited." Thus, Judge Sentelle argued, the court had to interpret the term "limited Times" to give it meaning. And the best interpretation, Judge Sentelle argued, would be to deny Congress the power to extend existing terms.

We asked the Court of Appeals for the D.C. Circuit as a whole to hear the case. Cases are ordinarily heard in panels of three, except for important cases or cases that raise issues specific to the circuit as a whole, where the court will sit "en banc" to hear the case.

The Court of Appeals rejected our request to hear the case en banc. This time, Judge Sentelle was joined by the most liberal member of the

D.C. Circuit, Judge David Tatel. Both the most conservative and the most liberal judges in the D.C. Circuit believed Congress had overstepped its bounds.

It was here that most expected *Eldred* v. *Ashcroft* would die, for the Supreme Court rarely reviews any decision by a court of appeals. (It hears about one hundred cases a year, out of more than five thousand appeals.) And it practically never reviews a decision that upholds a statute when no other court has yet reviewed the statute.

But in February 2002, the Supreme Court surprised the world by granting our petition to review the D.C. Circuit opinion. Argument was set for October of 2002. The summer would be spent writing briefs and preparing for argument.

It is over a year later as I write these words. It is still astonishingly hard. If you know anything at all about this story, you know that we lost the appeal. And if you know something more than just the minimum, you probably think there was no way this case could have been won. After our defeat, I received literally thousands of missives by well-wishers and supporters, thanking me for my work on behalf of this noble but doomed cause. And none from this pile was more significant to me than the e-mail from my client, Eric Eldred.

But my client and these friends were wrong. This case could have been won. It should have been won. And no matter how hard I try to retell this story to myself, I can never escape believing that my own mistake lost it.

The mistake was made early, though it became obvious only at the very end. Our case had been supported from the very beginning by an extraordinary lawyer, Geoffrey Stewart, and by the law firm he had moved to, Jones, Day, Reavis and Pogue. Jones Day took a great deal of heat from its copyright-protectionist clients for supporting us. They ignored this pressure (something that few law firms today would ever do), and throughout the case, they gave it everything they could.

There were three key lawyers on the case from Jones Day. Geoff Stewart was the first, but then Dan Bromberg and Don Ayer became quite involved. Bromberg and Ayer in particular had a common view about how this case would be won: We would only win, they repeatedly told me, if we could make the issue seem "important" to the Supreme Court. It had to seem as if dramatic harm were being done to free speech and free culture; otherwise, they would never vote against "the most powerful media companies in the world."

I hate this view of the law. Of course I thought the Sonny Bono Act was a dramatic harm to free speech and free culture. Of course I still think it is. But the idea that the Supreme Court decides the law based on how important they believe the issues are is just wrong. It might be "right" as in "true," I thought, but it is "wrong" as in "it just shouldn't be that way." As I believed that any faithful interpretation of what the framers of our Constitution did would yield the conclusion that the CTEA was unconstitutional, and as I believed that any faithful interpretation of what the First Amendment means would yield the conclusion that the power to extend existing copyright terms is unconstitutional, I was not persuaded that we had to sell our case like soap. Just as a law that bans the swastika is unconstitutional not because the Court likes Nazis but because such a law would violate the Constitution, so too, in my view, would the Court decide whether Congress's law was constitutional based on the Constitution, not based on whether they liked the values that the framers put in the Constitution.

In any case, I thought, the Court must already see the danger and the harm caused by this sort of law. Why else would they grant review? There was no reason to hear the case in the Supreme Court if they weren't convinced that this regulation was harmful. So in my view, we didn't need to persuade them that this law was bad, we needed to show why it was unconstitutional.

There was one way, however, in which I felt politics would matter and in which I thought a response was appropriate. I was convinced that the Court would not hear our arguments if it thought these were just the arguments of a group of lefty loons. This Supreme Court was not about to launch into a new field of judicial review if it seemed that this field of review was simply the preference of a small political minority. Although my focus in the case was not to demonstrate how bad the Sonny Bono Act was but to demonstrate that it was unconstitutional, my hope was to make this argument against a background of briefs that covered the full range of political views. To show that this claim against the CTEA was grounded in *law* and not politics, then, we tried to gather the widest range of credible critics—credible not because they were rich and famous, but because they, in the aggregate, demonstrated that this law was unconstitutional regardless of one's politics.

The first step happened all by itself. Phyllis Schlafly's organization, Eagle Forum, had been an opponent of the CTEA from the very beginning. Mrs. Schlafly viewed the CTEA as a sellout by Congress. In November 1998, she wrote a stinging editorial attacking the Republican Congress for allowing the law to pass. As she wrote, "Do you sometimes wonder why bills that create a financial windfall to narrow special interests slide easily through the intricate legislative process, while bills that benefit the general public seem to get bogged down?" The answer, as the editorial documented, was the power of money. Schlafly enumerated Disney's contributions to the key players on the committees. It was money, not justice, that gave Mickey Mouse twenty more years in Disney's control, Schlafly argued.

In the Court of Appeals, Eagle Forum was eager to file a brief supporting our position. Their brief made the argument that became the core claim in the Supreme Court: If Congress can extend the term of existing copyrights, there is no limit to Congress's power to set terms. That strong conservative argument persuaded a strong conservative judge, Judge Sentelle.

In the Supreme Court, the briefs on our side were about as diverse as it gets. They included an extraordinary historical brief by the Free

Software Foundation (home of the GNU project that made GNU/ Linux possible). They included a powerful brief about the costs of uncertainty by Intel. There were two law professors' briefs, one by copyright scholars and one by First Amendment scholars. There was an exhaustive and uncontroverted brief by the world's experts in the history of the Progress Clause. And of course, there was a new brief by Eagle Forum, repeating and strengthening its arguments.

Those briefs framed a legal argument. Then to support the legal argument, there were a number of powerful briefs by libraries and archives, including the Internet Archive, the American Association of Law Libraries, and the National Writers Union.

But two briefs captured the policy argument best. One made the argument I've already described: A brief by Hal Roach Studios argued that unless the law was struck, a whole generation of American film would disappear. The other made the economic argument absolutely clear.

This economists' brief was signed by seventeen economists, including five Nobel Prize winners, including Ronald Coase, James Buchanan, Milton Friedman, Kenneth Arrow, and George Akerlof. The economists, as the list of Nobel winners demonstrates, spanned the political spectrum. Their conclusions were powerful: There was no plausible claim that extending the terms of existing copyrights would do anything to increase incentives to create. Such extensions were nothing more than "rent-seeking"—the fancy term economists use to describe special-interest legislation gone wild.

The same effort at balance was reflected in the legal team we gathered to write our briefs in the case. The Jones Day lawyers had been with us from the start. But when the case got to the Supreme Court, we added three lawyers to help us frame this argument to this Court: Alan Morrison, a lawyer from Public Citizen, a Washington group that had made constitutional history with a series of seminal victories in the Supreme Court defending individual rights; my colleague and dean, Kathleen Sullivan, who had argued many cases in the Court, and who had advised us early on about a First Amendment strategy; and finally, former solicitor general Charles Fried.

Fried was a special victory for our side. Every other former solicitor general was hired by the other side to defend Congress's power to give media companies the special favor of extended copyright terms. Fried was the only one who turned down that lucrative assignment to stand up for something he believed in. He had been Ronald Reagan's chief lawyer in the Supreme Court. He had helped craft the line of cases that limited Congress's power in the context of the Commerce Clause. And while he had argued many positions in the Supreme Court that I personally disagreed with, his joining the cause was a vote of confidence in our argument.

The government, in defending the statute, had its collection of friends, as well. Significantly, however, none of these "friends" included historians or economists. The briefs on the other side of the case were written exclusively by major media companies, congressmen, and copyright holders.

The media companies were not surprising. They had the most to gain from the law. The congressmen were not surprising either—they were defending their power and, indirectly, the gravy train of contributions such power induced. And of course it was not surprising that the copyright holders would defend the idea that they should continue to have the right to control who did what with content they wanted to control.

Dr. Seuss's representatives, for example, argued that it was better for the Dr. Seuss estate to control what happened to Dr. Seuss's work— better than allowing it to fall into the public domain—because if this creativity were in the public domain, then people could use it to "glorify drugs or to create pornography."[14] That was also the motive of the Gershwin estate, which defended its "protection" of the work of George Gershwin. They refuse, for example, to license *Porgy and Bess* to anyone who refuses to use African Americans in the cast.[15] That's their view of how this part of American culture should be controlled, and they wanted this law to help them effect that control.

This argument made clear a theme that is rarely noticed in this debate. When Congress decides to extend the term of existing copyrights, Congress is making a choice about which speakers it will favor. Famous and beloved copyright owners, such as the Gershwin estate and Dr. Seuss, come to Congress and say, "Give us twenty years to control the speech about these icons of American culture. We'll do better with them than anyone else." Congress of course likes to reward the popular and famous by giving them what they want. But when Congress gives people an exclusive right to speak in a certain way, that's just what the First Amendment is traditionally meant to block.

We argued as much in a final brief. Not only would upholding the CTEA mean that there was no limit to the power of Congress to extend copyrights—extensions that would further concentrate the market; it would also mean that there was no limit to Congress's power to play favorites, through copyright, with who has the right to speak.

Between February and October, there was little I did beyond preparing for this case. Early on, as I said, I set the strategy.

The Supreme Court was divided into two important camps. One camp we called "the Conservatives." The other we called "the Rest." The Conservatives included Chief Justice Rehnquist, Justice O'Connor, Justice Scalia, Justice Kennedy, and Justice Thomas. These five had been the most consistent in limiting Congress's power. They were the five who had supported the *Lopez/Morrison* line of cases that said that an enumerated power had to be interpreted to assure that Congress's powers had limits.

The Rest were the four Justices who had strongly opposed limits on Congress's power. These four—Justice Stevens, Justice Souter, Justice Ginsburg, and Justice Breyer—had repeatedly argued that the Constitution gives Congress broad discretion to decide how best to implement its powers. In case after case, these justices had argued that the Court's role should be one of deference. Though the votes of these four justices were the votes that I personally had most consistently agreed with, they were also the votes that we were least likely to get.

In particular, the least likely was Justice Ginsburg's. In addition to her general view about deference to Congress (except where issues of gender are involved), she had been particularly deferential in the context of intellectual property protections. She and her daughter (an excellent and well-known intellectual property scholar) were cut from the same intellectual property cloth. We expected she would agree with the writings of her daughter: that Congress had the power in this context to do as it wished, even if what Congress wished made little sense.

Close behind Justice Ginsburg were two justices whom we also viewed as unlikely allies, though possible surprises. Justice Souter strongly favored deference to Congress, as did Justice Breyer. But both were also very sensitive to free speech concerns. And as we strongly believed, there was a very important free speech argument against these retrospective extensions.

The only vote we could be confident about was that of Justice Stevens. History will record Justice Stevens as one of the greatest judges on this Court. His votes are consistently eclectic, which just means that no simple ideology explains where he will stand. But he had consistently argued for limits in the context of intellectual property generally. We were fairly confident he would recognize limits here.

This analysis of "the Rest" showed most clearly where our focus had to be: on the Conservatives. To win this case, we had to crack open these five and get at least a majority to go our way. Thus, the single overriding argument that animated our claim rested on the Conservatives' most important jurisprudential innovation—the argument that Judge Sentelle had relied upon in the Court of Appeals, that Congress's power must be interpreted so that its enumerated powers have limits.

This then was the core of our strategy—a strategy for which I am responsible. We would get the Court to see that just as with the *Lopez* case, under the government's argument here, Congress would always have unlimited power to extend existing terms. If anything was plain about Congress's power under the Progress Clause, it was that this power was supposed to be "limited." Our aim would be to get the Court to reconcile *Eldred* with *Lopez:* If Congress's power to regulate commerce was limited, then so, too, must Congress's power to regulate copyright be limited.

The argument on the government's side came down to this: Congress has done it before. It should be allowed to do it again. The government claimed that from the very beginning, Congress has been extending the term of existing copyrights. So, the government argued, the Court should not now say that practice is unconstitutional.

There was some truth to the government's claim, but not much. We certainly agreed that Congress had extended existing terms in 1831 and in 1909. And of course, in 1962, Congress began extending existing terms regularly—eleven times in forty years.

But this "consistency" should be kept in perspective. Congress extended existing terms once in the first hundred years of the Republic. It then extended existing terms once again in the next fifty. Those rare extensions are in contrast to the now regular practice of extending existing terms. Whatever restraint Congress had had in the past, that restraint was now gone. Congress was now in a cycle of extensions; there was no reason to expect that cycle would end. This Court had not hesitated to intervene where Congress was in a similar cycle of extension. There was no reason it couldn't intervene here.

Oral argument was scheduled for the first week in October. I arrived in D.C. two weeks before the argument. During those two weeks, I was repeatedly "mooted" by lawyers who had volunteered to help in the case. Such "moots" are basically practice rounds, where wannabe justices fire questions at wannabe winners.

I was convinced that to win, I had to keep the Court focused on a single point: that if this extension is permitted, then there is no limit to the power to set terms. Going with the government would mean that terms would be effectively unlimited; going with us would give Congress a clear line to follow: Don't extend existing terms. The moots were an effective practice; I found ways to take every question back to this central idea.

One moot was before the lawyers at Jones Day. Don Ayer was the skeptic. He had served in the Reagan Justice Department with Solicitor General Charles Fried. He had argued many cases before the Supreme Court. And in his review of the moot, he let his concern speak:

"I'm just afraid that unless they really see the harm, they won't be willing to upset this practice that the government says has been a consistent practice for two hundred years. You have to make them see the harm—passionately get them to see the harm. For if they don't see that, then we haven't any chance of winning."

He may have argued many cases before this Court, I thought, but he didn't understand its soul. As a clerk, I had seen the Justices do the right thing—not because of politics but because it was right. As a law professor, I had spent my life teaching my students that this Court does the right thing—not because of politics but because it is right. As I listened to Ayer's plea for passion in pressing politics, I understood his point, and I rejected it. Our argument was right. That was enough. Let the politicians learn to see that it was also good.

The night before the argument, a line of people began to form in front of the Supreme Court. The case had become a focus of the press and of the movement to free culture. Hundreds stood in line for the chance to see the proceedings. Scores spent the night on the Supreme Court steps so that they would be assured a seat.

Not everyone has to wait in line. People who know the Justices can ask for seats they control. (I asked Justice Scalia's chambers for seats for my parents, for example.) Members of the Supreme Court bar can get a seat in a special section reserved for them. And senators and congressmen have a special place where they get to sit, too. And finally, of course, the press has a gallery, as do clerks working for the Justices on the Court. As we entered that morning, there was no place that was not taken. This was an argument about intellectual property law, yet the halls were filled. As I walked in to take my seat at the front of the Court, I saw my parents sitting on the left. As I sat down at the table, I saw Jack Valenti sitting in the special section ordinarily reserved for family of the Justices.

When the Chief Justice called me to begin my argument, I began where I intended to stay: on the question of the limits on Congress's power. This was a case about enumerated powers, I said, and whether those enumerated powers had any limit.

Justice O'Connor stopped me within one minute of my opening. The history was bothering her.

> JUSTICE O'CONNOR: Congress has extended the term so often through the years, and if you are right, don't we run the risk of upsetting previous extensions of time? I mean, this seems to be a practice that began with the very first act.

She was quite willing to concede "that this flies directly in the face of what the framers had in mind." But my response again and again was to emphasize limits on Congress's power.

> MR. LESSIG: Well, if it flies in the face of what the framers had in mind, then the question is, is there a way of interpreting their

words that gives effect to what they had in mind, and the answer is yes.

There were two points in this argument when I should have seen where the Court was going. The first was a question by Justice Kennedy, who observed,

JUSTICE KENNEDY: Well, I suppose implicit in the argument that the '76 act, too, should have been declared void, and that we might leave it alone because of the disruption, is that for all these years the act has impeded progress in science and the useful arts. I just don't see any empirical evidence for that.

Here follows my clear mistake. Like a professor correcting a student, I answered,

MR. LESSIG: Justice, we are not making an empirical claim at all. Nothing in our Copyright Clause claim hangs upon the empirical assertion about impeding progress. Our only argument is this is a structural limit necessary to assure that what would be an effectively perpetual term not be permitted under the copyright laws.

That was a correct answer, but it wasn't the right answer. The right answer was instead that there was an obvious and profound harm. Any number of briefs had been written about it. He wanted to hear it. And here was the place Don Ayer's advice should have mattered. This was a softball; my answer was a swing and a miss.

The second came from the Chief, for whom the whole case had been crafted. For the Chief Justice had crafted the *Lopez* ruling, and we hoped that he would see this case as its second cousin.

It was clear a second into his question that he wasn't at all sympathetic. To him, we were a bunch of anarchists. As he asked:

CHIEF JUSTICE: Well, but you want more than that. You want the right to copy verbatim other people's books, don't you?

MR. LESSIG: We want the right to copy verbatim works that should be in the public domain and would be in the public domain but for a statute that cannot be justified under ordinary First Amendment analysis or under a proper reading of the limits built into the Copyright Clause.

Things went better for us when the government gave its argument; for now the Court picked up on the core of our claim. As Justice Scalia asked Solicitor General Olson,

JUSTICE SCALIA: You say that the functional equivalent of an unlimited time would be a violation [of the Constitution], but that's precisely the argument that's being made by petitioners here, that a limited time which is extendable is the functional equivalent of an unlimited time.

When Olson was finished, it was my turn to give a closing rebuttal. Olson's flailing had revived my anger. But my anger still was directed to the academic, not the practical. The government was arguing as if this were the first case ever to consider limits on Congress's Copyright and Patent Clause power. Ever the professor and not the advocate, I closed by pointing out the long history of the Court imposing limits on Congress's power in the name of the Copyright and Patent Clause— indeed, the very first case striking a law of Congress as exceeding a specific enumerated power was based upon the Copyright and Patent Clause. All true. But it wasn't going to move the Court to my side.

As I left the court that day, I knew there were a hundred points I wished I could remake. There were a hundred questions I wished I had answered differently. But one way of thinking about this case left me optimistic.

The government had been asked over and over again, what is the limit? Over and over again, it had answered there is no limit. This was precisely the answer I wanted the Court to hear. For I could not imagine how the Court could understand that the government believed Congress's power was unlimited under the terms of the Copyright Clause, and sustain the government's argument. The solicitor general had made my argument for me. No matter how often I tried, I could not understand how the Court could find that Congress's power under the Commerce Clause was limited, but under the Copyright Clause, unlimited. In those rare moments when I let myself believe that we may have prevailed, it was because I felt this Court—in particular, the Conservatives—would feel itself constrained by the rule of law that it had established elsewhere.

The morning of January 15, 2003, I was five minutes late to the office and missed the 7:00 A.M. call from the Supreme Court clerk. Listening to the message, I could tell in an instant that she had bad news to report. The Supreme Court had affirmed the decision of the Court of Appeals. Seven justices had voted in the majority. There were two dissents.

A few seconds later, the opinions arrived by e-mail. I took the phone off the hook, posted an announcement to our blog, and sat down to see where I had been wrong in my reasoning.

My *reasoning*. Here was a case that pitted all the money in the world against *reasoning*. And here was the last naïve law professor, scouring the pages, looking for reasoning.

I first scoured the opinion, looking for how the Court would distinguish the principle in this case from the principle in *Lopez*. The argument was nowhere to be found. The case was not even cited. The argument that was the core argument of our case did not even appear in the Court's opinion.

Justice Ginsburg simply ignored the enumerated powers argument. Consistent with her view that Congress's power was not limited generally, she had found Congress's power not limited here.

Her opinion was perfectly reasonable—for her, and for Justice Souter. Neither believes in *Lopez*. It would be too much to expect them to write an opinion that recognized, much less explained, the doctrine they had worked so hard to defeat.

But as I realized what had happened, I couldn't quite believe what I was reading. I had said there was no way this Court could reconcile limited powers with the Commerce Clause and unlimited powers with the Progress Clause. It had never even occurred to me that they could reconcile the two simply *by not addressing the argument*. There was no inconsistency because they would not talk about the two together. There was therefore no principle that followed from the *Lopez* case: In that context, Congress's power would be limited, but in this context it would not.

Yet by what right did they get to choose which of the framers' values they would respect? By what right did they—the silent five—get to select the part of the Constitution they would enforce based on the values they thought important? We were right back to the argument that I said I hated at the start: I had failed to convince them that the issue here was important, and I had failed to recognize that however much I might hate a system in which the Court gets to pick the constitutional values that it will respect, that is the system we have.

Justices Breyer and Stevens wrote very strong dissents. Stevens's opinion was crafted internal to the law: He argued that the tradition of intellectual property law should not support this unjustified extension of terms. He based his argument on a parallel analysis that had governed in the context of patents (so had we). But the rest of the Court discounted the parallel—without explaining how the very same words in the Progress Clause could come to mean totally different things depending upon whether the words were about patents or copyrights. The Court let Justice Stevens's charge go unanswered.

Justice Breyer's opinion, perhaps the best opinion he has ever written, was external to the Constitution. He argued that the term of copyrights has become so long as to be effectively unlimited. We had said that under the current term, a copyright gave an author 99.8 percent of the value of a perpetual term. Breyer said we were wrong, that the actual number was 99.9997 percent of a perpetual term. Either way, the point was clear: If the Constitution said a term had to be "limited," and the existing term was so long as to be effectively unlimited, then it was unconstitutional.

These two justices understood all the arguments we had made. But because neither believed in the *Lopez* case, neither was willing to push it as a reason to reject this extension. The case was decided without anyone having addressed the argument that we had carried from Judge Sentelle. It was *Hamlet* without the Prince.

Defeat brings depression. They say it is a sign of health when depression gives way to anger. My anger came quickly, but it didn't cure the depression. This anger was of two sorts.

It was first anger with the five "Conservatives." It would have been one thing for them to have explained why the principle of *Lopez* didn't apply in this case. That wouldn't have been a very convincing argument, I don't believe, having read it made by others, and having tried to make it myself. But it at least would have been an act of integrity. These justices in particular have repeatedly said that the proper mode of interpreting the Constitution is "originalism"—to first understand the framers' text, interpreted in their context, in light of the structure of the Constitution. That method had produced *Lopez* and many other "originalist" rulings. Where was their "originalism" now?

Here, they had joined an opinion that never once tried to explain what the framers had meant by crafting the Progress Clause as they did; they joined an opinion that never once tried to explain how the structure of that clause would affect the interpretation of Congress's power. And they joined an opinion that didn't even try to explain why this grant of power could be unlimited, whereas the Commerce Clause would be limited. In short, they had joined an opinion that did not apply to, and was inconsistent with, their own method for interpreting the Constitution. This opinion may well have yielded a result that they liked. It did not produce a reason that was consistent with their own principles.

My anger with the Conservatives quickly yielded to anger with myself. For I had let a view of the law that I liked interfere with a view of the law as it is.

Most lawyers, and most law professors, have little patience for idealism about courts in general and this Supreme Court in particular. Most have a much more pragmatic view. When Don Ayer said that this case would be won based on whether I could convince the Justices that the framers' values were important, I fought the idea, because I didn't want to believe that that is how this Court decides. I insisted on arguing this case as if it were a simple application of a set of principles. I had an argument that followed in logic. I didn't need to waste my time showing it should also follow in popularity.

As I read back over the transcript from that argument in October, I can see a hundred places where the answers could have taken the conversation in different directions, where the truth about the harm that this unchecked power will cause could have been made clear to this Court. Justice Kennedy in good faith wanted to be shown. I, idiotically, corrected his question. Justice Souter in good faith wanted to be shown the First Amendment harms. I, like a math teacher, reframed the question to make the logical point. I had shown them how they could strike this law of Congress if they wanted to. There were a hundred places where I could have helped them want to, yet my stubbornness, my refusal to give in, stopped me. I have stood before hundreds of audiences trying to persuade; I have used passion in that effort to persuade; but I refused to stand before this audience and try to persuade with the passion I had used elsewhere. It was not the basis on which a court should decide the issue.

Would it have been different if I had argued it differently? Would it have been different if Don Ayer had argued it? Or Charles Fried? Or Kathleen Sullivan?

My friends huddled around me to insist it would not. The Court was not ready, my friends insisted. This was a loss that was destined. It would take a great deal more to show our society why our framers were right. And when we do that, we will be able to show that Court.

Maybe, but I doubt it. These Justices have no financial interest in doing anything except the right thing. They are not lobbied. They have little reason to resist doing right. I can't help but think that if I had stepped down from this pretty picture of dispassionate justice, I could have persuaded.

And even if I couldn't, then that doesn't excuse what happened in January. For at the start of this case, one of America's leading intellectual property professors stated publicly that my bringing this case was a mistake. "The Court is not ready," Peter Jaszi said; this issue should not be raised until it is.

After the argument and after the decision, Peter said to me, and publicly, that he was wrong. But if indeed that Court could not have been persuaded, then that is all the evidence that's needed to know that here again Peter was right. Either I was not ready to argue this case in a way that would do some good or they were not ready to hear this case in a way that would do some good. Either way, the decision to bring this case—a decision I had made four years before—was wrong.

While the reaction to the Sonny Bono Act itself was almost unanimously negative, the reaction to the Court's decision was mixed. No one, at least in the press, tried to say that extending the term of copyright was a good idea. We had won that battle over ideas. Where the decision was praised, it was praised by papers that had been skeptical of the Court's activism in other cases. Deference was a good thing, even if it left standing a silly law. But where the decision was attacked, it was attacked because it left standing a silly and harmful law. *The New York Times* wrote in its editorial,

> In effect, the Supreme Court's decision makes it likely that we are seeing the beginning of the end of public domain and the birth of copyright perpetuity. The public domain has been a grand experiment, one that should not be allowed to die. The ability to draw freely on the entire creative output of humanity is one of the reasons we live in a time of such fruitful creative ferment.

The best responses were in the cartoons. There was a gaggle of hilarious images—of Mickey in jail and the like. The best, from my view of the case, was Ruben Bolling's, reproduced on the next page. The "powerful and wealthy" line is a bit unfair. But the punch in the face felt exactly like that.

The image that will always stick in my head is that evoked by the quote from *The New York Times*. That "grand experiment" we call the "public domain" is over? When I can make light of it, I think, "Honey, I shrunk the Constitution." But I can rarely make light of it. We had in our Constitution a commitment to free culture. In the case that I fathered, the Supreme Court effectively renounced that commitment. A better lawyer would have made them see differently.

TOM the DANCING BUG

BY RUBEN BOLLING

DIST. BY UNIVERSAL PRESS SYNDICATE ©2008 R.BOLLING 633 www.tomthedancingbug.com

Panel 1: SUPERMAN IS PATROLLING THE CITY, WHEN HE HEARS A HIGH-PITCHED PLEA!

HELP! SUPERMAN!

Panel 2: THAT CRY CAME FROM THIS BUILDING... WHO'S THERE?

Panel 3: HA-HA! WELCOME TO MY DOMAIN, SUPERMAN! MY **PUBLIC DOMAIN!** WHERE I AM YOUR! **MASTER!**

Panel 4: THAT'S BECAUSE WHEN CONGRESS'S ENDLESS EXTENSIONS OF **COPYRIGHT TERMS** ARE DECLARED **UNCONSTITUTIONAL,** YOU'LL ALL BE MY--OR ANYONE'S-- **HELPLESS PLAYTHINGS!**

Panel 5: COPYRIGHT... FADING! CAN'T...RESIST UNAUTHORIZED...USE! IF HE CAN CAPTURE **SUPERMAN,** WHO CAN SAVE US?!

Panel 6: AND NOW I'LL FORCE YOU ALL TO PERFORM "**GONE WITH THE WIND**"! OH...ASHLEY... OH NO! **JUDGE SCALIA!!** CRASH

Panel 7: **JUDGE SCALIA**

JUDGE SCALIA, CRUSADING SUPREME COURT JUSTICE, WHO FIGHTS A NEVER-ENDING BATTLE TO PROTECT THE POWERFUL AND WEALTHY.

Panel 8: GO! RUN BACK TO YOUR CORPORATIONS!

Panel 9: B-BUT **YOU** MUST AGREE THAT THE CONSTITUTION PLAINLY LIMITS CONGRESS'S POWER... URK POW FRANKLY, PUNK, I DON'T GIVE A DAMN! THE END

CHAPTER FOURTEEN: Eldred II

The day *Eldred* was decided, fate would have it that I was to travel to Washington, D.C. (The day the rehearing petition in *Eldred* was denied—meaning the case was really finally over—fate would have it that I was giving a speech to technologists at Disney World.) This was a particularly long flight to my least favorite city. The drive into the city from Dulles was delayed because of traffic, so I opened up my computer and wrote an op-ed piece.

It was an act of contrition. During the whole of the flight from San Francisco to Washington, I had heard over and over again in my head the same advice from Don Ayer: You need to make them see why it is important. And alternating with that command was the question of Justice Kennedy: "For all these years the act has impeded progress in science and the useful arts. I just don't see any empirical evidence for that." And so, having failed in the argument of constitutional principle, finally, I turned to an argument of politics.

The New York Times published the piece. In it, I proposed a simple fix: Fifty years after a work has been published, the copyright owner would be required to register the work and pay a small fee. If he paid the fee, he got the benefit of the full term of copyright. If he did not, the work passed into the public domain.

We called this the Eldred Act, but that was just to give it a name. Eric Eldred was kind enough to let his name be used once again, but as he said early on, it won't get passed unless it has another name.

Or another two names. For depending upon your perspective, this is either the "Public Domain Enhancement Act" or the "Copyright Term Deregulation Act." Either way, the essence of the idea is clear and obvious: Remove copyright where it is doing nothing except blocking access and the spread of knowledge. Leave it for as long as Congress allows for those works where its worth is at least $1. But for everything else, let the content go.

The reaction to this idea was amazingly strong. Steve Forbes endorsed it in an editorial. I received an avalanche of e-mail and letters expressing support. When you focus the issue on lost creativity, people can see the copyright system makes no sense. As a good Republican might say, here government regulation is simply getting in the way of innovation and creativity. And as a good Democrat might say, here the government is blocking access and the spread of knowledge for no good reason. Indeed, there is no real difference between Democrats and Republicans on this issue. Anyone can recognize the stupid harm of the present system.

Indeed, many recognized the obvious benefit of the registration requirement. For one of the hardest things about the current system for people who want to license content is that there is no obvious place to look for the current copyright owners. Since registration is not required, since marking content is not required, since no formality at all is required, it is often impossibly hard to locate copyright owners to ask permission to use or license their work. This system would lower these costs, by establishing at least one registry where copyright owners could be identified.

As I described in chapter 10, formalities in copyright law were removed in 1976, when Congress followed the Europeans by abandoning any formal requirement before a copyright is granted.[1] The Europeans are said to view copyright as a "natural right." Natural rights don't need forms to exist. Traditions, like the Anglo-American tradition that required copyright owners to follow form if their rights were to be protected, did not, the Europeans thought, properly respect the dignity of the author. My right as a creator turns on my creativity, not upon the special favor of the government.

That's great rhetoric. It sounds wonderfully romantic. But it is absurd copyright policy. It is absurd especially for authors, because a world without formalities harms the creator. The ability to spread "Walt Disney creativity" is destroyed when there is no simple way to know what's protected and what's not.

The fight against formalities achieved its first real victory in Berlin in 1908. International copyright lawyers amended the Berne Convention in 1908, to require copyright terms of life plus fifty years, as well as the abolition of copyright formalities. The formalities were hated because the stories of inadvertent loss were increasingly common. It was as if a Charles Dickens character ran all copyright offices, and the failure to dot an *i* or cross a *t* resulted in the loss of widows' only income.

These complaints were real and sensible. And the strictness of the formalities, especially in the United States, was absurd. The law should always have ways of forgiving innocent mistakes. There is no reason copyright law couldn't, as well. Rather than abandoning formalities totally, the response in Berlin should have been to embrace a more equitable system of registration.

Even that would have been resisted, however, because registration in the nineteenth and twentieth centuries was still expensive. It was also a hassle. The abolishment of formalities promised not only to save the starving widows, but also to lighten an unnecessary regulatory burden imposed upon creators.

In addition to the practical complaint of authors in 1908, there was a moral claim as well. There was no reason that creative property should be a second-class form of property. If a carpenter builds a table, his rights over the table don't depend upon filing a form with the government. He has a property right over the table "naturally," and he can assert that right against anyone who would steal the table, whether or not he has informed the government of his ownership of the table.

This argument is correct, but its implications are misleading. For the argument in favor of formalities does not depend upon creative property being second-class property. The argument in favor of formalities turns upon the special problems that creative property presents. The law of formalities responds to the special physics of creative property, to assure that it can be efficiently and fairly spread.

No one thinks, for example, that land is second-class property just because you have to register a deed with a court if your sale of land is to be effective. And few would think a car is second-class property just because you must register the car with the state and tag it with a license. In both of those cases, everyone sees that there is an important reason to secure registration—both because it makes the markets more efficient and because it better secures the rights of the owner. Without a registration system for land, landowners would perpetually have to guard their property. With registration, they can simply point the police to a deed. Without a registration system for cars, auto theft would be much easier. With a registration system, the thief has a high burden to sell a stolen car. A slight burden is placed on the property owner, but those burdens produce a much better system of protection for property generally.

It is similarly special physics that makes formalities important in copyright law. Unlike a carpenter's table, there's nothing in nature that makes it relatively obvious who might own a particular bit of creative property. A recording of Lyle Lovett's latest album can exist in a billion places without anything necessarily linking it back to a particular owner. And like a car, there's no way to buy and sell creative property with confidence unless there is some simple way to authenticate who is the author and what rights he has. Simple transactions are destroyed in a world without formalities. Complex, expensive, *lawyer* transactions take their place.

This was the understanding of the problem with the Sonny Bono Act that we tried to demonstrate to the Court. This was the part it didn't "get." Because we live in a system without formalities, there is no way easily to build upon or use culture from our past. If copyright terms were, as Justice Story said they would be, "short," then this wouldn't matter much. For fourteen years, under the framers' system, a work would be presumptively controlled. After fourteen years, it would be presumptively uncontrolled.

But now that copyrights can be just about a century long, the inability to know what is protected and what is not protected becomes a huge and obvious burden on the creative process. If the only way a library can offer an Internet exhibit about the New Deal is to hire a lawyer to clear the rights to every image and sound, then the copyright system is burdening creativity in a way that has never been seen before *because there are no formalities.*

The Eldred Act was designed to respond to exactly this problem. If it is worth $1 to you, then register your work and you can get the longer term. Others will know how to contact you and, therefore, how to get your permission if they want to use your work. And you will get the benefit of an extended copyright term.

If it isn't worth it to you to register to get the benefit of an extended term, then it shouldn't be worth it for the government to defend your monopoly over that work either. The work should pass into the public domain where anyone can copy it, or build archives with it, or create a movie based on it. It should become free if it is not worth $1 to you.

Some worry about the burden on authors. Won't the burden of registering the work mean that the $1 is really misleading? Isn't the hassle worth more than $1? Isn't that the real problem with registration?

It is. The hassle is terrible. The system that exists now is awful. I completely agree that the Copyright Office has done a terrible job (no doubt because they are terribly funded) in enabling simple and cheap registrations. Any real solution to the problem of formalities must address the real problem of *governments* standing at the core of any system of formalities. In this book, I offer such a solution. That solution essentially remakes the Copyright Office. For now, assume it was Amazon that ran the registration system. Assume it was one-click registration. The Eldred Act would propose a simple, one-click registration fifty years after a work was published. Based upon historical data, that system would move up to 98 percent of commercial work, commercial work that no longer had a commercial life, into the public domain within fifty years. What do you think?

When Steve Forbes endorsed the idea, some in Washington began to pay attention. Many people contacted me pointing to representatives who might be willing to introduce the Eldred Act. And I had a few who directly suggested that they might be willing to take the first step.

One representative, Zoe Lofgren of California, went so far as to get the bill drafted. The draft solved any problem with international law. It imposed the simplest requirement upon copyright owners possible. In May 2003, it looked as if the bill would be introduced. On May 16, I posted on the Eldred Act blog, "we are close." There was a general reaction in the blog community that something good might happen here.

But at this stage, the lobbyists began to intervene. Jack Valenti and the MPAA general counsel came to the congresswoman's office to give the view of the MPAA. Aided by his lawyer, as Valenti told me, Valenti informed the congresswoman that the MPAA would oppose the Eldred Act. The reasons are embarrassingly thin. More importantly, their thinness shows something clear about what this debate is really about.

The MPAA argued first that Congress had "firmly rejected the central concept in the proposed bill"—that copyrights be renewed. That was true, but irrelevant, as Congress's "firm rejection" had occurred long before the Internet made subsequent uses much more likely. Second, they argued that the proposal would harm poor copyright own-ers—apparently those who could not afford the $1 fee. Third, they ar-gued that Congress had determined that extending a copyright term would encourage restoration work. Maybe in the case of the small per-centage of work covered by copyright law that is still commercially valuable, but again this was irrelevant, as the proposal would not cut off the extended term unless the $1 fee was not paid. Fourth, the MPAA argued that the bill would impose "enormous" costs, since a registration system is not free. True enough, but those costs are certainly less than the costs of clearing the rights for a copyright whose owner is not known. Fifth, they worried about the risks if the copyright to a story underlying a film were to pass into the public domain. But what risk is that? If it is in the public domain, then the film is a valid derivative use.

Finally, the MPAA argued that existing law enabled copyright owners to do this if they wanted. But the whole point is that there are thousands of copyright owners who don't even know they have a copy-right to give. Whether they are free to give away their copyright or not—a controversial claim in any case—unless they know about a copyright, they're not likely to.

At the beginning of this book, I told two stories about the law re-acting to changes in technology. In the one, common sense prevailed. In the other, common sense was delayed. The difference between the two stories was the power of the opposition—the power of the side that fought to defend the status quo. In both cases, a new technology threat-ened old interests. But in only one case did those interest's have the power to protect themselves against this new competitive threat.

I used these two cases as a way to frame the war that this book has been about. For here, too, a new technology is forcing the law to react. And here, too, we should ask, is the law following or resisting common sense? If common sense supports the law, what explains this common sense?

When the issue is piracy, it is right for the law to back the copyright owners. The commercial piracy that I described is wrong and harmful, and the law should work to eliminate it. When the issue is p2p sharing, it is easy to understand why the law backs the owners still: Much of this sharing is wrong, even if much is harmless. When the issue is copyright terms for the Mickey Mouses of the world, it is possible still to understand why the law favors Hollywood: Most people don't recognize the reasons for limiting copyright terms; it is thus still possible to see good faith within the resistance.

But when the copyright owners oppose a proposal such as the Eldred Act, then, finally, there is an example that lays bare the naked self-interest driving this war. This act would free an extraordinary range of content that is otherwise unused. It wouldn't interfere with any copyright owner's desire to exercise continued control over his content. It would simply liberate what Kevin Kelly calls the "Dark Content" that fills archives around the world. So when the warriors oppose a change like this, we should ask one simple question:

What does this industry really want?

With very little effort, the warriors could protect their content. So the effort to block something like the Eldred Act is not really about protecting *their* content. The effort to block the Eldred Act is an effort to assure that nothing more passes into the public domain. It is another step to assure that the public domain will never compete, that there will be no use of content that is not commercially controlled, and that there will be no commercial use of content that doesn't require *their* permission first.

The opposition to the Eldred Act reveals how extreme the other side is. The most powerful and sexy and well loved of lobbies really has as its aim not the protection of "property" but the rejection of a tradition. Their aim is not simply to protect what is theirs. *Their aim is to assure that all there is is what is theirs.*

It is not hard to understand why the warriors take this view. It is not hard to see why it would benefit them if the competition of the public domain tied to the Internet could somehow be quashed. Just as RCA feared the competition of FM, they fear the competition of a public domain connected to a public that now has the means to create with it and to share its own creation.

What is hard to understand is why the public takes this view. It is as if the law made airplanes trespassers. The MPAA stands with the Causbys and demands that their remote and useless property rights be respected, so that these remote and forgotten copyright holders might block the progress of others.

All this seems to follow easily from this untroubled acceptance of the "property" in intellectual property. Common sense supports it, and so long as it does, the assaults will rain down upon the technologies of the Internet. The consequence will be an increasing "permission society." The past can be cultivated only if you can identify the owner and gain permission to build upon his work. The future will be controlled by this dead (and often unfindable) hand of the past.

CONCLUSION

There are more than 35 million people with the AIDS virus worldwide. Twenty-five million of them live in sub-Saharan Africa. Seventeen million have already died. Seventeen million Africans is proportional percentage-wise to seven million Americans. More importantly, it is seventeen million Africans.

There is no cure for AIDS, but there are drugs to slow its progression. These antiretroviral therapies are still experimental, but they have already had a dramatic effect. In the United States, AIDS patients who regularly take a cocktail of these drugs increase their life expectancy by ten to twenty years. For some, the drugs make the disease almost invisible.

These drugs are expensive. When they were first introduced in the United States, they cost between $10,000 and $15,000 per person per year. Today, some cost $25,000 per year. At these prices, of course, no African nation can afford the drugs for the vast majority of its population: $15,000 is thirty times the per capita gross national product of Zimbabwe. At these prices, the drugs are totally unavailable.[1]

These prices are not high because the ingredients of the drugs are expensive. These prices are high because the drugs are protected by patents. The drug companies that produced these life-saving mixes enjoy at least a twenty-year monopoly for their inventions. They use that monopoly power to extract the most they can from the market. That power is in turn used to keep the prices high.

There are many who are skeptical of patents, especially drug patents. I am not. Indeed, of all the areas of research that might be supported by patents, drug research is, in my view, the clearest case where patents are needed. The patent gives the drug company some assurance that if it is successful in inventing a new drug to treat a disease, it will be able to earn back its investment and more. This is socially an extremely valuable incentive. I am the last person who would argue that the law should abolish it, at least without other changes.

But it is one thing to support patents, even drug patents. It is another thing to determine how best to deal with a crisis. And as African leaders began to recognize the devastation that AIDS was bringing, they started looking for ways to import HIV treatments at costs significantly below the market price.

In 1997, South Africa tried one tack. It passed a law to allow the importation of patented medicines that had been produced or sold in another nation's market with the consent of the patent owner. For example, if the drug was sold in India, it could be imported into Africa from India. This is called "parallel importation," and it is generally permitted under international trade law and is specifically permitted within the European Union.[2]

However, the United States government opposed the bill. Indeed, more than opposed. As the International Intellectual Property Association characterized it, "The U.S. government pressured South Africa . . . not to permit compulsory licensing or parallel imports."[3] Through the Office of the United States Trade Representative, the government asked South Africa to change the law—and to add pressure to that request, in 1998, the USTR listed South Africa for possible trade sanctions. That same year, more than forty pharmaceutical companies began proceedings in the South African courts to challenge the government's actions. The United States was then joined by other governments from the EU. Their claim, and the claim of the pharmaceutical companies, was that South Africa was violating its obligations under international law by discriminating against a particular kind of patent—pharmaceutical patents. The demand of these governments, with the United States in the lead, was that South Africa respect these patents as it respects any other patent, regardless of any effect on the treatment of AIDS within South Africa.[4]

We should place the intervention by the United States in context. No doubt patents are not the most important reason that Africans don't have access to drugs. Poverty and the total absence of an effective health care infrastructure matter more. But whether patents are the most important reason or not, the price of drugs has an effect on their demand, and patents affect price. And so, whether massive or marginal, there was an effect from our government's intervention to stop the flow of medications into Africa.

By stopping the flow of HIV treatment into Africa, the United States government was not saving drugs for United States citizens. This is not like wheat (if they eat it, we can't); instead, the flow that the United States intervened to stop was, in effect, a flow of knowledge: information about how to take chemicals that exist within Africa, and turn those chemicals into drugs that would save 15 to 30 million lives.

Nor was the intervention by the United States going to protect the profits of United States drug companies—at least, not substantially. It was not as if these countries were in the position to buy the drugs for the prices the drug companies were charging. Again, the Africans are wildly too poor to afford these drugs at the offered prices. Stopping the parallel import of these drugs would not substantially increase the sales by U.S. companies.

Instead, the argument in favor of restricting this flow of information, which was needed to save the lives of millions, was an argument about the sanctity of property.[5] It was because "intellectual property" would be violated that these drugs should not flow into Africa. It was a principle about the importance of "intellectual property" that led these government actors to intervene against the South African response to AIDS.

Now just step back for a moment. There will be a time thirty years from now when our children look back at us and ask, how could we have let this happen? How could we allow a policy to be pursued whose direct cost would be to speed the death of 15 to 30 million Africans, and whose only real benefit would be to uphold the "sanctity" of an idea? What possible justification could there ever be for a policy that results in so many deaths? What exactly is the insanity that would allow so many to die for such an abstraction?

Some blame the drug companies. I don't. They are corporations. Their managers are ordered by law to make money for the corporation. They push a certain patent policy not because of ideals, but because it is the policy that makes them the most money. And it only makes them the most money because of a certain corruption within our political system— a corruption the drug companies are certainly not responsible for.

The corruption is our own politicians' failure of integrity. For the drug companies would love—they say, and I believe them—to sell their drugs as cheaply as they can to countries in Africa and elsewhere. There are issues they'd have to resolve to make sure the drugs didn't get back into the United States, but those are mere problems of technology. They could be overcome.

A different problem, however, could not be overcome. This is the fear of the grandstanding politician who would call the presidents of the drug companies before a Senate or House hearing, and ask, "How is it you can sell this HIV drug in Africa for only $1 a pill, but the same drug would cost an American $1,500?" Because there is no "sound bite" answer to that question, its effect would be to induce regulation of prices in America. The drug companies thus avoid this spiral by avoiding the first step. They reinforce the idea that property should be sacred. They adopt a rational strategy in an irrational context, with the unintended consequence that perhaps millions die. And that rational strategy thus becomes framed in terms of this ideal—the sanctity of an idea called "intellectual property."

So when the common sense of your child confronts you, what will you say? When the common sense of a generation finally revolts against what we have done, how will we justify what we have done? What is the argument?

A sensible patent policy could endorse and strongly support the patent system without having to reach everyone everywhere in exactly the same way. Just as a sensible copyright policy could endorse and strongly support a copyright system without having to regulate the spread of culture perfectly and forever, a sensible patent policy could endorse and strongly support a patent system without having to block the spread of drugs to a country not rich enough to afford market prices in any case. A sensible policy, in other words, could be a balanced policy. For most of our history, both copyright and patent policies were balanced in just this sense.

But we as a culture have lost this sense of balance. We have lost the critical eye that helps us see the difference between truth and extremism. A certain property fundamentalism, having no connection to our tradition, now reigns in this culture—bizarrely, and with consequences more grave to the spread of ideas and culture than almost any other single policy decision that we as a democracy will make.

A simple idea blinds us, and under the cover of darkness, much happens that most of us would reject if any of us looked. So uncritically do we accept the idea of property in ideas that we don't even notice how monstrous it is to deny ideas to a people who are dying without them. So uncritically do we accept the idea of property in culture that we don't even question when the control of that property removes our ability, as a people, to develop our culture democratically. Blindness becomes our common sense. And the challenge for anyone who would reclaim the right to cultivate our culture is to find a way to make this common sense open its eyes.

So far, common sense sleeps. There is no revolt. Common sense does not yet see what there could be to revolt about. The extremism that now dominates this debate fits with ideas that seem natural, and that fit is reinforced by the RCAs of our day. They wage a frantic war to fight "piracy," and devastate a culture for creativity. They defend the idea of "creative property," while transforming real creators into modern-day sharecroppers. They are insulted by the idea that rights should be balanced, even though each of the major players in this content war was itself a beneficiary of a more balanced ideal. The hypocrisy reeks. Yet in a city like Washington, hypocrisy is not even noticed. Powerful lobbies, complex issues, and MTV attention spans produce the "perfect storm" for free culture.

In August 2003, a fight broke out in the United States about a decision by the World Intellectual Property Organization to cancel a meeting.[6] At the request of a wide range of interests, WIPO had decided to hold a meeting to discuss "open and collaborative projects to create public goods." These are projects that have been successful in producing public goods without relying exclusively upon a proprietary use of intellectual property. Examples include the Internet and the World Wide Web, both of which were developed on the basis of protocols in the public domain. It included an emerging trend to support open academic journals, including the Public Library of Science project that I describe in the Afterword. It included a project to develop single nucleotide polymorphisms (SNPs), which are thought to have great significance in biomedical research. (That nonprofit project comprised a consortium of the Wellcome Trust and pharmaceutical and technological companies, including Amersham Biosciences, AstraZeneca,

Aventis, Bayer, Bristol-Myers Squibb, Hoffmann-La Roche, Glaxo-SmithKline, IBM, Motorola, Novartis, Pfizer, and Searle.) It included the Global Positioning System, which Ronald Reagan set free in the early 1980s. And it included "open source and free software."

The aim of the meeting was to consider this wide range of projects from one common perspective: that none of these projects relied upon intellectual property extremism. Instead, in all of them, intellectual property was balanced by agreements to keep access open or to impose limitations on the way in which proprietary claims might be used.

From the perspective of this book, then, the conference was ideal.[7] The projects within its scope included both commercial and noncommercial work. They primarily involved science, but from many perspectives. And WIPO was an ideal venue for this discussion, since WIPO is the preeminent international body dealing with intellectual property issues.

Indeed, I was once publicly scolded for not recognizing this fact about WIPO. In February 2003, I delivered a keynote address to a preparatory conference for the World Summit on the Information Society (WSIS). At a press conference before the address, I was asked what I would say. I responded that I would be talking a little about the importance of balance in intellectual property for the development of an information society. The moderator for the event then promptly interrupted to inform me and the assembled reporters that no question about intellectual property would be discussed by WSIS, since those questions were the exclusive domain of WIPO. In the talk that I had prepared, I had actually made the issue of intellectual property relatively minor. But after this astonishing statement, I made intellectual property the sole focus of my talk. There was no way to talk about an "Information Society" unless one also talked about the range of information and culture that would be free. My talk did not make my immoderate moderator very happy. And she was no doubt correct that the scope of intellectual property protections was ordinarily the stuff of

WIPO. But in my view, there couldn't be too much of a conversation about how much intellectual property is needed, since in my view, the very idea of balance in intellectual property had been lost.

So whether or not WSIS can discuss balance in intellectual property, I had thought it was taken for granted that WIPO could and should. And thus the meeting about "open and collaborative projects to create public goods" seemed perfectly appropriate within the WIPO agenda.

But there is one project within that list that is highly controversial, at least among lobbyists. That project is "open source and free software." Microsoft in particular is wary of discussion of the subject. From its perspective, a conference to discuss open source and free software would be like a conference to discuss Apple's operating system. Both open source and free software compete with Microsoft's software. And internationally, many governments have begun to explore requirements that they use open source or free software, rather than "proprietary software," for their own internal uses.

I don't mean to enter that debate here. It is important only to make clear that the distinction is not between commercial and noncommercial software. There are many important companies that depend fundamentally upon open source and free software, IBM being the most prominent. IBM is increasingly shifting its focus to the GNU/Linux operating system, the most famous bit of "free software"—and IBM is emphatically a commercial entity. Thus, to support "open source and free software" is not to oppose commercial entities. It is, instead, to support a mode of software development that is different from Microsoft's.[8]

More important for our purposes, to support "open source and free software" is not to oppose copyright. "Open source and free software" is not software in the public domain. Instead, like Microsoft's software, the copyright owners of free and open source software insist quite strongly that the terms of their software license be respected by adopters of free and open source software. The terms of that license are no doubt different from the terms of a proprietary software license. Free software licensed under the General Public License (GPL), for example, requires that the source code for the software be made available by anyone who modifies and redistributes the software. But that requirement is effective only if copyright governs software. If copyright did not govern software, then free software could not impose the same kind of requirements on its adopters. It thus depends upon copyright law just as Microsoft does.

It is therefore understandable that as a proprietary software developer, Microsoft would oppose this WIPO meeting, and understandable that it would use its lobbyists to get the United States government to oppose it, as well. And indeed, that is just what was reported to have happened. According to Jonathan Krim of the *Washington Post*, Microsoft's lobbyists succeeded in getting the United States government to veto the meeting.[9] And without U.S. backing, the meeting was canceled.

I don't blame Microsoft for doing what it can to advance its own interests, consistent with the law. And lobbying governments is plainly consistent with the law. There was nothing surprising about its lobbying here, and nothing terribly surprising about the most powerful software producer in the United States having succeeded in its lobbying efforts.

What was surprising was the United States government's reason for opposing the meeting. Again, as reported by Krim, Lois Boland, acting director of international relations for the U.S. Patent and Trademark Office, explained that "open-source software runs counter to the mission of WIPO, which is to promote intellectual-property rights." She is quoted as saying, "To hold a meeting which has as its purpose to disclaim or waive such rights seems to us to be contrary to the goals of WIPO."

These statements are astonishing on a number of levels.

First, they are just flat wrong. As I described, most open source and free software relies fundamentally upon the intellectual property right called "copyright." Without it, restrictions imposed by those licenses wouldn't work. Thus, to say it "runs counter" to the mission of promoting intellectual property rights reveals an extraordinary gap in understanding—the sort of mistake that is excusable in a first-year law student, but an embarrassment from a high government official dealing with intellectual property issues.

Second, who ever said that WIPO's exclusive aim was to "promote" intellectual property maximally? As I had been scolded at the preparatory conference of WSIS, WIPO is to consider not only how best to protect intellectual property, but also what the best balance of intellectual property is. As every economist and lawyer knows, the hard question in intellectual property law is to find that balance. But that there should be limits is, I had thought, uncontested. One wants to ask Ms. Boland, are generic drugs (drugs based on drugs whose patent has expired) contrary to the WIPO mission? Does the public domain weaken intellectual property? Would it have been better if the protocols of the Internet had been patented?

Third, even if one believed that the purpose of WIPO was to maximize intellectual property rights, in our tradition, intellectual property rights are held by individuals and corporations. They get to decide what to do with those rights because, again, they are *their* rights. If they want to "waive" or "disclaim" their rights, that is, within our tradition, totally appropriate. When Bill Gates gives away more than $20 billion to do good in the world, that is not inconsistent with the objectives of the property system. That is, on the contrary, just what a property system is supposed to be about: giving individuals the right to decide what to do with *their* property.

When Ms. Boland says that there is something wrong with a meeting "which has as its purpose to disclaim or waive such rights," she's saying that WIPO has an interest in interfering with the choices of the individuals who own intellectual property rights. That somehow, WIPO's objective should be to stop an individual from "waiving" or "disclaiming" an intellectual property right. That the interest of WIPO is not just that intellectual property rights be maximized, but that they also should be exercised in the most extreme and restrictive way possible.

There is a history of just such a property system that is well known in the Anglo-American tradition. It is called "feudalism." Under feudalism, not only was property held by a relatively small number of individuals and entities. And not only were the rights that ran with that property powerful and extensive. But the feudal system had a strong interest in assuring that property holders within that system not weaken feudalism by liberating people or property within their control to the free market. Feudalism depended upon maximum control and concentration. It fought any freedom that might interfere with that control.

As Peter Drahos and John Braithwaite relate, this is precisely the choice we are now making about intellectual property.[10] We will have an information society. That much is certain. Our only choice now is whether that information society will be *free* or *feudal*. The trend is toward the feudal.

When this battle broke, I blogged it. A spirited debate within the comment section ensued. Ms. Boland had a number of supporters who tried to show why her comments made sense. But there was one comment that was particularly depressing for me. An anonymous poster wrote,

> George, you misunderstand Lessig: He's only talking about the world as it should be ("the goal of WIPO, and the goal of any government, should be to promote the right balance of intellectual-property rights, not simply to promote intellectual property rights"), not as it is. If we were talking about the world as it is, then of course Boland didn't say anything wrong. But in the world

as Lessig would have it, then of course she did. Always pay attention to the distinction between Lessig's world and ours.

I missed the irony the first time I read it. I read it quickly and thought the poster was supporting the idea that seeking balance was what our government should be doing. (Of course, my criticism of Ms. Boland was not about whether she was seeking balance or not; my criticism was that her comments betrayed a first-year law student's mistake. I have no illusion about the extremism of our government, whether Republican or Democrat. My only illusion apparently is about whether our government should speak the truth or not.)

Obviously, however, the poster was not supporting that idea. Instead, the poster was ridiculing the very idea that in the real world, the "goal" of a government should be "to promote the right balance" of intellectual property. That was obviously silly to him. And it obviously betrayed, he believed, my own silly utopianism. "Typical for an academic," the poster might well have continued.

I understand criticism of academic utopianism. I think utopianism is silly, too, and I'd be the first to poke fun at the absurdly unrealistic ideals of academics throughout history (and not just in our own country's history).

But when it has become silly to suppose that the role of our government should be to "seek balance," then count me with the silly, for that means that this has become quite serious indeed. If it should be obvious to everyone that the government does not seek balance, that the government is simply the tool of the most powerful lobbyists, that the idea of holding the government to a different standard is absurd, that the idea of demanding of the government that it speak truth and not lies is just naïve, then who have we, the most powerful democracy in the world, become?

It might be crazy to expect a high government official to speak the truth. It might be crazy to believe that government policy will be something more than the handmaiden of the most powerful interests.

It might be crazy to argue that we should preserve a tradition that has been part of our tradition for most of our history—free culture. If this is crazy, then let there be more crazies. Soon.

There are moments of hope in this struggle. And moments that surprise. When the FCC was considering relaxing ownership rules, which would thereby further increase the concentration in media ownership, an extraordinary bipartisan coalition formed to fight this change. For perhaps the first time in history, interests as diverse as the NRA, the ACLU, Moveon.org, William Safire, Ted Turner, and CodePink Women for Peace organized to oppose this change in FCC policy. An astonishing 700,000 letters were sent to the FCC, demanding more hearings and a different result.

This activism did not stop the FCC, but soon after, a broad coalition in the Senate voted to reverse the FCC decision. The hostile hearings leading up to that vote revealed just how powerful this movement had become. There was no substantial support for the FCC's decision, and there was broad and sustained support for fighting further concentration in the media.

But even this movement misses an important piece of the puzzle. Largeness as such is not bad. Freedom is not threatened just because some become very rich, or because there are only a handful of big players. The poor quality of Big Macs or Quarter Pounders does not mean that you can't get a good hamburger from somewhere else.

The danger in media concentration comes not from the concentration, but instead from the feudalism that this concentration, tied to the change in copyright, produces. It is not just that there are a few powerful companies that control an ever expanding slice of the media. It is that this concentration can call upon an equally bloated range of rights—property rights of a historically extreme form—that makes their bigness bad.

It is therefore significant that so many would rally to demand competition and increased diversity. Still, if the rally is understood as being about bigness alone, it is not terribly surprising. We Americans have a long history of fighting "big," wisely or not. That we could be motivated to fight "big" again is not something new.

It would be something new, and something very important, if an equal number could be rallied to fight the increasing extremism built within the idea of "intellectual property." Not because balance is alien to our tradition; indeed, as I've argued, balance is our tradition. But because the muscle to think critically about the scope of anything called "property" is not well exercised within this tradition anymore.

If we were Achilles, this would be our heel. This would be the place of our tragedy.

As I write these final words, the news is filled with stories about the RIAA lawsuits against almost three hundred individuals.[11] Eminem has just been sued for "sampling" someone else's music.[12] The story about Bob Dylan "stealing" from a Japanese author has just finished making the rounds.[13] An insider from Hollywood—who insists he must remain anonymous—reports "an amazing conversation with these studio guys. They've got extraordinary [old] content that they'd love to use but can't because they can't begin to clear the rights. They've got scores of kids who could do amazing things with the content, but it would take scores of lawyers to clean it first." Congressmen are talking about deputizing computer viruses to bring down computers thought to violate the law. Universities are threatening expulsion for kids who use a computer to share content.

Yet on the other side of the Atlantic, the BBC has just announced that it will build a "Creative Archive," from which British citizens can download BBC content, and rip, mix, and burn it.[14] And in Brazil, the culture minister, Gilberto Gil, himself a folk hero of Brazilian music, has joined with Creative Commons to release content and free licenses in that Latin American country.[15]

I've told a dark story. The truth is more mixed. A technology has given us a new freedom. Slowly, some begin to understand that this freedom need not mean anarchy. We can carry a free culture into the twenty-first century, without artists losing and without the potential of digital technology being destroyed. It will take some thought, and more importantly, it will take some will to transform the RCAs of our day into the Causbys.

Common sense must revolt. It must act to free culture. Soon, if this potential is ever to be realized.

AFTERWORD

At least some who have read this far will agree with me that something must be done to change where we are heading. The balance of this book maps what might be done.

I divide this map into two parts: that which anyone can do now, and that which requires the help of lawmakers. If there is one lesson that we can draw from the history of remaking common sense, it is that it requires remaking how many people think about the very same issue.

That means this movement must begin in the streets. It must recruit a significant number of parents, teachers, librarians, creators, authors, musicians, filmmakers, scientists—all to tell this story in their own words, and to tell their neighbors why this battle is so important.

Once this movement has its effect in the streets, it has some hope of having an effect in Washington. We are still a democracy. What people think matters. Not as much as it should, at least when an RCA stands opposed, but still, it matters. And thus, in the second part below, I sketch changes that Congress could make to better secure a free culture.

US, NOW

Common sense is with the copyright warriors because the debate so far has been framed at the extremes—as a grand either/or: either property or anarchy, either total control or artists won't be paid. If that really is the choice, then the warriors should win.

The mistake here is the error of the excluded middle. There are extremes in this debate, but the extremes are not all that there is. There are those who believe in maximal copyright—"All Rights Reserved"—and those who reject copyright—"No Rights Reserved." The "All Rights Reserved" sorts believe that you should ask permission before you "use" a copyrighted work in any way. The "No Rights Reserved" sorts believe you should be able to do with content as you wish, regardless of whether you have permission or not.

When the Internet was first born, its initial architecture effectively tilted in the "no rights reserved" direction. Content could be copied perfectly and cheaply; rights could not easily be controlled. Thus, regardless of anyone's desire, the effective regime of copyright under the original design of the Internet was "no rights reserved." Content was "taken" regardless of the rights. Any rights were effectively unprotected.

This initial character produced a reaction (opposite, but not quite equal) by copyright owners. That reaction has been the topic of this book. Through legislation, litigation, and changes to the network's design, copyright holders have been able to change the essential character of the environment of the original Internet. If the original architecture made the effective default "no rights reserved," the future architecture will make the effective default "all rights reserved." The architecture and law that surround the Internet's design will increasingly produce an environment where all use of content requires permission. The "cut and paste" world that defines the Internet today will become a "get permission to cut and paste" world that is a creator's nightmare.

What's needed is a way to say something in the middle—neither "all rights reserved" nor "no rights reserved" but "some rights reserved"—and thus a way to respect copyrights but enable creators to free content as they see fit. In other words, we need a way to restore a set of freedoms that we could just take for granted before.

Rebuilding Freedoms Previously Presumed: Examples

If you step back from the battle I've been describing here, you will recognize this problem from other contexts. Think about privacy. Before the Internet, most of us didn't have to worry much about data about our lives that we broadcast to the world. If you walked into a bookstore and browsed through some of the works of Karl Marx, you didn't need to worry about explaining your browsing habits to your neighbors or boss. The "privacy" of your browsing habits was assured.

What made it assured?

Well, if we think in terms of the modalities I described in chapter 10, your privacy was assured because of an inefficient architecture for gathering data and hence a market constraint (cost) on anyone who wanted to gather that data. If you were a suspected spy for North Korea, working for the CIA, no doubt your privacy would not be assured. But that's because the CIA would (we hope) find it valuable enough to spend the thousands required to track you. But for most of us (again, we can hope), spying doesn't pay. The highly inefficient architecture of real space means we all enjoy a fairly robust amount of privacy. That privacy is guaranteed to us by friction. Not by law (there is no law protecting "privacy" in public places), and in many places, not by norms (snooping and gossip are just fun), but instead, by the costs that friction imposes on anyone who would want to spy.

Enter the Internet, where the cost of tracking browsing in particular has become quite tiny. If you're a customer at Amazon, then as you browse the pages, Amazon collects the data about what you've looked at. You know this because at the side of the page, there's a list of "recently viewed" pages. Now, because of the architecture of the Net and the function of cookies on the Net, it is easier to collect the data than not. The friction has disappeared, and hence any "privacy" protected by the friction disappears, too.

Amazon, of course, is not the problem. But we might begin to worry about libraries. If you're one of those crazy lefties who thinks that people should have the "right" to browse in a library without the government knowing which books you look at (I'm one of those lefties, too), then this change in the technology of monitoring might concern you. If it becomes simple to gather and sort who does what in electronic spaces, then the friction-induced privacy of yesterday disappears.

It is this reality that explains the push of many to define "privacy" on the Internet. It is the recognition that technology can remove what friction before gave us that leads many to push for laws to do what friction did.[1] And whether you're in favor of those laws or not, it is the pattern that is important here. We must take affirmative steps to secure a kind of freedom that was passively provided before. A change in technology now forces those who believe in privacy to affirmatively act where, before, privacy was given by default.

A similar story could be told about the birth of the free software movement. When computers with software were first made available commercially, the software—both the source code and the binaries—was free. You couldn't run a program written for a Data General machine on an IBM machine, so Data General and IBM didn't care much about controlling their software.

That was the world Richard Stallman was born into, and while he was a researcher at MIT, he grew to love the community that developed when one was free to explore and tinker with the software that ran on machines. Being a smart sort himself, and a talented programmer, Stallman grew to depend upon the freedom to add to or modify other people's work.

In an academic setting, at least, that's not a terribly radical idea. In a math department, anyone would be free to tinker with a proof that someone offered. If you thought you had a better way to prove a theorem, you could take what someone else did and change it. In a classics department, if you believed a colleague's translation of a recently discovered text was flawed, you were free to improve it. Thus, to Stallman, it seemed obvious that you should be free to tinker with and improve the code that ran a machine. This, too, was knowledge. Why shouldn't it be open for criticism like anything else?

No one answered that question. Instead, the architecture of revenue for computing changed. As it became possible to import programs from one system to another, it became economically attractive (at least in the view of some) to hide the code of your program. So, too, as companies started selling peripherals for mainframe systems. If I could just take your printer driver and copy it, then that would make it easier for me to sell a printer to the market than it was for you.

Thus, the practice of proprietary code began to spread, and by the early 1980s, Stallman found himself surrounded by proprietary code.

The world of free software had been erased by a change in the economics of computing. And as he believed, if he did nothing about it, then the freedom to change and share software would be fundamentally weakened.

Therefore, in 1984, Stallman began a project to build a free operating system, so that at least a strain of free software would survive. That was the birth of the GNU project, into which Linus Torvalds's "Linux" kernel was added to produce the GNU/Linux operating system.

Stallman's technique was to use copyright law to build a world of software that must be kept free. Software licensed under the Free Software Foundation's GPL cannot be modified and distributed unless the source code for that software is made available as well. Thus, anyone building upon GPL'd software would have to make their buildings free as well. This would assure, Stallman believed, that an ecology of code would develop that remained free for others to build upon. His fundamental goal was freedom; innovative creative code was a byproduct.

Stallman was thus doing for software what privacy advocates now do for privacy. He was seeking a way to rebuild a kind of freedom that was taken for granted before. Through the affirmative use of licenses that bind copyrighted code, Stallman was affirmatively reclaiming a space where free software would survive. He was actively protecting what before had been passively guaranteed.

Finally, consider a very recent example that more directly resonates with the story of this book. This is the shift in the way academic and scientific journals are produced.

As digital technologies develop, it is becoming obvious to many that printing thousands of copies of journals every month and sending them to libraries is perhaps not the most efficient way to distribute knowledge. Instead, journals are increasingly becoming electronic, and libraries and their users are given access to these electronic journals through password-protected sites. Something similar to this has been happening in law for almost thirty years: Lexis and Westlaw have had electronic versions of case reports available to subscribers to their service. Although a Supreme Court opinion is not copyrighted, and anyone is free to go to a library and read it, Lexis and Westlaw are also free to charge users for the privilege of gaining access to that Supreme Court opinion through their respective services.

There's nothing wrong in general with this, and indeed, the ability to charge for access to even public domain materials is a good incentive for people to develop new and innovative ways to spread knowledge. The law has agreed, which is why Lexis and Westlaw have been allowed to flourish. And if there's nothing wrong with selling the public domain, then there could be nothing wrong, in principle, with selling access to material that is not in the public domain.

But what if the only way to get access to social and scientific data was through proprietary services? What if no one had the ability to browse this data except by paying for a subscription?

As many are beginning to notice, this is increasingly the reality with scientific journals. When these journals were distributed in paper form, libraries could make the journals available to anyone who had access to the library. Thus, patients with cancer could become cancer experts because the library gave them access. Or patients trying to understand the risks of a certain treatment could research those risks by reading all available articles about that treatment. This freedom was therefore a function of the institution of libraries (norms) and the technology of paper journals (architecture)—namely, that it was very hard to control access to a paper journal.

As journals become electronic, however, the publishers are demanding that libraries not give the general public access to the journals. This means that the freedoms provided by print journals in public libraries begin to disappear. Thus, as with privacy and with software, a changing technology and market shrink a freedom taken for granted before.

This shrinking freedom has led many to take affirmative steps to restore the freedom that has been lost. The Public Library of Science (PLoS), for example, is a nonprofit corporation dedicated to making scientific research available to anyone with a Web connection. Authors of scientific work submit that work to the Public Library of Science. That work is then subject to peer review. If accepted, the work is then deposited in a public, electronic archive and made permanently available for free. PLoS also sells a print version of its work, but the copyright for the print journal does not inhibit the right of anyone to redistribute the work for free.

This is one of many such efforts to restore a freedom taken for granted before, but now threatened by changing technology and markets. There's no doubt that this alternative competes with the traditional publishers and their efforts to make money from the exclusive distribution of content. But competition in our tradition is presumptively a good—especially when it helps spread knowledge and science.

Rebuilding Free Culture: One Idea

The same strategy could be applied to culture, as a response to the increasing control effected through law and technology.

Enter the Creative Commons. The Creative Commons is a non-profit corporation established in Massachusetts, but with its home at Stanford University. Its aim is to build a layer of *reasonable* copyright on top of the extremes that now reign. It does this by making it easy for people to build upon other people's work, by making it simple for creators to express the freedom for others to take and build upon their work. Simple tags, tied to human-readable descriptions, tied to bullet-proof licenses, make this possible.

Simple—which means without a middleman, or without a lawyer. By developing a free set of licenses that people can attach to their content, Creative Commons aims to mark a range of content that can easily, and reliably, be built upon. These tags are then linked to machine-readable versions of the license that enable computers automatically to identify content that can easily be shared. These three expressions together—a legal license, a human-readable description, and machine-readable tags—constitute a Creative Commons license. A Creative Commons license constitutes a grant of freedom to anyone who accesses the license, and more importantly, an expression of the ideal that the person associated with the license believes in something different than the "All" or "No" extremes. Content is marked with the CC mark, which does not mean that copyright is waived, but that certain freedoms are given.

These freedoms are beyond the freedoms promised by fair use. Their precise contours depend upon the choices the creator makes. The creator can choose a license that permits any use, so long as attribution is given. She can choose a license that permits only noncommercial use. She can choose a license that permits any use so long as the same freedoms are given to other uses ("share and share alike"). Or any use so long as no derivative use is made. Or any use at all within developing nations. Or any sampling use, so long as full copies are not made. Or lastly, any educational use.

These choices thus establish a range of freedoms beyond the default of copyright law. They also enable freedoms that go beyond traditional fair use. And most importantly, they express these freedoms in a way that subsequent users can use and rely upon without the need to hire a lawyer. Creative Commons thus aims to build a layer of content, governed by a layer of reasonable copyright law, that others can build upon. Voluntary choice of individuals and creators will make this content available. And that content will in turn enable us to rebuild a public domain.

This is just one project among many within the Creative Commons. And of course, Creative Commons is not the only organization pursuing such freedoms. But the point that distinguishes the Creative Commons from many is that we are not interested only in talking about a public domain or in getting legislators to help build a public domain. Our aim is to build a movement of consumers and producers of content ("content conducers," as attorney Mia Garlick calls them) who help build the public domain and, by their work, demonstrate the importance of the public domain to other creativity.

The aim is not to fight the "All Rights Reserved" sorts. The aim is to complement them. The problems that the law creates for us as a culture are produced by insane and unintended consequences of laws written centuries ago, applied to a technology that only Jefferson could have imagined. The rules may well have made sense against a background of technologies from centuries ago, but they do not make sense against the background of digital technologies. New rules—with different freedoms, expressed in ways so that humans without lawyers can use them—are needed. Creative Commons gives people a way effectively to begin to build those rules.

Why would creators participate in giving up total control? Some participate to better spread their content. Cory Doctorow, for example, is a science fiction author. His first novel, *Down and Out in the Magic Kingdom*, was released on-line and for free, under a Creative Commons license, on the same day that it went on sale in bookstores.

Why would a publisher ever agree to this? I suspect his publisher reasoned like this: There are two groups of people out there: (1) those who will buy Cory's book whether or not it's on the Internet, and (2) those who may never hear of Cory's book, if it isn't made available for free on the Internet. Some part of (1) will download Cory's book instead of buying it. Call them bad-(1)s. Some part of (2) will download Cory's book, like it, and then decide to buy it. Call them (2)-goods. If there are more (2)-goods than bad-(1)s, the strategy of releasing Cory's book free on-line will probably *increase* sales of Cory's book.

Indeed, the experience of his publisher clearly supports that conclusion. The book's first printing was exhausted months before the publisher had expected. This first novel of a science fiction author was a total success.

The idea that free content might increase the value of nonfree content was confirmed by the experience of another author. Peter Wayner, who wrote a book about the free software movement titled *Free for All*, made an electronic version of his book free on-line under a Creative Commons license after the book went out of print. He then monitored used book store prices for the book. As predicted, as the number of downloads increased, the used book price for his book increased, as well.

These are examples of using the Commons to better spread proprietary content. I believe that is a wonderful and common use of the Commons. There are others who use Creative Commons licenses for other reasons. Many who use the "sampling license" do so because anything else would be hypocritical. The sampling license says that others are free, for commercial or noncommercial purposes, to sample content from the licensed work; they are just not free to make full copies of the licensed work available to others. This is consistent with their own art—they, too, sample from others. Because the *legal* costs of sampling are so high (Walter Leaphart, manager of the rap group Public Enemy, which was born sampling the music of others, has stated that he does not "allow" Public Enemy to sample anymore, because the legal costs are so high[2]), these artists release into the creative environment content that others can build upon, so that their form of creativity might grow.

Finally, there are many who mark their content with a Creative Commons license just because they want to express to others the importance of balance in this debate. If you just go along with the system as it is, you are effectively saying you believe in the "All Rights Reserved" model. Good for you, but many do not. Many believe that however appropriate that rule is for Hollywood and freaks, it is not an appropriate description of how most creators view the rights associated with their content. The Creative Commons license expresses this notion of "Some Rights Reserved," and gives many the chance to say it to others.

In the first six months of the Creative Commons experiment, over 1 million objects were licensed with these free-culture licenses. The next step is partnerships with middleware content providers to help them build into their technologies simple ways for users to mark their content with Creative Commons freedoms. Then the next step is to watch and celebrate creators who build content based upon content set free.

These are first steps to rebuilding a public domain. They are not mere arguments; they are action. Building a public domain is the first step to showing people how important that domain is to creativity and innovation. Creative Commons relies upon voluntary steps to achieve this rebuilding. They will lead to a world in which more than voluntary steps are possible.

Creative Commons is just one example of voluntary efforts by individuals and creators to change the mix of rights that now govern the creative field. The project does not compete with copyright; it complements it. Its aim is not to defeat the rights of authors, but to make it easier for authors and creators to exercise their rights more flexibly and cheaply. That difference, we believe, will enable creativity to spread more easily.

THEM, SOON

We will not reclaim a free culture by individual action alone. It will also take important reforms of laws. We have a long way to go before the politicians will listen to these ideas and implement these reforms. But that also means that we have time to build awareness around the changes that we need.

In this chapter, I outline five kinds of changes: four that are general, and one that's specific to the most heated battle of the day, music. Each is a step, not an end. But any of these steps would carry us a long way to our end.

1. More Formalities

If you buy a house, you have to record the sale in a deed. If you buy land upon which to build a house, you have to record the purchase in a deed. If you buy a car, you get a bill of sale and register the car. If you buy an airplane ticket, it has your name on it.

These are all formalities associated with property. They are requirements that we all must bear if we want our property to be protected.

In contrast, under current copyright law, you automatically get a copyright, regardless of whether you comply with any formality. You don't have to register. You don't even have to mark your content. The default is control, and "formalities" are banished.

Why?

As I suggested in chapter 10, the motivation to abolish formalities was a good one. In the world before digital technologies, formalities imposed a burden on copyright holders without much benefit. Thus, it was progress when the law relaxed the formal requirements that a copyright owner must bear to protect and secure his work. Those formalities were getting in the way.

But the Internet changes all this. Formalities today need not be a burden. Rather, the world without formalities is the world that burdens creativity. Today, there is no simple way to know who owns what, or with whom one must deal in order to use or build upon the creative work of others. There are no records, there is no system to trace— there is no simple way to know how to get permission. Yet given the massive increase in the scope of copyright's rule, getting permission is a necessary step for any work that builds upon our past. And thus, the *lack* of formalities forces many into silence where they otherwise could speak.

The law should therefore change this requirement[1]—but it should not change it by going back to the old, broken system. We should require formalities, but we should establish a system that will create the incentives to minimize the burden of these formalities.

The important formalities are three: marking copyrighted work, registering copyrights, and renewing the claim to copyright. Traditionally, the first of these three was something the copyright owner did; the second two were something the government did. But a revised system of formalities would banish the government from the process, except for the sole purpose of approving standards developed by others.

REGISTRATION AND RENEWAL

Under the old system, a copyright owner had to file a registration with the Copyright Office to register or renew a copyright. When filing that registration, the copyright owner paid a fee. As with most government agencies, the Copyright Office had little incentive to minimize the burden of registration; it also had little incentive to minimize the fee. And as the Copyright Office is not a main target of government policymaking, the office has historically been terribly underfunded. Thus, when people who know something about the process hear this idea about formalities, their first reaction is panic—nothing could be worse than forcing people to deal with the mess that is the Copyright Office.

Yet it is always astonishing to me that we, who come from a tradition of extraordinary innovation in governmental design, can no longer think innovatively about how governmental functions can be designed. Just because there is a public purpose to a government role, it doesn't follow that the government must actually administer the role. Instead, we should be creating incentives for private parties to serve the public, subject to standards that the government sets.

In the context of registration, one obvious model is the Internet. There are at least 32 million Web sites registered around the world. Domain name owners for these Web sites have to pay a fee to keep their registration alive. In the main top-level domains (.com, .org, .net), there is a central registry. The actual registrations are, however, performed by many competing registrars. That competition drives the cost of registering down, and more importantly, it drives the ease with which registration occurs up.

We should adopt a similar model for the registration and renewal of copyrights. The Copyright Office may well serve as the central registry, but it should not be in the registrar business. Instead, it should establish a database, and a set of standards for registrars. It should approve registrars that meet its standards. Those registrars would then compete with one another to deliver the cheapest and simplest systems for registering and renewing copyrights. That competition would substantially lower the burden of this formality—while producing a database of registrations that would facilitate the licensing of content.

MARKING

It used to be that the failure to include a copyright notice on a creative work meant that the copyright was forfeited. That was a harsh punishment for failing to comply with a regulatory rule—akin to imposing the death penalty for a parking ticket in the world of creative rights. Here again, there is no reason that a marking requirement needs to be enforced in this way. And more importantly, there is no reason a marking requirement needs to be enforced uniformly across all media.

The aim of marking is to signal to the public that this work is copyrighted and that the author wants to enforce his rights. The mark also makes it easy to locate a copyright owner to secure permission to use the work.

One of the problems the copyright system confronted early on was that different copyrighted works had to be differently marked. It wasn't clear how or where a statue was to be marked, or a record, or a film. A new marking requirement could solve these problems by recognizing the differences in media, and by allowing the system of marking to evolve as technologies enable it to. The system could enable a special signal from the failure to mark—not the loss of the copyright, but the loss of the right to punish someone for failing to get permission first.

Let's start with the last point. If a copyright owner allows his work to be published without a copyright notice, the consequence of that failure need not be that the copyright is lost. The consequence could instead be that anyone has the right to use this work, until the copyright owner complains and demonstrates that it is his work and he doesn't give permission.[2] The meaning of an unmarked work would therefore be "use unless someone complains." If someone does complain, then the obligation would be to stop using the work in any new work from then on though no penalty would attach for existing uses. This would create a strong incentive for copyright owners to mark their work.

That in turn raises the question about how work should best be marked. Here again, the system needs to adjust as the technologies evolve. The best way to ensure that the system evolves is to limit the Copyright Office's role to that of approving standards for marking content that have been crafted elsewhere.

For example, if a recording industry association devises a method for marking CDs, it would propose that to the Copyright Office. The Copyright Office would hold a hearing, at which other proposals could be made. The Copyright Office would then select the proposal that it judged preferable, and it would base that choice *solely* upon the consideration of which method could best be integrated into the registration and renewal system. We would not count on the government to innovate; but we would count on the government to keep the product of innovation in line with its other important functions.

Finally, marking content clearly would simplify registration requirements. If photographs were marked by author and year, there would be little reason not to allow a photographer to reregister, for example, all photographs taken in a particular year in one quick step. The aim of the formality is not to burden the creator; the system itself should be kept as simple as possible.

The objective of formalities is to make things clear. The existing system does nothing to make things clear. Indeed, it seems designed to make things unclear.

If formalities such as registration were reinstated, one of the most difficult aspects of relying upon the public domain would be removed. It would be simple to identify what content is presumptively free; it would be simple to identify who controls the rights for a particular kind of content; it would be simple to assert those rights, and to renew that assertion at the appropriate time.

2. Shorter Terms

The term of copyright has gone from fourteen years to ninety-five years for corporate authors, and life of the author plus seventy years for natural authors.

In *The Future of Ideas*, I proposed a seventy-five-year term, granted in five-year increments with a requirement of renewal every five years. That seemed radical enough at the time. But after we lost *Eldred* v. *Ashcroft*, the proposals became even more radical. *The Economist* endorsed a proposal for a fourteen-year copyright term.[3] Others have proposed tying the term to the term for patents.

I agree with those who believe that we need a radical change in copyright's term. But whether fourteen years or seventy-five, there are four principles that are important to keep in mind about copyright terms.

(1) *Keep it short:* The term should be as long as necessary to give incentives to create, but no longer. If it were tied to very strong protections for authors (so authors were able to reclaim rights from publishers), rights to the same work (not derivative works) might be extended further. The key is not to tie the work up with legal regulations when it no longer benefits an author.

(2) *Keep it simple:* The line between the public domain and protected content must be kept clear. Lawyers like the fuzziness of "fair use," and the distinction between "ideas" and "expression." That kind of law gives them lots of work. But our framers had a simpler idea in mind: protected versus unprotected. The value of short terms is that there is little need to build exceptions into copyright when the term itself is kept short. A clear and active "lawyer-free zone" makes the complexities of "fair use" and "idea/expression" less necessary to navigate.

(3) *Keep it alive:* Copyright should have to be renewed. Especially if the maximum term is long, the copyright owner should be required to signal periodically that he wants the protection continued. This need not be an onerous burden, but there is no reason this monopoly protection has to be granted for free. On average, it takes ninety minutes for a veteran to apply for a pension.[4] If we make veterans suffer that burden, I don't see why we couldn't require authors to spend ten minutes every fifty years to file a single form.

(4) *Keep it prospective:* Whatever the term of copyright should be, the clearest lesson that economists teach is that a term once given should not be extended. It might have been a mistake in 1923 for the law to offer authors only a fifty-six-year term. I don't think so, but it's possible. If it was a mistake, then the consequence was that we got fewer authors to create in 1923 than we otherwise would have. But we can't correct that mistake today by increasing the term. No matter what we do today, we will not increase the number of authors who wrote in 1923. Of course, we can increase the reward that those who write now get (or alternatively, increase the copyright burden that smothers many works that are today invisible). But increasing their reward will not increase their creativity in 1923. What's not done is not done, and there's nothing we can do about that now.

These changes together should produce an *average* copyright term that is much shorter than the current term. Until 1976, the average term was just 32.2 years. We should be aiming for the same.

No doubt the extremists will call these ideas "radical." (After all, I call them "extremists.") But again, the term I recommended was longer than the term under Richard Nixon. How "radical" can it be to ask for a more generous copyright law than Richard Nixon presided over?

3. Free Use Vs. Fair Use

As I observed at the beginning of this book, property law originally granted property owners the right to control their property from the ground to the heavens. The airplane came along. The scope of property rights quickly changed. There was no fuss, no constitutional challenge. It made no sense anymore to grant that much control, given the emergence of that new technology.

Our Constitution gives Congress the power to give authors "exclusive right" to "their writings." Congress has given authors an exclusive right to "their writings" plus any derivative writings (made by others) that are sufficiently close to the author's original work. Thus, if I write a book, and you base a movie on that book, I have the power to deny you the right to release that movie, even though that movie is not "my writing."

Congress granted the beginnings of this right in 1870, when it expanded the exclusive right of copyright to include a right to control translations and dramatizations of a work.[5] The courts have expanded it slowly through judicial interpretation ever since. This expansion has been commented upon by one of the law's greatest judges, Judge Benjamin Kaplan.

> So inured have we become to the extension of the monopoly to a large range of so-called derivative works, that we no longer sense the oddity of accepting such an enlargement of copyright while yet intoning the abracadabra of idea and expression.[6]

I think it's time to recognize that there are airplanes in this field and the expansiveness of these rights of derivative use no longer make sense. More precisely, they don't make sense for the period of time that a copyright runs. And they don't make sense as an amorphous grant. Consider each limitation in turn.

Term: If Congress wants to grant a derivative right, then that right should be for a much shorter term. It makes sense to protect John

Grisham's right to sell the movie rights to his latest novel (or at least I'm willing to assume it does); but it does not make sense for that right to run for the same term as the underlying copyright. The derivative right could be important in inducing creativity; it is not important long after the creative work is done.

Scope: Likewise should the scope of derivative rights be narrowed. Again, there are some cases in which derivative rights are important. Those should be specified. But the law should draw clear lines around regulated and unregulated uses of copyrighted material. When all "reuse" of creative material was within the control of businesses, perhaps it made sense to require lawyers to negotiate the lines. It no longer makes sense for lawyers to negotiate the lines. Think about all the creative possibilities that digital technologies enable; now imagine pouring molasses into the machines. That's what this general requirement of permission does to the creative process. Smothers it.

This was the point that Alben made when describing the making of the Clint Eastwood CD. While it makes sense to require negotiation for foreseeable derivative rights—turning a book into a movie, or a poem into a musical score—it doesn't make sense to require negotiation for the unforeseeable. Here, a statutory right would make much more sense.

In each of these cases, the law should mark the uses that are protected, and the presumption should be that other uses are not protected. This is the reverse of the recommendation of my colleague Paul Goldstein.[7] His view is that the law should be written so that expanded protections follow expanded uses.

Goldstein's analysis would make perfect sense if the cost of the legal system were small. But as we are currently seeing in the context of the Internet, the uncertainty about the scope of protection, and the incentives to protect existing architectures of revenue, combined with a strong copyright, weaken the process of innovation.

The law could remedy this problem either by removing protection beyond the part explicitly drawn or by granting reuse rights upon certain statutory conditions. Either way, the effect would be to free a great deal of culture to others to cultivate. And under a statutory rights regime, that reuse would earn artists more income.

4. Liberate the Music—Again

The battle that got this whole war going was about music, so it wouldn't be fair to end this book without addressing the issue that is, to most people, most pressing—music. There is no other policy issue that better teaches the lessons of this book than the battles around the sharing of music.

The appeal of file-sharing music was the crack cocaine of the Internet's growth. It drove demand for access to the Internet more powerfully than any other single application. It was the Internet's killer app—possibly in two senses of that word. It no doubt was the application that drove demand for bandwidth. It may well be the application that drives demand for regulations that in the end kill innovation on the network.

The aim of copyright, with respect to content in general and music in particular, is to create the incentives for music to be composed, performed, and, most importantly, spread. The law does this by giving an exclusive right to a composer to control public performances of his work, and to a performing artist to control copies of her performance.

File-sharing networks complicate this model by enabling the spread of content for which the performer has not been paid. But of course, that's not all the file-sharing networks do. As I described in chapter 5, they enable four different kinds of sharing:

A. There are some who are using sharing networks as substitutes for purchasing CDs.
B. There are also some who are using sharing networks to sample, on the way to purchasing CDs.

C. There are many who are using file-sharing networks to get access to content that is no longer sold but is still under copyright or that would have been too cumbersome to buy off the Net.

D. There are many who are using file-sharing networks to get access to content that is not copyrighted or to get access that the copyright owner plainly endorses.

Any reform of the law needs to keep these different uses in focus. It must avoid burdening type D even if it aims to eliminate type A. The eagerness with which the law aims to eliminate type A, moreover, should depend upon the magnitude of type B. As with VCRs, if the net effect of sharing is actually not very harmful, the need for regulation is significantly weakened.

As I said in chapter 5, the actual harm caused by sharing is controversial. For the purposes of this chapter, however, I assume the harm is real. I assume, in other words, that type A sharing is significantly greater than type B, and is the dominant use of sharing networks.

Nonetheless, there is a crucial fact about the current technological context that we must keep in mind if we are to understand how the law should respond.

Today, file sharing is addictive. In ten years, it won't be. It is addictive today because it is the easiest way to gain access to a broad range of content. It won't be the easiest way to get access to a broad range of content in ten years. Today, access to the Internet is cumbersome and slow—we in the United States are lucky to have broadband service at 1.5 MBs, and very rarely do we get service at that speed both up and down. Although wireless access is growing, most of us still get access across wires. Most only gain access through a machine with a keyboard. The idea of the always on, always connected Internet is mainly just an idea.

But it will become a reality, and that means the way we get access to the Internet today is a technology in transition. Policy makers should not make policy on the basis of technology in transition. They should make policy on the basis of where the technology is going. The question should not be, how should the law regulate sharing in this world? The question should be, what law will we require when the network becomes the network it is clearly becoming? That network is one in which every machine with electricity is essentially on the Net; where everywhere you are—except maybe the desert or the Rockies—you can instantaneously be connected to the Internet. Imagine the Internet as ubiquitous as the best cell-phone service, where with the flip of a device, you are connected.

In that world, it will be extremely easy to connect to services that give you access to content on the fly—such as Internet radio, content that is streamed to the user when the user demands. Here, then, is the critical point: When it is *extremely* easy to connect to services that give access to content, it will be *easier* to connect to services that give you access to content than it will be to download and store content *on the many devices you will have for playing content*. It will be easier, in other words, to subscribe than it will be to be a database manager, as everyone in the download-sharing world of Napster-like technologies essentially is. Content services will compete with content sharing, even if the services charge money for the content they give access to. Already cell-phone services in Japan offer music (for a fee) streamed over cell phones (enhanced with plugs for headphones). The Japanese are paying for this content even though "free" content is available in the form of MP3s across the Web.[8]

This point about the future is meant to suggest a perspective on the present: It is emphatically temporary. The "problem" with file sharing—to the extent there is a real problem—is a problem that will increasingly disappear as it becomes easier to connect to the Internet. And thus it is an extraordinary mistake for policy makers today to be "solving" this problem in light of a technology that will be gone tomorrow. The question should not be how to regulate the Internet to eliminate file sharing (the Net will evolve that problem away). The question instead should be how to assure that artists get paid, during this transition between twentieth-century models for doing business and twenty-first-century technologies.

The answer begins with recognizing that there are different "problems" here to solve. Let's start with type D content—uncopyrighted content or copyrighted content that the artist wants shared. The "problem" with this content is to make sure that the technology that would enable this kind of sharing is not rendered illegal. You can think of it this way: Pay phones are used to deliver ransom demands, no doubt. But there are many who need to use pay phones who have nothing to do with ransoms. It would be wrong to ban pay phones in order to eliminate kidnapping.

Type C content raises a different "problem." This is content that was, at one time, published and is no longer available. It may be unavailable because the artist is no longer valuable enough for the record label he signed with to carry his work. Or it may be unavailable because the work is forgotten. Either way, the aim of the law should be to facilitate the access to this content, ideally in a way that returns something to the artist.

Again, the model here is the used book store. Once a book goes out of print, it may still be available in libraries and used book stores. But libraries and used book stores don't pay the copyright owner when someone reads or buys an out-of-print book. That makes total sense, of course, since any other system would be so burdensome as to eliminate the possibility of used book stores' existing. But from the author's perspective, this "sharing" of his content without his being compensated is less than ideal.

The model of used book stores suggests that the law could simply deem out-of-print music fair game. If the publisher does not make copies of the music available for sale, then commercial and noncommercial providers would be free, under this rule, to "share" that content, even though the sharing involved making a copy. The copy here would be incidental to the trade; in a context where commercial publishing has ended, trading music should be as free as trading books.

Alternatively, the law could create a statutory license that would ensure that artists get something from the trade of their work. For example, if the law set a low statutory rate for the commercial sharing of content that was not offered for sale by a commercial publisher, and if that rate were automatically transferred to a trust for the benefit of the artist, then businesses could develop around the idea of trading this content, and artists would benefit from this trade.

This system would also create an incentive for publishers to keep works available commercially. Works that are available commercially would not be subject to this license. Thus, publishers could protect the right to charge whatever they want for content if they kept the work commercially available. But if they don't keep it available, and instead, the computer hard disks of fans around the world keep it alive, then any royalty owed for such copying should be much less than the amount owed a commercial publisher.

The hard case is content of types A and B, and again, this case is hard only because the extent of the problem will change over time, as the technologies for gaining access to content change. The law's solution should be as flexible as the problem is, understanding that we are in the middle of a radical transformation in the technology for delivering and accessing content.

So here's a solution that will at first seem very strange to both sides in this war, but which upon reflection, I suggest, should make some sense.

Stripped of the rhetoric about the sanctity of property, the basic claim of the content industry is this: A new technology (the Internet) has harmed a set of rights that secure copyright. If those rights are to be protected, then the content industry should be compensated for that harm. Just as the technology of tobacco harmed the health of millions of Americans, or the technology of asbestos caused grave illness to thousands of miners, so, too, has the technology of digital networks harmed the interests of the content industry.

I love the Internet, and so I don't like likening it to tobacco or asbestos. But the analogy is a fair one from the perspective of the law. And it suggests a fair response: Rather than seeking to destroy the Internet, or the p2p technologies that are currently harming content providers on the Internet, we should find a relatively simple way to compensate those who are harmed.

The idea would be a modification of a proposal that has been floated by Harvard law professor William Fisher.[9] Fisher suggests a very clever way around the current impasse of the Internet. Under his plan, all content capable of digital transmission would (1) be marked with a digital watermark (don't worry about how easy it is to evade these marks; as you'll see, there's no incentive to evade them). Once the content is marked, then entrepreneurs would develop (2) systems to monitor how many items of each content were distributed. On the basis of those numbers, then (3) artists would be compensated. The compensation would be paid for by (4) an appropriate tax.

Fisher's proposal is careful and comprehensive. It raises a million questions, most of which he answers well in his upcoming book, *Promises to Keep*. The modification that I would make is relatively simple: Fisher imagines his proposal replacing the existing copyright system. I imagine it complementing the existing system. The aim of the proposal would be to facilitate compensation to the extent that harm could be shown. This compensation would be temporary, aimed at facilitating a transition between regimes. And it would require renewal after a period of years. If it continues to make sense to facilitate free exchange of content, supported through a taxation system, then it can be continued. If this form of protection is no longer necessary, then the system could lapse into the old system of controlling access.

Fisher would balk at the idea of allowing the system to lapse. His aim is not just to ensure that artists are paid, but also to ensure that the system supports the widest range of "semiotic democracy" possible. But the aims of semiotic democracy would be satisfied if the other changes I described were accomplished—in particular, the limits on derivative uses. A system that simply charges for access would not greatly burden semiotic democracy if there were few limitations on what one was allowed to do with the content itself.

No doubt it would be difficult to calculate the proper measure of "harm" to an industry. But the difficulty of making that calculation would be outweighed by the benefit of facilitating innovation. This background system to compensate would also not need to interfere with innovative proposals such as Apple's MusicStore. As experts predicted when Apple launched the MusicStore, it could beat "free" by being easier than free is. This has proven correct: Apple has sold millions of songs at even the very high price of 99 cents a song. (At 99 cents, the cost is the equivalent of a per-song CD price, though the labels have none of the costs of a CD to pay.) Apple's move was countered by Real Networks, offering music at just 79 cents a song. And no doubt there will be a great deal of competition to offer and sell music on-line.

This competition has already occurred against the background of "free" music from p2p systems. As the sellers of cable television have known for thirty years, and the sellers of bottled water for much more than that, there is nothing impossible at all about "competing with free." Indeed, if anything, the competition spurs the competitors to offer new and better products. This is precisely what the competitive market was to be about. Thus in Singapore, though piracy is rampant, movie theaters are often luxurious—with "first class" seats, and meals served while you watch a movie—as they struggle and succeed in finding ways to compete with "free."

This regime of competition, with a backstop to assure that artists don't lose, would facilitate a great deal of innovation in the delivery of content. That competition would continue to shrink type A sharing. It would inspire an extraordinary range of new innovators—ones who would have a right to the content, and would no longer fear the uncertain and barbarically severe punishments of the law.

In summary, then, my proposal is this:

The Internet is in transition. We should not be regulating a technology in transition. We should instead be regulating to minimize the harm to interests affected by this technological change, while enabling, and encouraging, the most efficient technology we can create. We can minimize that harm while maximizing the benefit to innovation by

1. guaranteeing the right to engage in type D sharing;
2. permitting noncommercial type C sharing without liability, and commercial type C sharing at a low and fixed rate set by statute;
3. while in this transition, taxing and compensating for type A sharing, to the extent actual harm is demonstrated.

But what if "piracy" doesn't disappear? What if there is a competitive market providing content at a low cost, but a significant number of consumers continue to "take" content for nothing? Should the law do something then?

Yes, it should. But, again, what it should do depends upon how the facts develop. These changes may not eliminate type A sharing. But the real issue is not whether it eliminates sharing in the abstract. The real issue is its effect on the market. Is it better (a) to have a technology that is 95 percent secure and produces a market of size *x*, or (b) to have a technology that is 50 percent secure but produces a market of five times *x*? Less secure might produce more unauthorized sharing, but it is likely to also produce a much bigger market in authorized sharing. The most important thing is to assure artists' compensation without breaking the Internet. Once that's assured, then it may well be appropriate to find ways to track down the petty pirates.

But we're a long way away from whittling the problem down to this subset of type A sharers. And our focus until we're there should not be on finding ways to break the Internet. Our focus until we're there should be on how to make sure the artists are paid, while protecting the space for innovation and creativity that the Internet is.

5. Fire Lots of Lawyers

I'm a lawyer. I make lawyers for a living. I believe in the law. I believe in the law of copyright. Indeed, I have devoted my life to working in law, not because there are big bucks at the end but because there are ideals at the end that I would love to live.

Yet much of this book has been a criticism of lawyers, or the role lawyers have played in this debate. The law speaks to ideals, but it is my view that our profession has become too attuned to the client. And in a world where the rich clients have one strong view, the unwillingness of the profession to question or counter that one strong view queers the law.

The evidence of this bending is compelling. I'm attacked as a "radical" by many within the profession, yet the positions that I am advocating are precisely the positions of some of the most moderate and significant figures in the history of this branch of the law. Many, for example, thought crazy the challenge that we brought to the Copyright Term Extension Act. Yet just thirty years ago, the dominant scholar and practitioner in the field of copyright, Melville Nimmer, thought it obvious.[10]

However, my criticism of the role that lawyers have played in this debate is not just about a professional bias. It is more importantly about our failure to actually reckon the costs of the law.

Economists are supposed to be good at reckoning costs and benefits. But more often than not, economists, with no clue about how the legal system actually functions, simply assume that the transaction costs of the legal system are slight.[11] They see a system that has been around for hundreds of years, and they assume it works the way their elementary school civics class taught them it works.

But the legal system doesn't work. Or more accurately, it doesn't work for anyone except those with the most resources. Not because the system is corrupt. I don't think our legal system (at the federal level, at least) is at all corrupt. I mean simply because the costs of our legal system are so astonishingly high that justice can practically never be done. These costs distort free culture in many ways. A lawyer's time is billed at the largest firms at more than $400 per hour. How much time should such a lawyer spend reading cases carefully, or researching obscure strands of authority? The answer is the increasing reality: very little. The law depended upon the careful articulation and development of doctrine, but the careful articulation and development of legal doctrine depends upon careful work. Yet that careful work costs too much, except in the most high-profile and costly cases.

The costliness and clumsiness and randomness of this system mock our tradition. And lawyers, as well as academics, should consider it their duty to change the way the law works—or better, to change the law so that it works. It is wrong that the system works well only for the top 1 percent of the clients. It could be made radically more efficient, and inexpensive, and hence radically more just.

But until that reform is complete, we as a society should keep the law away from areas that we know it will only harm. And that is precisely what the law will too often do if too much of our culture is left to its review.

Think about the amazing things your kid could do or make with digital technology—the film, the music, the Web page, the blog. Or think about the amazing things your community could facilitate with digital technology—a wiki, a barn raising, activism to change something. Think about all those creative things, and then imagine cold molasses poured onto the machines. This is what any regime that requires permission produces. Again, this is the reality of Brezhnev's Russia.

The law should regulate in certain areas of culture—but it should regulate culture only where that regulation does good. Yet lawyers rarely test their power, or the power they promote, against this simple pragmatic question: "Will it do good?" When challenged about the expanding reach of the law, the lawyer answers, "Why not?"

We should ask, "Why?" Show me why your regulation of culture is needed. Show me how it does good. And until you can show me both, keep your lawyers away.

NOTES

Throughout this text, there are references to links on the World Wide Web. As anyone who has tried to use the Web knows, these links can be highly unstable. I have tried to remedy the instability by redirecting readers to the original source through the Web site associated with this book. For each link below, you can go to **http://free-culture.cc/notes** and locate the original source by clicking on the number after the # sign. If the original link remains alive, you will be redirected to that link. If the original link has disappeared, you will be redirected to an appropriate reference for the material.

PREFACE

1. David Pogue, "Don't Just Chat, Do Something," *New York Times*, 30 January 2000.
2. Richard M. Stallman, *Free Software, Free Societies* 57 (Joshua Gay, ed. 2002).
3. William Safire, "The Great Media Gulp," *New York Times*, 22 May 2003.

INTRODUCTION

1. St. George Tucker, *Blackstone's Commentaries* 3 (South Hackensack, N.J.: Rothman Reprints, 1969), 18.
2. United States v. Causby, U.S. 328 (1946): 256, 261. The Court did find that there could be a "taking" if the government's use of its land effectively destroyed the value of the Causbys' land. This example was suggested to me by Keith Aoki's wonderful piece, "(Intellectual) Property and Sovereignty:

Notes Toward a Cultural Geography of Authorship," *Stanford Law Review* 48 (1996): 1293, 1333. See also Paul Goldstein, *Real Property* (Mineola, N.Y.: Foundation Press, 1984), 1112–13.

3. Lawrence Lessing, *Man of High Fidelity: Edwin Howard Armstrong* (Philadelphia: J. B. Lipincott Company, 1956), 209.

4. See "Saints: The Heroes and Geniuses of the Electronic Era," First Electronic Church of America, at www.webstationone.com/fecha, available at link #1.

5. Lessing, 226.

6. Lessing, 256.

7. Amanda Lenhart, "The Ever-Shifting Internet Population: A New Look at Internet Access and the Digital Divide," Pew Internet and American Life Project, 15 April 2003: 6, available at link #2.

8. This is not the only purpose of copyright, though it is the overwhelmingly primary purpose of the copyright established in the federal constitution. State copyright law historically protected not just the commercial interest in publication, but also a privacy interest. By granting authors the exclusive right to first publication, state copyright law gave authors the power to control the spread of facts about them. See Samuel D. Warren and Louis D. Brandeis, "The Right to Privacy," *Harvard Law Review* 4 (1890): 193, 198–200.

9. See Jessica Litman, *Digital Copyright* (New York: Prometheus Books, 2001), ch. 13.

10. Amy Harmon, "Black Hawk Download: Moving Beyond Music, Pirates Use New Tools to Turn the Net into an Illicit Video Club," *New York Times*, 17 January 2002.

11. Neil W. Netanel, "Copyright and a Democratic Civil Society," *Yale Law Journal* 106 (1996): 283.

"PIRACY"

1. *Bach v. Longman*, 98 Eng. Rep. 1274 (1777) (Mansfield).

2. See Rochelle Dreyfuss, "Expressive Genericity: Trademarks as Language in the Pepsi Generation," *Notre Dame Law Review* 65 (1990): 397.

3. Lisa Bannon, "The Birds May Sing, but Campers Can't Unless They Pay Up," *Wall Street Journal*, 21 August 1996, available at link #3; Jonathan Zittrain, "Calling Off the Copyright War: In Battle of Property vs. Free Speech, No One Wins," *Boston Globe*, 24 November 2002.

4. In *The Rise of the Creative Class* (New York: Basic Books, 2002), Richard Florida documents a shift in the nature of labor toward a labor of creativity. His work, however, doesn't directly address the legal conditions under which that creativity is enabled or stifled. I certainly agree with him about the importance and significance of this change, but I also believe the conditions under which it will be enabled are much more tenuous.

CHAPTER ONE: CREATORS

1. Leonard Maltin, *Of Mice and Magic: A History of American Animated Cartoons* (New York: Penguin Books, 1987), 34–35.
2. I am grateful to David Gerstein and his careful history, described at link #4. According to Dave Smith of the Disney Archives, Disney paid royalties to use the music for five songs in *Steamboat Willie:* "Steamboat Bill," "The Simpleton" (Delille), "Mischief Makers" (Carbonara), "Joyful Hurry No. 1" (Baron), and "Gawky Rube" (Lakay). A sixth song, "The Turkey in the Straw," was already in the public domain. Letter from David Smith to Harry Surden, 10 July 2003, on file with author.
3. He was also a fan of the public domain. See Chris Sprigman, "The Mouse that Ate the Public Domain," Findlaw, 5 March 2002, at link #5.
4. Until 1976, copyright law granted an author the possibility of two terms: an initial term and a renewal term. I have calculated the "average" term by determining the weighted average of total registrations for any particular year, and the proportion renewing. Thus, if 100 copyrights are registered in year 1, and only 15 are renewed, and the renewal term is 28 years, then the average term is 32.2 years. For the renewal data and other relevant data, see the Web site associated with this book, available at link #6.
5. For an excellent history, see Scott McCloud, *Reinventing Comics* (New York: Perennial, 2000).
6. See Salil K. Mehra, "Copyright and Comics in Japan: Does Law Explain Why All the Comics My Kid Watches Are Japanese Imports?" *Rutgers Law Review* 55 (2002): 155, 182. "[T]here might be a collective economic rationality that would lead manga and anime artists to forgo bringing legal actions for infringement. One hypothesis is that all manga artists may be better off collectively if they set aside their individual self-interest and decide not to press their legal rights. This is essentially a prisoner's dilemma solved."
7. The term *intellectual property* is of relatively recent origin. See Siva Vaidhyanathan, *Copyrights and Copywrongs,* 11 (New York: New York University Press, 2001). See also Lawrence Lessig, *The Future of Ideas* (New York: Random House, 2001), 293 n. 26. The term accurately describes a set of "property" rights—copyright, patents, trademark, and trade-secret—but the nature of those rights is very different.

CHAPTER TWO: "MERE COPYISTS"

1. Reese V. Jenkins, *Images and Enterprise* (Baltimore: Johns Hopkins University Press, 1975), 112.
2. Brian Coe, *The Birth of Photography* (New York: Taplinger Publishing, 1977), 53.
3. Jenkins, 177.
4. Based on a chart in Jenkins, p. 178.

5. Coe, 58.
6. For illustrative cases, see, for example, *Pavesich* v. *N.E. Life Ins. Co.*, 50 S.E. 68 (Ga. 1905); *Foster-Milburn Co.* v. *Chinn*, 123090 S.W. 364, 366 (Ky. 1909); *Corliss* v. *Walker*, 64 F. 280 (Mass. Dist. Ct. 1894).
7. Samuel D. Warren and Louis D. Brandeis, "The Right to Privacy," *Harvard Law Review* 4 (1890): 193.
8. See Melville B. Nimmer, "The Right of Publicity," *Law and Contemporary Problems* 19 (1954): 203; William L. Prosser, "Privacy," *California Law Review* 48 (1960) 398–407; *White* v. *Samsung Electronics America, Inc.*, 971 F. 2d 1395 (9th Cir. 1992), cert. denied, 508 U.S. 951 (1993).
9. H. Edward Goldberg, "Essential Presentation Tools: Hardware and Software You Need to Create Digital Multimedia Presentations," cadalyst, 1 February 2002, available at link #7.
10. Judith Van Evra, *Television and Child Development* (Hillsdale, N.J.: Lawrence Erlbaum Associates, 1990); "Findings on Family and TV Study," *Denver Post*, 25 May 1997, B6.
11. Interview with Elizabeth Daley and Stephanie Barish, 13 December 2002.
12. See Scott Steinberg, "Crichton Gets Medieval on PCs," E!online, 4 November 2000, available at link #8; "Timeline," 22 November 2000, available at link #9.
13. Interview with Daley and Barish.
14. Ibid.
15. See, for example, Alexis de Tocqueville, *Democracy in America*, bk. 1, trans. Henry Reeve (New York: Bantam Books, 2000), ch. 16.
16. Bruce Ackerman and James Fishkin, "Deliberation Day," *Journal of Political Philosophy* 10 (2) (2002): 129.
17. Cass Sunstein, *Republic.com* (Princeton: Princeton University Press, 2001), 65–80, 175, 182, 183, 192.
18. Noah Shachtman, "With Incessant Postings, a Pundit Stirs the Pot," *New York Times*, 16 January 2003, G5.
19. Telephone interview with David Winer, 16 April 2003.
20. John Schwartz, "Loss of the Shuttle: The Internet; A Wealth of Information Online," *New York Times*, 2 February 2003, A28; Staci D. Kramer, "Shuttle Disaster Coverage Mixed, but Strong Overall," Online Journalism Review, 2 February 2003, available at link #10.
21. See Michael Falcone, "Does an Editor's Pencil Ruin a Web Log?" *New York Times*, 29 September 2003, C4. ("Not all news organizations have been as accepting of employees who blog. Kevin Sites, a CNN correspondent in Iraq who started a blog about his reporting of the war on March 9, stopped posting 12 days later at his bosses' request. Last year Steve Olafson, a *Houston Chronicle* reporter, was fired for keeping a personal Web log,

published under a pseudonym, that dealt with some of the issues and people he was covering.")

22. See, for example, Edward Felten and Andrew Appel, "Technological Access Control Interferes with Noninfringing Scholarship," *Communications of the Association for Computer Machinery* 43 (2000): 9.

CHAPTER THREE: CATALOGS

1. Tim Goral, "Recording Industry Goes After Campus P-2-P Networks: Suit Alleges $97.8 Billion in Damages," *Professional Media Group LCC* 6 (2003): 5, available at 2003 WL 55179443.
2. Occupational Employment Survey, U.S. Dept. of Labor (2001) (27–2042—Musicians and Singers). See also National Endowment for the Arts, *More Than One in a Blue Moon* (2000).
3. Douglas Lichtman makes a related point in "KaZaA and Punishment," *Wall Street Journal*, 10 September 2003, A24.

CHAPTER FOUR: "PIRATES"

1. I am grateful to Peter DiMauro for pointing me to this extraordinary history. See also Siva Vaidhyanathan, *Copyrights and Copywrongs*, 87–93, which details Edison's "adventures" with copyright and patent.
2. J. A. Aberdeen, *Hollywood Renegades: The Society of Independent Motion Picture Producers* (Cobblestone Entertainment, 2000) and expanded texts posted at "The Edison Movie Monopoly: The Motion Picture Patents Company vs. the Independent Outlaws," available at link #11. For a discussion of the economic motive behind both these limits and the limits imposed by Victor on phonographs, see Randal C. Picker, "From Edison to the Broadcast Flag: Mechanisms of Consent and Refusal and the Propertization of Copyright" (September 2002), University of Chicago Law School, James M. Olin Program in Law and Economics, Working Paper No. 159.
3. Marc Wanamaker, "The First Studios," *The Silents Majority*, archived at link #12.
4. To Amend and Consolidate the Acts Respecting Copyright: Hearings on S. 6330 and H.R. 19853 Before the (Joint) Committees on Patents, 59th Cong. 59, 1st sess. (1906) (statement of Senator Alfred B. Kittredge, of South Dakota, chairman), reprinted in *Legislative History of the 1909 Copyright Act*, E. Fulton Brylawski and Abe Goldman, eds. (South Hackensack, N.J.: Rothman Reprints, 1976).
5. To Amend and Consolidate the Acts Respecting Copyright, 223 (statement of Nathan Burkan, attorney for the Music Publishers Association).
6. To Amend and Consolidate the Acts Respecting Copyright, 226 (statement of Nathan Burkan, attorney for the Music Publishers Association).

7. To Amend and Consolidate the Acts Respecting Copyright, 23 (statement of John Philip Sousa, composer).

8. To Amend and Consolidate the Acts Respecting Copyright, 283–84 (statement of Albert Walker, representative of the Auto-Music Perforating Company of New York).

9. To Amend and Consolidate the Acts Respecting Copyright, 376 (prepared memorandum of Philip Mauro, general patent counsel of the American Graphophone Company Association).

10. Copyright Law Revision: Hearings on S. 2499, S. 2900, H.R. 243, and H.R. 11794 Before the (Joint) Committee on Patents, 60th Cong., 1st sess., 217 (1908) (statement of Senator Reed Smoot, chairman), reprinted in *Legislative History of the 1909 Copyright Act,* E. Fulton Brylawski and Abe Goldman, eds. (South Hackensack, N.J.: Rothman Reprints, 1976).

11. Copyright Law Revision: Report to Accompany H.R. 2512, House Committee on the Judiciary, 90th Cong., 1st sess., House Document no. 83, 66 (8 March 1967). I am grateful to Glenn Brown for drawing my attention to this report.

12. See 17 *United States Code,* sections 106 and 110. At the beginning, record companies printed "Not Licensed for Radio Broadcast" and other messages purporting to restrict the ability to play a record on a radio station. Judge Learned Hand rejected the argument that a warning attached to a record might restrict the rights of the radio station. See *RCA Manufacturing Co.* v. *Whiteman,* 114 F. 2d 86 (2nd Cir. 1940). See also Randal C. Picker, "From Edison to the Broadcast Flag: Mechanisms of Consent and Refusal and the Propertization of Copyright," *University of Chicago Law Review* 70 (2003): 281.

13. Copyright Law Revision—CATV: Hearing on S. 1006 Before the Subcommittee on Patents, Trademarks, and Copyrights of the Senate Committee on the Judiciary, 89th Cong., 2nd sess., 78 (1966) (statement of Rosel H. Hyde, chairman of the Federal Communications Commission).

14. Copyright Law Revision—CATV, 116 (statement of Douglas A. Anello, general counsel of the National Association of Broadcasters).

15. Copyright Law Revision—CATV, 126 (statement of Ernest W. Jennes, general counsel of the Association of Maximum Service Telecasters, Inc.).

16. Copyright Law Revision—CATV, 169 (joint statement of Arthur B. Krim, president of United Artists Corp., and John Sinn, president of United Artists Television, Inc.).

17. Copyright Law Revision—CATV, 209 (statement of Charlton Heston, president of the Screen Actors Guild).

18. Copyright Law Revision—CATV, 216 (statement of Edwin M. Zimmerman, acting assistant attorney general).

19. See, for example, National Music Publisher's Association, *The Engine of Free Expression: Copyright on the Internet—The Myth of Free Information,* avail-

able at link #13. "The threat of piracy—the use of someone else's creative work without permission or compensation—has grown with the Internet."

CHAPTER FIVE: "PIRACY"

1. See IFPI (International Federation of the Phonographic Industry), *The Recording Industry Commercial Piracy Report 2003*, July 2003, available at link #14. See also Ben Hunt, "Companies Warned on Music Piracy Risk," *Financial Times*, 14 February 2003, 11.

2. See Peter Drahos with John Braithwaite, *Information Feudalism: Who Owns the Knowledge Economy?* (New York: The New Press, 2003), 10–13, 209. The Trade-Related Aspects of Intellectual Property Rights (TRIPS) agreement obligates member nations to create administrative and enforcement mechanisms for intellectual property rights, a costly proposition for developing countries. Additionally, patent rights may lead to higher prices for staple industries such as agriculture. Critics of TRIPS question the disparity between burdens imposed upon developing countries and benefits conferred to industrialized nations. TRIPS does permit governments to use patents for public, noncommercial uses without first obtaining the patent holder's permission. Developing nations may be able to use this to gain the benefits of foreign patents at lower prices. This is a promising strategy for developing nations within the TRIPS framework.

3. For an analysis of the economic impact of copying technology, see Stan Liebowitz, *Rethinking the Network Economy* (New York: Amacom, 2002), 144–90. "In some instances . . . the impact of piracy on the copyright holder's ability to appropriate the value of the work will be negligible. One obvious instance is the case where the individual engaging in pirating would not have purchased an original even if pirating were not an option." Ibid., 149.

4. *Bach v. Longman*, 98 Eng. Rep. 1274 (1777).

5. See Clayton M. Christensen, *The Innovator's Dilemma: The Revolutionary National Bestseller That Changed the Way We Do Business* (New York: HarperBusiness, 2000). Professor Christensen examines why companies that give rise to and dominate a product area are frequently unable to come up with the most creative, paradigm-shifting uses for their own products. This job usually falls to outside innovators, who reassemble existing technology in inventive ways. For a discussion of Christensen's ideas, see Lawrence Lessig, *Future*, 89–92, 139.

6. See Carolyn Lochhead, "Silicon Valley Dream, Hollywood Nightmare," *San Francisco Chronicle*, 24 September 2002, A1; "Rock 'n' Roll Suicide," *New Scientist*, 6 July 2002, 42; Benny Evangelista, "Napster Names CEO, Secures New Financing," *San Francisco Chronicle*, 23 May 2003, C1; "Napster's Wake-Up Call," *Economist*, 24 June 2000, 23; John Naughton, "Hollywood at War with the Internet" (London) *Times*, 26 July 2002, 18.

7. See Ipsos-Insight, *TEMPO: Keeping Pace with Online Music Distribution*

(September 2002), reporting that 28 percent of Americans aged twelve and older have downloaded music off of the Internet and 30 percent have listened to digital music files stored on their computers.

8. Amy Harmon, "Industry Offers a Carrot in Online Music Fight," *New York Times*, 6 June 2003, A1.

9. See Liebowitz, *Rethinking the Network Economy*,148–49.

10. See Cap Gemini Ernst & Young, *Technology Evolution and the Music Industry's Business Model Crisis* (2003), 3. This report describes the music industry's effort to stigmatize the budding practice of cassette taping in the 1970s, including an advertising campaign featuring a cassette-shape skull and the caption "Home taping is killing music."

At the time digital audio tape became a threat, the Office of Technical Assessment conducted a survey of consumer behavior. In 1988, 40 percent of consumers older than ten had taped music to a cassette format. U.S. Congress, Office of Technology Assessment, *Copyright and Home Copying: Technology Challenges the Law*, OTA-CIT-422 (Washington, D.C.: U.S. Government Printing Office, October 1989), 145–56.

11. U.S. Congress, *Copyright and Home Copying*, 4.

12. See Recording Industry Association of America, *2002 Yearend Statistics*, available at link #15. A later report indicates even greater losses. See Recording Industry Association of America, *Some Facts About Music Piracy*, 25 June 2003, available at link #16: "In the past four years, unit shipments of recorded music have fallen by 26 percent from 1.16 billion units in 1999 to 860 million units in 2002 in the United States (based on units shipped). In terms of sales, revenues are down 14 percent, from $14.6 billion in 1999 to $12.6 billion last year (based on U.S. dollar value of shipments). The music industry worldwide has gone from a $39 billion industry in 2000 down to a $32 billion industry in 2002 (based on U.S. dollar value of shipments)."

13. Jane Black, "Big Music's Broken Record," BusinessWeek online, 13 February 2003, available at link #17.

14. Ibid.

15. By one estimate, 75 percent of the music released by the major labels is no longer in print. See Online Entertainment and Copyright Law—Coming Soon to a Digital Device Near You: Hearing Before the Senate Committee on the Judiciary, 107th Cong., 1st sess. (3 April 2001) (prepared statement of the Future of Music Coalition), available at link #18.

16. While there are not good estimates of the number of used record stores in existence, in 2002, there were 7,198 used book dealers in the United States, an increase of 20 percent since 1993. See Book Hunter Press, *The Quiet Revolution: The Expansion of the Used Book Market* (2002), available at link #19. Used records accounted for $260 million in sales in 2002. See National Association of Recording Merchandisers, "2002 Annual Survey Results," available at link #20.

17. See Transcript of Proceedings, In Re: Napster Copyright Litigation at 34-35 (N.D. Cal., 11 July 2001), nos. MDL-00-1369 MHP, C 99-5183 MHP, available at link #21. For an account of the litigation and its toll on Napster, see Joseph Menn, *All the Rave: The Rise and Fall of Shawn Fanning's Napster* (New York: Crown Business, 2003), 269–82.
18. Copyright Infringements (Audio and Video Recorders): Hearing on S. 1758 Before the Senate Committee on the Judiciary, 97th Cong., 1st and 2nd sess., 459 (1982) (testimony of Jack Valenti, president, Motion Picture Association of America, Inc.).
19. Copyright Infringements (Audio and Video Recorders), 475.
20. *Universal City Studios, Inc.* v. *Sony Corp. of America*, 480 F. Supp. 429, 438 (C.D. Cal., 1979).
21. Copyright Infringements (Audio and Video Recorders), 485 (testimony of Jack Valenti).
22. *Universal City Studios, Inc.* v. *Sony Corp. of America*, 659 F. 2d 963 (9th Cir. 1981).
23. *Sony Corp. of America* v. *Universal City Studios, Inc.*, 464 U.S. 417, 431 (1984).
24. These are the most important instances in our history, but there are other cases as well. The technology of digital audio tape (DAT), for example, was regulated by Congress to minimize the risk of piracy. The remedy Congress imposed did burden DAT producers, by taxing tape sales and controlling the technology of DAT. See Audio Home Recording Act of 1992 (Title 17 of the *United States Code*), Pub. L. No. 102-563, 106 Stat. 4237, codified at 17 U.S.C. §1001. Again, however, this regulation did not eliminate the opportunity for free riding in the sense I've described. See Lessig, *Future*, 71. See also Picker, "From Edison to the Broadcast Flag," *University of Chicago Law Review* 70 (2003): 293–96.
25. *Sony Corp. of America* v. *Universal City Studios, Inc.*, 464 U.S. 417, 432 (1984).
26. John Schwartz, "New Economy: The Attack on Peer-to-Peer Software Echoes Past Efforts," *New York Times*, 22 September 2003, C3.

"PROPERTY"

1. Letter from Thomas Jefferson to Isaac McPherson (13 August 1813) in *The Writings of Thomas Jefferson*, vol. 6 (Andrew A. Lipscomb and Albert Ellery Bergh, eds., 1903), 330, 333–34.
2. As the legal realists taught American law, all property rights are intangible. A property right is simply a right that an individual has against the world to do or not do certain things that may or may not attach to a physical object. The right itself is intangible, even if the object to which it is (metaphorically) attached is tangible. See Adam Mossoff, "What Is Property? Putting the Pieces Back Together," *Arizona Law Review* 45 (2003): 373, 429 n. 241.

CHAPTER SIX: FOUNDERS

1. Jacob Tonson is typically remembered for his associations with prominent eighteenth-century literary figures, especially John Dryden, and for his handsome "definitive editions" of classic works. In addition to *Romeo and Juliet*, he published an astonishing array of works that still remain at the heart of the English canon, including collected works of Shakespeare, Ben Jonson, John Milton, and John Dryden. See Keith Walker, "Jacob Tonson, Bookseller," *American Scholar* 61:3 (1992): 424–31.

2. Lyman Ray Patterson, *Copyright in Historical Perspective* (Nashville: Vanderbilt University Press, 1968), 151–52.

3. As Siva Vaidhyanathan nicely argues, it is erroneous to call this a "copyright law." See Vaidhyanathan, *Copyrights and Copywrongs*, 40.

4. Philip Wittenberg, *The Protection and Marketing of Literary Property* (New York: J. Messner, Inc., 1937), 31.

5. A Letter to a Member of Parliament concerning the Bill now depending in the House of Commons, for making more effectual an Act in the Eighth Year of the Reign of Queen Anne, entitled, An Act for the Encouragement of Learning, by Vesting the Copies of Printed Books in the Authors or Purchasers of such Copies, during the Times therein mentioned (London, 1735), in Brief Amici Curiae of Tyler T. Ochoa et al., 8, *Eldred v. Ashcroft*, 537 U.S. 186 (2003) (No. 01-618).

6. Lyman Ray Patterson, "Free Speech, Copyright, and Fair Use," *Vanderbilt Law Review* 40 (1987): 28. For a wonderfully compelling account, see Vaidhyanathan, 37–48.

7. For a compelling account, see David Saunders, *Authorship and Copyright* (London: Routledge, 1992), 62–69.

8. Mark Rose, *Authors and Owners* (Cambridge: Harvard University Press, 1993), 92.

9. Ibid., 93.

10. Lyman Ray Patterson, *Copyright in Historical Perspective,* 167 (quoting Borwell).

11. Howard B. Abrams, "The Historic Foundation of American Copyright Law: Exploding the Myth of Common Law Copyright," *Wayne Law Review* 29 (1983): 1152.

12. Ibid., 1156.

13. Rose, 97.

14. Ibid.

CHAPTER SEVEN: RECORDERS

1. For an excellent argument that such use is "fair use," but that lawyers don't permit recognition that it is "fair use," see Richard A. Posner with William F. Patry, "Fair Use and Statutory Reform in the Wake of *Eldred*" (draft on file with author), University of Chicago Law School, 5 August 2003.

CHAPTER EIGHT: TRANSFORMERS

1. Technically, the rights that Alben had to clear were mainly those of publicity—rights an artist has to control the commercial exploitation of his image. But these rights, too, burden "Rip, Mix, Burn" creativity, as this chapter evinces.

2. U.S. Department of Commerce Office of Acquisition Management, *Seven Steps to Performance-Based Services Acquisition,* available at link #22.

CHAPTER NINE: COLLECTORS

1. The temptations remain, however. Brewster Kahle reports that the White House changes its own press releases without notice. A May 13, 2003, press release stated, "Combat Operations in Iraq Have Ended." That was later changed, without notice, to "Major Combat Operations in Iraq Have Ended." E-mail from Brewster Kahle, 1 December 2003.

2. Doug Herrick, "Toward a National Film Collection: Motion Pictures at the Library of Congress," *Film Library Quarterly* 13 nos. 2–3 (1980): 5; Anthony Slide, *Nitrate Won't Wait: A History of Film Preservation in the United States* (Jefferson, N.C.: McFarland & Co., 1992), 36.

3. Dave Barns, "Fledgling Career in Antique Books: Woodstock Landlord, Bar Owner Starts a New Chapter by Adopting Business," *Chicago Tribune,* 5 September 1997, at Metro Lake 1L. Of books published between 1927 and 1946, only 2.2 percent were in print in 2002. R. Anthony Reese, "The First Sale Doctrine in the Era of Digital Networks," *Boston College Law Review* 44 (2003): 593 n. 51.

CHAPTER TEN: "PROPERTY"

1. Home Recording of Copyrighted Works: Hearings on H.R. 4783, H.R. 4794, H.R. 4808, H.R. 5250, H.R. 5488, and H.R. 5705 Before the Subcommittee on Courts, Civil Liberties, and the Administration of Justice of the Committee on the Judiciary of the House of Representatives, 97th Cong., 2nd sess. (1982): 65 (testimony of Jack Valenti).

2. Lawyers speak of "property" not as an absolute thing, but as a bundle of rights that are sometimes associated with a particular object. Thus, my "property right" to my car gives me the right to exclusive use, but not the right to drive at 150 miles an hour. For the best effort to connect the ordinary meaning of "property" to "lawyer talk," see Bruce Ackerman, *Private Property and the Constitution* (New Haven: Yale University Press, 1977), 26–27.

3. By describing the way law affects the other three modalities, I don't mean to suggest that the other three don't affect law. Obviously, they do. Law's only distinction is that it alone speaks as if it has a right self-consciously to change the other three. The right of the other three is more timidly expressed. See Lawrence Lessig, *Code: And Other Laws of Cyberspace* (New

York: Basic Books, 1999): 90–95; Lawrence Lessig, "The New Chicago School," *Journal of Legal Studies,* June 1998.

4. Some people object to this way of talking about "liberty." They object because their focus when considering the constraints that exist at any particular moment are constraints imposed exclusively by the government. For instance, if a storm destroys a bridge, these people think it is meaningless to say that one's liberty has been restrained. A bridge has washed out, and it's harder to get from one place to another. To talk about this as a loss of freedom, they say, is to confuse the stuff of politics with the vagaries of ordinary life.

   I don't mean to deny the value in this narrower view, which depends upon the context of the inquiry. I do, however, mean to argue against any insistence that this narrower view is the only proper view of liberty. As I argued in *Code,* we come from a long tradition of political thought with a broader focus than the narrow question of what the government did when. John Stuart Mill defended freedom of speech, for example, from the tyranny of narrow minds, not from the fear of government prosecution; John Stuart Mill, *On Liberty* (Indiana: Hackett Publishing Co., 1978), 19. John R. Commons famously defended the economic freedom of labor from constraints imposed by the market; John R. Commons, "The Right to Work," in Malcom Rutherford and Warren J. Samuels, eds., *John R. Commons: Selected Essays* (London: Routledge: 1997), 62. The Americans with Disabilities Act increases the liberty of people with physical disabilities by changing the architecture of certain public places, thereby making access to those places easier; 42 *United States Code,* section 12101 (2000). Each of these interventions to change existing conditions changes the liberty of a particular group. The effect of those interventions should be accounted for in order to understand the effective liberty that each of these groups might face.

5. See Geoffrey Smith, "Film vs. Digital: Can Kodak Build a Bridge?" BusinessWeek online, 2 August 1999, available at link #23. For a more recent analysis of Kodak's place in the market, see Chana R. Schoenberger, "Can Kodak Make Up for Lost Moments?" Forbes.com, 6 October 2003, available at link #24.

6. Fred Warshofsky, *The Patent Wars* (New York: Wiley, 1994), 170–71.

7. See, for example, James Boyle, "A Politics of Intellectual Property: Environmentalism for the Net?" *Duke Law Journal* 47 (1997): 87.

8. William W. Crosskey, *Politics and the Constitution in the History of the United States* (London: Cambridge University Press, 1953), vol. 1, 485–86: "extinguish[ing], by plain implication of 'the supreme Law of the Land,' *the perpetual rights which authors had, or were supposed by some to have, under the Common Law*" (emphasis added).

9. Although 13,000 titles were published in the United States from 1790 to

1799, only 556 copyright registrations were filed; John Tebbel, *A History of Book Publishing in the United States*, vol. 1, *The Creation of an Industry, 1630–1865* (New York: Bowker, 1972), 141. Of the 21,000 imprints recorded before 1790, only twelve were copyrighted under the 1790 act; William J. Maher, *Copyright Term, Retrospective Extension and the Copyright Law of 1790 in Historical Context*, 7–10 (2002), available at link #25. Thus, the overwhelming majority of works fell immediately into the public domain. Even those works that were copyrighted fell into the public domain quickly, because the term of copyright was short. The initial term of copyright was fourteen years, with the option of renewal for an additional fourteen years. Copyright Act of May 31, 1790, §1, 1 stat. 124.

10. Few copyright holders ever chose to renew their copyrights. For instance, of the 25,006 copyrights registered in 1883, only 894 were renewed in 1910. For a year-by-year analysis of copyright renewal rates, see Barbara A. Ringer, "Study No. 31: Renewal of Copyright," *Studies on Copyright*, vol. 1 (New York: Practicing Law Institute, 1963), 618. For a more recent and comprehensive analysis, see William M. Landes and Richard A. Posner, "Indefinitely Renewable Copyright," *University of Chicago Law Review* 70 (2003): 471, 498–501, and accompanying figures.

11. See Ringer, ch. 9, n. 2.

12. These statistics are understated. Between the years 1910 and 1962 (the first year the renewal term was extended), the average term was never more than thirty-two years, and averaged thirty years. See Landes and Posner, "Indefinitely Renewable Copyright," loc. cit.

13. See Thomas Bender and David Sampliner, "Poets, Pirates, and the Creation of American Literature," 29 *New York University Journal of International Law and Politics* 255 (1997), and James Gilraeth, ed., Federal Copyright Records, 1790–1800 (U.S. G.P.O., 1987).

14. Jonathan Zittrain, "The Copyright Cage," *Legal Affairs*, July/August 2003, available at link #26.

15. Professor Rubenfeld has presented a powerful constitutional argument about the difference that copyright law should draw (from the perspective of the First Amendment) between mere "copies" and derivative works. See Jed Rubenfeld, "The Freedom of Imagination: Copyright's Constitutionality," *Yale Law Journal* 112 (2002): 1–60 (see especially pp. 53–59).

16. This is a simplification of the law, but not much of one. The law certainly regulates more than "copies"—a public performance of a copyrighted song, for example, is regulated even though performance per se doesn't make a copy; 17 *United States Code*, section 106(4). And it certainly sometimes doesn't regulate a "copy"; 17 *United States Code*, section 112(a). But the presumption under the existing law (which regulates "copies;" 17 *United States Code*, section 102) is that if there is a copy, there is a right.

17. Thus, my argument is not that in each place that copyright law extends,

we should repeal it. It is instead that we should have a good argument for its extending where it does, and should not determine its reach on the basis of arbitrary and automatic changes caused by technology.

18. I don't mean "nature" in the sense that it couldn't be different, but rather that its present instantiation entails a copy. Optical networks need not make copies of content they transmit, and a digital network could be designed to delete anything it copies so that the same number of copies remain.

19. See David Lange, "Recognizing the Public Domain," *Law and Contemporary Problems* 44 (1981): 172–73.

20. Ibid. See also Vaidhyanathan, *Copyrights and Copywrongs*, 1–3.

21. In principle, a contract might impose a requirement on me. I might, for example, buy a book from you that includes a contract that says I will read it only three times, or that I promise to read it three times. But that obligation (and the limits for creating that obligation) would come from the contract, not from copyright law, and the obligations of contract would not necessarily pass to anyone who subsequently acquired the book.

22. See Pamela Samuelson, "Anticircumvention Rules: Threat to Science," *Science* 293 (2001): 2028; Brendan I. Koerner, "Play Dead: Sony Muzzles the Techies Who Teach a Robot Dog New Tricks," *American Prospect,* 1 January 2002; "Court Dismisses Computer Scientists' Challenge to DMCA," *Intellectual Property Litigation Reporter,* 11 December 2001; Bill Holland, "Copyright Act Raising Free-Speech Concerns," *Billboard,* 26 May 2001; Janelle Brown, "Is the RIAA Running Scared?" Salon.com, 26 April 2001; Electronic Frontier Foundation, "Frequently Asked Questions about *Felten and USENIX* v. *RIAA* Legal Case," available at link #27.

23. *Sony Corporation of America* v. *Universal City Studios, Inc.,* 464 U.S. 417, 455 fn. 27 (1984). Rogers never changed his view about the VCR. See James Lardner, *Fast Forward: Hollywood, the Japanese, and the Onslaught of the VCR* (New York: W. W. Norton, 1987), 270–71.

24. For an early and prescient analysis, see Rebecca Tushnet, "Legal Fictions, Copyright, Fan Fiction, and a New Common Law," *Loyola of Los Angeles Entertainment Law Journal* 17 (1997): 651.

25. FCC Oversight: Hearing Before the Senate Commerce, Science and Transportation Committee, 108th Cong., 1st sess. (22 May 2003) (statement of Senator John McCain).

26. Lynette Holloway, "Despite a Marketing Blitz, CD Sales Continue to Slide," *New York Times,* 23 December 2002.

27. Molly Ivins, "Media Consolidation Must Be Stopped," *Charleston Gazette,* 31 May 2003.

28. James Fallows, "The Age of Murdoch," *Atlantic Monthly* (September 2003): 89.

29. Leonard Hill, "The Axis of Access," remarks before Weidenbaum Center Forum, "Entertainment Economics: The Movie Industry," St. Louis, Mis-

souri, 3 April 2003 (transcript of prepared remarks available at link #28; for the Lear story, not included in the prepared remarks, see link #29).

30. NewsCorp./DirecTV Merger and Media Consolidation: Hearings on Media Ownership Before the Senate Commerce Committee, 108th Cong., 1st sess. (2003) (testimony of Gene Kimmelman on behalf of Consumers Union and the Consumer Federation of America), available at link #30. Kimmelman quotes Victoria Riskin, president of Writers Guild of America, West, in her Remarks at FCC En Banc Hearing, Richmond, Virginia, 27 February 2003.

31. Ibid.

32. "Barry Diller Takes on Media Deregulation," *Now with Bill Moyers*, Bill Moyers, 25 April 2003, edited transcript available at link #31.

33. Clayton M. Christensen, *The Innovator's Dilemma: The Revolutionary National Bestseller that Changed the Way We Do Business* (Cambridge: Harvard Business School Press, 1997). Christensen acknowledges that the idea was first suggested by Dean Kim Clark. See Kim B. Clark, "The Interaction of Design Hierarchies and Market Concepts in Technological Evolution," *Research Policy* 14 (1985): 235–51. For a more recent study, see Richard Foster and Sarah Kaplan, *Creative Destruction: Why Companies That Are Built to Last Underperform the Market—and How to Successfully Transform Them* (New York: Currency/Doubleday, 2001).

34. The Marijuana Policy Project, in February 2003, sought to place ads that directly responded to the Nick and Norm series on stations within the Washington, D.C., area. Comcast rejected the ads as "against [their] policy." The local NBC affiliate, WRC, rejected the ads without reviewing them. The local ABC affiliate, WJOA, originally agreed to run the ads and accepted payment to do so, but later decided not to run the ads and returned the collected fees. Interview with Neal Levine, 15 October 2003.

These restrictions are, of course, not limited to drug policy. See, for example, Nat Ives, "On the Issue of an Iraq War, Advocacy Ads Meet with Rejection from TV Networks," *New York Times*, 13 March 2003, C4. Outside of election-related air time there is very little that the FCC or the courts are willing to do to even the playing field. For a general overview, see Rhonda Brown, "Ad Hoc Access: The Regulation of Editorial Advertising on Television and Radio," *Yale Law and Policy Review* 6 (1988): 449–79, and for a more recent summary of the stance of the FCC and the courts, see *Radio-Television News Directors Association* v. *FCC*, 184 F. 3d 872 (D.C. Cir. 1999). Municipal authorities exercise the same authority as the networks. In a recent example from San Francisco, the San Francisco transit authority rejected an ad that criticized its Muni diesel buses. Phillip Matier and Andrew Ross, "Antidiesel Group Fuming After Muni Rejects Ad," SFGate.com, 16 June 2003, available at link #32. The ground was that the criticism was "too controversial."

35. Siva Vaidhyanathan captures a similar point in his "four surrenders" of copyright law in the digital age. See Vaidhyanathan, 159–60.

36. It was the single most important contribution of the legal realist movement to demonstrate that all property rights are always crafted to balance public and private interests. See Thomas C. Grey, "The Disintegration of Property," in *Nomos XXII: Property*, J. Roland Pennock and John W. Chapman, eds. (New York: New York University Press, 1980).

CHAPTER ELEVEN: CHIMERA

1. H. G. Wells, "The Country of the Blind" (1904, 1911). See H. G. Wells, *The Country of the Blind and Other Stories*, Michael Sherborne, ed. (New York: Oxford University Press, 1996).

2. For an excellent summary, see the report prepared by GartnerG2 and the Berkman Center for Internet and Society at Harvard Law School, "Copyright and Digital Media in a Post-Napster World," 27 June 2003, available at link #33. Reps. John Conyers Jr. (D-Mich.) and Howard L. Berman (D-Calif.) have introduced a bill that would treat unauthorized on-line copying as a felony offense with punishments ranging as high as five years imprisonment; see Jon Healey, "House Bill Aims to Up Stakes on Piracy," *Los Angeles Times*, 17 July 2003, available at link #34. Civil penalties are currently set at $150,000 per copied song. For a recent (and unsuccessful) legal challenge to the RIAA's demand that an ISP reveal the identity of a user accused of sharing more than 600 songs through a family computer, see *RIAA* v. *Verizon Internet Services (In re. Verizon Internet Services)*, 240 F. Supp. 2d 24 (D.D.C. 2003). Such a user could face liability ranging as high as $90 million. Such astronomical figures furnish the RIAA with a powerful arsenal in its prosecution of file sharers. Settlements ranging from $12,000 to $17,500 for four students accused of heavy file sharing on university networks must have seemed a mere pittance next to the $98 billion the RIAA could seek should the matter proceed to court. See Elizabeth Young, "Downloading Could Lead to Fines," redandblack.com, 26 August 2003, available at link #35. For an example of the RIAA's targeting of student file sharing, and of the subpoenas issued to universities to reveal student file-sharer identities, see James Collins, "RIAA Steps Up Bid to Force BC, MIT to Name Students," *Boston Globe*, 8 August 2003, D3, available at link #36.

3. WIPO and the DMCA One Year Later: Assessing Consumer Access to Digital Entertainment on the Internet and Other Media: Hearing Before the Subcommittee on Telecommunications, Trade, and Consumer Protection, House Committee on Commerce, 106th Cong. 29 (1999) (statement of Peter Harter, vice president, Global Public Policy and Standards, EMusic.com), available in LEXIS, Federal Document Clearing House Congressional Testimony File.

CHAPTER TWELVE: HARMS

1. See Lynne W. Jeter, *Disconnected: Deceit and Betrayal at WorldCom* (Hoboken, N.J.: John Wiley & Sons, 2003), 176, 204; for details of the settlement, see MCI press release, "MCI Wins U.S. District Court Approval for SEC Settlement" (7 July 2003), available at link #37.

2. The bill, modeled after California's tort reform model, was passed in the House of Representatives but defeated in a Senate vote in July 2003. For an overview, see Tanya Albert, "Measure Stalls in Senate: 'We'll Be Back,' Say Tort Reformers," amednews.com, 28 July 2003, available at link #38, and "Senate Turns Back Malpractice Caps," CBSNews.com, 9 July 2003, available at link #39. President Bush has continued to urge tort reform in recent months.

3. See Danit Lidor, "Artists Just Wanna Be Free," *Wired*, 7 July 2003, available at link #40. For an overview of the exhibition, see link #41.

4. See Joseph Menn, "Universal, EMI Sue Napster Investor," *Los Angeles Times*, 23 April 2003. For a parallel argument about the effects on innovation in the distribution of music, see Janelle Brown, "The Music Revolution Will Not Be Digitized," Salon.com, 1 June 2001, available at link #42. See also Jon Healey, "Online Music Services Besieged," *Los Angeles Times*, 28 May 2001.

5. Rafe Needleman, "Driving in Cars with MP3s," *Business 2.0*, 16 June 2003, available at link #43. I am grateful to Dr. Mohammad Al-Ubaydli for this example.

6. "Copyright and Digital Media in a Post-Napster World," GartnerG2 and the Berkman Center for Internet and Society at Harvard Law School (2003), 33–35, available at link #44.

7. GartnerG2, 26–27.

8. See David McGuire, "Tech Execs Square Off Over Piracy," Newsbytes, 28 February 2002 (Entertainment).

9. Jessica Litman, *Digital Copyright* (Amherst, N.Y.: Prometheus Books, 2001).

10. The only circuit court exception is found in *Recording Industry Association of America (RIAA)* v. *Diamond Multimedia Systems*, 180 F. 3d 1072 (9th Cir. 1999). There the court of appeals for the Ninth Circuit reasoned that makers of a portable MP3 player were not liable for contributory copyright infringement for a device that is unable to record or redistribute music (a device whose only copying function is to render portable a music file already stored on a user's hard drive).

At the district court level, the only exception is found in *Metro-Goldwyn-Mayer Studios, Inc.* v. *Grokster, Ltd.*, 259 F. Supp. 2d 1029 (C.D. Cal., 2003), where the court found the link between the distributor and any given user's conduct too attenuated to make the distributor liable for contributory or vicarious infringement liability.

11. For example, in July 2002, Representative Howard Berman introduced the Peer-to-Peer Piracy Prevention Act (H.R. 5211), which would immunize copyright holders from liability for damage done to computers when the copyright holders use technology to stop copyright infringement. In August 2002, Representative Billy Tauzin introduced a bill to mandate that technologies capable of rebroadcasting digital copies of films broadcast on TV (i.e., computers) respect a "broadcast flag" that would disable copying of that content. And in March of the same year, Senator Fritz Hollings introduced the Consumer Broadband and Digital Television Promotion Act, which mandated copyright protection technology in all digital media devices. See GartnerG2, "Copyright and Digital Media in a Post-Napster World," 27 June 2003, 33–34, available at link #44.

12. Lessing, 239.

13. Ibid., 229.

14. This example was derived from fees set by the original Copyright Arbitration Royalty Panel (CARP) proceedings, and is drawn from an example offered by Professor William Fisher. Conference Proceedings, iLaw (Stanford), 3 July 2003, on file with author. Professors Fisher and Zittrain submitted testimony in the CARP proceeding that was ultimately rejected. See Jonathan Zittrain, Digital Performance Right in Sound Recordings and Ephemeral Recordings, Docket No. 2000-9, CARP DTRA 1 and 2, available at link #45.

For an excellent analysis making a similar point, see Randal C. Picker, "Copyright as Entry Policy: The Case of Digital Distribution," *Antitrust Bulletin* (Summer/Fall 2002): 461: "This was not confusion, these are just old-fashioned entry barriers. Analog radio stations are protected from digital entrants, reducing entry in radio and diversity. Yes, this is done in the name of getting royalties to copyright holders, but, absent the play of powerful interests, that could have been done in a media-neutral way."

15. Mike Graziano and Lee Rainie, "The Music Downloading Deluge," Pew Internet and American Life Project (24 April 2001), available at link #46. The Pew Internet and American Life Project reported that 37 million Americans had downloaded music files from the Internet by early 2001.

16. Alex Pham, "The Labels Strike Back: N.Y. Girl Settles RIAA Case," *Los Angeles Times*, 10 September 2003, Business.

17. Jeffrey A. Miron and Jeffrey Zwiebel, "Alcohol Consumption During Prohibition," *American Economic Review* 81, no. 2 (1991): 242.

18. National Drug Control Policy: Hearing Before the House Government Reform Committee, 108th Cong., 1st sess. (5 March 2003) (statement of John P. Walters, director of National Drug Control Policy).

19. See James Andreoni, Brian Erard, and Jonathon Feinstein, "Tax Compliance," *Journal of Economic Literature* 36 (1998): 818 (survey of compliance literature).

20. See Frank Ahrens, "RIAA's Lawsuits Meet Surprised Targets; Single Mother in Calif., 12-Year-Old Girl in N.Y. Among Defendants," *Washington Post*, 10 September 2003, E1; Chris Cobbs, "Worried Parents Pull Plug on File 'Stealing'; With the Music Industry Cracking Down on File Swapping, Parents are Yanking Software from Home PCs to Avoid Being Sued," *Orlando Sentinel Tribune*, 30 August 2003, C1; Jefferson Graham, "Recording Industry Sues Parents," *USA Today*, 15 September 2003, 4D; John Schwartz, "She Says She's No Music Pirate. No Snoop Fan, Either," *New York Times*, 25 September 2003, C1; Margo Varadi, "Is Brianna a Criminal?" *Toronto Star*, 18 September 2003, P7.

21. See "Revealed: How RIAA Tracks Downloaders: Music Industry Discloses Some Methods Used," CNN.com, available at link #47.

22. See Jeff Adler, "Cambridge: On Campus, Pirates Are Not Penitent," *Boston Globe*, 18 May 2003, City Weekly, 1; Frank Ahrens, "Four Students Sued over Music Sites; Industry Group Targets File Sharing at Colleges," *Washington Post*, 4 April 2003, E1; Elizabeth Armstrong, "Students 'Rip, Mix, Burn' at Their Own Risk," *Christian Science Monitor*, 2 September 2003, 20; Robert Becker and Angela Rozas, "Music Pirate Hunt Turns to Loyola; Two Students Names Are Handed Over; Lawsuit Possible," *Chicago Tribune*, 16 July 2003, 1C; Beth Cox, "RIAA Trains Antipiracy Guns on Universities," *Internet News*, 30 January 2003, available at link #48; Benny Evangelista, "Download Warning 101: Freshman Orientation This Fall to Include Record Industry Warnings Against File Sharing," *San Francisco Chronicle*, 11 August 2003, E11; "Raid, Letters Are Weapons at Universities," *USA Today*, 26 September 2000, 3D.

CHAPTER THIRTEEN: ELDRED

1. There's a parallel here with pornography that is a bit hard to describe, but it's a strong one. One phenomenon that the Internet created was a world of noncommercial pornographers—people who were distributing porn but were not making money directly or indirectly from that distribution. Such a class didn't exist before the Internet came into being because the costs of distributing porn were so high. Yet this new class of distributors got special attention in the Supreme Court, when the Court struck down the Communications Decency Act of 1996. It was partly because of the burden on noncommercial speakers that the statute was found to exceed Congress's power. The same point could have been made about noncommercial publishers after the advent of the Internet. The Eric Eldreds of the world before the Internet were extremely few. Yet one would think it at least as important to protect the Eldreds of the world as to protect noncommercial pornographers.

2. The full text is: "Sonny [Bono] wanted the term of copyright protection to last forever. I am informed by staff that such a change would violate the

Constitution. I invite all of you to work with me to strengthen our copyright laws in all of the ways available to us. As you know, there is also Jack Valenti's proposal for a term to last forever less one day. Perhaps the Committee may look at that next Congress," 144 Cong. Rec. H9946, 9951-2 (October 7, 1998).

3. Associated Press, "Disney Lobbying for Copyright Extension No Mickey Mouse Effort; Congress OKs Bill Granting Creators 20 More Years," *Chicago Tribune*, 17 October 1998, 22.

4. See Nick Brown, "Fair Use No More?: Copyright in the Information Age," available at link #49.

5. Alan K. Ota, "Disney in Washington: The Mouse That Roars," *Congressional Quarterly This Week*, 8 August 1990, available at link #50.

6. *United States* v. *Lopez*, 514 U.S. 549, 564 (1995).

7. *United States* v. *Morrison*, 529 U.S. 598 (2000).

8. If it is a principle about enumerated powers, then the principle carries from one enumerated power to another. The animating point in the context of the Commerce Clause was that the interpretation offered by the government would allow the government unending power to regulate commerce—the limitation to interstate commerce notwithstanding. The same point is true in the context of the Copyright Clause. Here, too, the government's interpretation would allow the government unending power to regulate copyrights—the limitation to "limited times" notwithstanding.

9. Brief of the Nashville Songwriters Association, *Eldred* v. *Ashcroft*, 537 U.S. 186 (2003) (No. 01-618), n.10, available at link #51.

10. The figure of 2 percent is an extrapolation from the study by the Congressional Research Service, in light of the estimated renewal ranges. See Brief of Petitioners, *Eldred* v. *Ashcroft*, 7, available at link #52.

11. See David G. Savage, "High Court Scene of Showdown on Copyright Law," *Los Angeles Times*, 6 October 2002; David Streitfeld, "Classic Movies, Songs, Books at Stake; Supreme Court Hears Arguments Today on Striking Down Copyright Extension," *Orlando Sentinel Tribune*, 9 October 2002.

12. Brief of Hal Roach Studios and Michael Agee as Amicus Curiae Supporting the Petitoners, *Eldred* v. *Ashcroft*, 537 U.S. 186 (2003) (No. 01-618), 12. See also Brief of Amicus Curiae filed on behalf of Petitioners by the Internet Archive, *Eldred* v. *Ashcroft*, available at link #53.

13. Jason Schultz, "The Myth of the 1976 Copyright 'Chaos' Theory," 20 December 2002, available at link #54.

14. Brief of Amici Dr. Seuss Enterprise et al., *Eldred* v. *Ashcroft*, 537 U.S. 186 (2003) (No. 01-618), 19.

15. Dinitia Smith, "Immortal Words, Immortal Royalties? Even Mickey Mouse Joins the Fray," *New York Times*, 28 March 1998, B7.

CHAPTER FOURTEEN: ELDRED II

1. Until the 1908 Berlin Act of the Berne Convention, national copyright legislation sometimes made protection depend upon compliance with formalities such as registration, deposit, and affixation of notice of the author's claim of copyright. However, starting with the 1908 act, every text of the Convention has provided that "the enjoyment and the exercise" of rights guaranteed by the Convention "shall not be subject to any formality." The prohibition against formalities is presently embodied in Article 5(2) of the Paris Text of the Berne Convention. Many countries continue to impose some form of deposit or registration requirement, albeit not as a condition of copyright. French law, for example, requires the deposit of copies of works in national repositories, principally the National Museum. Copies of books published in the United Kingdom must be deposited in the British Library. The German Copyright Act provides for a Registrar of Authors where the author's true name can be filed in the case of anonymous or pseudonymous works. Paul Goldstein, *International Intellectual Property Law, Cases and Materials* (New York: Foundation Press, 2001), 153–54.

CONCLUSION

1. Commission on Intellectual Property Rights, "Final Report: Integrating Intellectual Property Rights and Development Policy" (London, 2002), available at link #55. According to a World Health Organization press release issued 9 July 2002, only 230,000 of the 6 million who need drugs in the developing world receive them—and half of them are in Brazil.

2. See Peter Drahos with John Braithwaite, *Information Feudalism: Who Owns the Knowledge Economy?* (New York: The New Press, 2003), 37.

3. International Intellectual Property Institute (IIPI), *Patent Protection and Access to HIV/AIDS Pharmaceuticals in Sub-Saharan Africa, a Report Prepared for the World Intellectual Property Organization* (Washington, D.C., 2000), 14, available at link #56. For a firsthand account of the struggle over South Africa, see Hearing Before the Subcommittee on Criminal Justice, Drug Policy, and Human Resources, House Committee on Government Reform, H. Rep., 1st sess., Ser. No. 106-126 (22 July 1999), 150–57 (statement of James Love).

4. International Intellectual Property Institute (IIPI), *Patent Protection and Access to HIV/AIDS Pharmaceuticals in Sub-Saharan Africa, a Report Prepared for the World Intellectual Property Organization* (Washington, D.C., 2000), 15.

5. See Sabin Russell, "New Crusade to Lower AIDS Drug Costs: Africa's Needs at Odds with Firms' Profit Motive," *San Francisco Chronicle*, 24 May 1999, A1, available at link #57 ("compulsory licenses and gray mar-

kets pose a threat to the entire system of intellectual property protection"); Robert Weissman, "AIDS and Developing Countries: Democratizing Access to Essential Medicines," *Foreign Policy in Focus* 4:23 (August 1999), available at link #58 (describing U.S. policy); John A. Harrelson, "TRIPS, Pharmaceutical Patents, and the HIV/AIDS Crisis: Finding the Proper Balance Between Intellectual Property Rights and Compassion, a Synopsis," *Widener Law Symposium Journal* (Spring 2001): 175.

6. Jonathan Krim, "The Quiet War over Open-Source," *Washington Post,* 21 August 2003, E1, available at link #59; William New, "Global Group's Shift on 'Open Source' Meeting Spurs Stir," *National Journal's Technology Daily,* 19 August 2003, available at link #60; William New, "U.S. Official Opposes 'Open Source' Talks at WIPO," *National Journal's Technology Daily,* 19 August 2003, available at link #61.

7. I should disclose that I was one of the people who asked WIPO for the meeting.

8. Microsoft's position about free and open source software is more sophisticated. As it has repeatedly asserted, it has no problem with "open source" software or software in the public domain. Microsoft's principal opposition is to "free software" licensed under a "copyleft" license, meaning a license that requires the licensee to adopt the same terms on any derivative work. See Bradford L. Smith, "The Future of Software: Enabling the Marketplace to Decide," *Government Policy Toward Open Source Software* (Washington, D.C.: AEI-Brookings Joint Center for Regulatory Studies, American Enterprise Institute for Public Policy Research, 2002), 69, available at link #62. See also Craig Mundie, Microsoft senior vice president, *The Commercial Software Model,* discussion at New York University Stern School of Business (3 May 2001), available at link #63.

9. Krim, "The Quiet War over Open-Source," available at link #64.

10. See Drahos with Braithwaite, *Information Feudalism,* 210–20.

11. John Borland, "RIAA Sues 261 File Swappers," CNET News.com, 8 September 2003, available at link #65; Paul R. La Monica, "Music Industry Sues Swappers," CNN/Money, 8 September 2003, available at link #66; Soni Sangha and Phyllis Furman with Robert Gearty, "Sued for a Song, N.Y.C. 12-Yr-Old Among 261 Cited as Sharers," *New York Daily News,* 9 September 2003, 3; Frank Ahrens, "RIAA's Lawsuits Meet Surprised Targets; Single Mother in Calif., 12-Year-Old Girl in N.Y. Among Defendants," *Washington Post,* 10 September 2003, E1; Katie Dean, "Schoolgirl Settles with RIAA," *Wired News,* 10 September 2003, available at link #67.

12. Jon Wiederhorn, "Eminem Gets Sued . . . by a Little Old Lady," mtv.com, 17 September 2003, available at link #68.

13. Kenji Hall, Associated Press, "Japanese Book May Be Inspiration for Dylan Songs," Kansascity.com, 9 July 2003, available at link #69.

14. "BBC Plans to Open Up Its Archive to the Public," BBC press release, 24 August 2003, available at link #70.
15. "Creative Commons and Brazil," Creative Commons Weblog, 6 August 2003, available at link #71.

US, NOW

1. See, for example, Marc Rotenberg, "Fair Information Practices and the Architecture of Privacy (What Larry Doesn't Get)," *Stanford Technology Law Review* 1 (2001): par. 6–18, available at link #72 (describing examples in which technology defines privacy policy). See also Jeffrey Rosen, *The Naked Crowd: Reclaiming Security and Freedom in an Anxious Age* (New York: Random House, 2004) (mapping tradeoffs between technology and privacy).
2. *Willful Infringement: A Report from the Front Lines of the Real Culture Wars* (2003), produced by Jed Horovitz, directed by Greg Hittelman, a Fiat Lucre production, available at link #72.

THEM, SOON

1. The proposal I am advancing here would apply to American works only. Obviously, I believe it would be beneficial for the same idea to be adopted by other countries as well.
2. There would be a complication with derivative works that I have not solved here. In my view, the law of derivatives creates a more complicated system than is justified by the marginal incentive it creates.
3. "A Radical Rethink," *Economist*, 366:8308 (25 January 2003): 15, available at link #74.
4. Department of Veterans Affairs, Veteran's Application for Compensation and/or Pension, VA Form 21-526 (OMB Approved No. 2900-0001), available at link #75.
5. Benjamin Kaplan, *An Unhurried View of Copyright* (New York: Columbia University Press, 1967), 32.
6. Ibid., 56.
7. Paul Goldstein, *Copyright's Highway: From Gutenberg to the Celestial Jukebox* (Stanford: Stanford University Press, 2003), 187–216.
8. See, for example, "Music Media Watch," The J@pan Inc. Newsletter, 3 April 2002, available at link #76.
9. William Fisher, *Digital Music: Problems and Possibilities* (last revised: 10 October 2000), available at link #77; William Fisher, *Promises to Keep: Technology, Law, and the Future of Entertainment* (forthcoming) (Stanford: Stanford University Press, 2004), ch. 6, available at link #78. Professor Netanel has proposed a related idea that would exempt noncommercial sharing from the reach of copyright and would establish compensation to artists to balance any loss. See Neil Weinstock Netanel, "Impose a Noncommercial Use Levy to Allow Free P2P File Sharing," available at link

#79. For other proposals, see Lawrence Lessig, "Who's Holding Back Broadband?" *Washington Post,* 8 January 2002, A17; Philip S. Corwin on behalf of Sharman Networks, A Letter to Senator Joseph R. Biden, Jr., Chairman of the Senate Foreign Relations Committee, 26 February 2002, available at link #80; Serguei Osokine, *A Quick Case for Intellectual Property Use Fee (IPUF),* 3 March 2002, available at link #81; Jefferson Graham, "Kazaa, Verizon Propose to Pay Artists Directly," *USA Today,* 13 May 2002, available at link #82; Steven M. Cherry, "Getting Copyright Right," IEEE Spectrum Online, 1 July 2002, available at link #83; Declan Mc-Cullagh, "Verizon's Copyright Campaign," CNET News.com, 27 August 2002, available at link #84.

Fisher's proposal is very similar to Richard Stallman's proposal for DAT. Unlike Fisher's, Stallman's proposal would not pay artists directly proportionally, though more popular artists would get more than the less popular. As is typical with Stallman, his proposal predates the current debate by about a decade. See link #85.

10. Lawrence Lessig, "Copyright's First Amendment" (Melville B. Nimmer Memorial Lecture), *UCLA Law Review* 48 (2001): 1057, 1069–70.

11. A good example is the work of Professor Stan Liebowitz. Liebowitz is to be commended for his careful review of data about infringement, leading him to question his own publicly stated position—twice. He initially predicted that downloading would substantially harm the industry. He then revised his view in light of the data, and he has since revised his view again. Compare Stan J. Liebowitz, *Rethinking the Network Economy: The True Forces That Drive the Digital Marketplace* (New York: Amacom, 2002), 173 (reviewing his original view but expressing skepticism) with Stan J. Liebowitz, "Will MP3s Annihilate the Record Industry?" working paper, June 2003, available at link #86.

Liebowitz's careful analysis is extremely valuable in estimating the effect of file-sharing technology. In my view, however, he underestimates the costs of the legal system. See, for example, *Rethinking,* 174–76.

ACKNOWLEDGMENTS

This book is the product of a long and as yet unsuccessful struggle that began when I read of Eric Eldred's war to keep books free. Eldred's work helped launch a movement, the free culture movement, and it is to him that this book is dedicated.

I received guidance in various places from friends and academics, including Glenn Brown, Peter DiCola, Jennifer Mnookin, Richard Posner, Mark Rose, and Kathleen Sullivan. And I received correction and guidance from many amazing students at Stanford Law School and Stanford University. They included Andrew B. Coan, John Eden, James P. Fellers, Christopher Guzelian, Erica Goldberg, Robert Hallman, Andrew Harris, Matthew Kahn, Brian Link, Ohad Mayblum, Alina Ng, and Erica Platt. I am particularly grateful to Catherine Crump and Harry Surden, who helped direct their research, and to Laura Lynch, who brilliantly managed the army that they assembled, and provided her own critical eye on much of this.

Yuko Noguchi helped me to understand the laws of Japan as well as its culture. I am thankful to her, and to the many in Japan who helped me prepare this book: Joi Ito, Takayuki Matsutani, Naoto Misaki, Michihiro Sasaki, Hiromichi Tanaka, Hiroo Yamagata, and Yoshihiro

Yonezawa. I am thankful as well as to Professor Nobuhiro Nakayama, and the Tokyo University Business Law Center, for giving me the chance to spend time in Japan, and to Tadashi Shiraishi and Kiyokazu Yamagami for their generous help while I was there.

These are the traditional sorts of help that academics regularly draw upon. But in addition to them, the Internet has made it possible to receive advice and correction from many whom I have never even met. Among those who have responded with extremely helpful advice to requests on my blog about the book are Dr. Mohammad Al-Ubaydli, David Gerstein, and Peter DiMauro, as well as a long list of those who had specific ideas about ways to develop my argument. They included Richard Bondi, Steven Cherry, David Coe, Nik Cubrilovic, Bob Devine, Charles Eicher, Thomas Guida, Elihu M. Gerson, Jeremy Hunsinger, Vaughn Iverson, John Karabaic, Jeff Keltner, James Lindenschmidt, K. L. Mann, Mark Manning, Nora McCauley, Jeffrey McHugh, Evan McMullen, Fred Norton, John Pormann, Pedro A. D. Rezende, Shabbir Safdar, Saul Schleimer, Clay Shirky, Adam Shostack, Kragen Sitaker, Chris Smith, Bruce Steinberg, Andrzej Jan Taramina, Sean Walsh, Matt Wasserman, Miljenko Williams, "Wink," Roger Wood, "Ximmbo da Jazz," and Richard Yanco. (I apologize if I have missed anyone; with computers come glitches, and a crash of my e-mail system meant I lost a bunch of great replies.)

Richard Stallman and Michael Carroll each read the whole book in draft, and each provided extremely helpful correction and advice. Michael helped me to see more clearly the significance of the regulation of derivitive works. And Richard corrected an embarrassingly large number of errors. While my work is in part inspired by Stallman's, he does not agree with me in important places throughout this book.

Finally, and forever, I am thankful to Bettina, who has always insisted that there would be unending happiness away from these battles, and who has always been right. This slow learner is, as ever, grateful for her perpetual patience and love.

INDEX

ABC, 164, 321*n*
academic journals, 262, 280–82
Adobe eBook Reader, 148–53
advertising, 36, 45–46, 127, 145–46, 167–68, 321*n*
Africa, medications for HIV patients in, 257–61
Agee, Michael, 223–24, 225
agricultural patents, 313*n*
Aibo robotic dog, 153–55, 156, 157, 160
AIDS medications, 257–60
air traffic, land ownership vs., 1–3
Akerlof, George, 232
Alben, Alex, 100–104, 105, 198–99, 295, 317*n*
alcohol prohibition, 200
Alice's Adventures in Wonderland (Carroll), 152–53
Allen, Paul, 100
All in the Family, 164, 165
Amazon, 278
American Association of Law Libraries, 232
American Graphophone Company, 56
Americans with Disabilities Act (1990), 318*n*
Andromeda, 203

Anello, Douglas, 60
animated cartoons, 21–24
antiretroviral drugs, 257–61
Apple Corporation, 203, 264, 302
architecture, constraint effected through, 122, 123, 124, 318*n*
archive.org, 112
    see also Internet Archive
archives, digital, 108–15, 173, 222, 226–27
Aristotle, 150
Armstrong, Edwin Howard, 3–6, 184, 196
Arrow, Kenneth, 232
art, underground, 186
artists:
    publicity rights on images of, 317*n*
    recording industry payments to, 52, 58–59, 74, 195, 196–97, 199, 301, 329*n*–30*n*
    retrospective compilations on, 100–104
ASCAP, 18
Asia, commercial piracy in, 63, 64, 65, 302
AT&T, 6
Ayer, Don, 230, 237, 239, 244, 248

Bacon, Francis, 93
Barish, Stephanie, 38, 39, 46

Barlow, Joel, 8
Barnes & Noble, 147
Barry, Hank, 189, 191
BBC, 270
Beatles, 57
Beckett, Thomas, 92
Bell, Alexander Graham, 3
Berlin Act (1908), 327n
Berman, Howard L., 322n, 324n
Berne Convention (1908), 250, 327n
Bernstein, Leonard, 72
Betamax, 75–76
biomedical research, 262–63
Black, Jane, 70
blogs (Web-logs), 41, 42–45, 310n-11n
BMG, 162
BMW, 191
Boies, David, 105
Boland, Lois, 265, 266–68
Bolling, Ruben, 246, 247
Bono, Mary, 215, 326n
Bono, Sonny, 215, 325n
books:
    English copyright law developed for,
        85–94
    free on-line releases of, 72–73, 284–85
    on Internet, 143, 144, 148–53
    out of print, 72, 113, 134, 299, 317n
    resales of, 72, 134, 299, 314n
    three types of uses of, 141–43
    total number of, 114
booksellers, English, 88–94, 316n
Boswell, James, 91
bots, 108, 161
Boyle, James, 129
Braithwaite, John, 267
Branagh, Kenneth, 85, 88
Brandeis, Louis, 34
Brazil, free culture in, 270
Breyer, Stephen, 234, 235, 242, 243
Brezhnev, Leonid, 128
British Parliament, 86, 87, 89–90, 91–92,
    94
broadcast flag, 193, 324n
Bromberg, Dan, 230
Brown, John Seely, 45, 46, 47, 127
browsing, 145, 147, 277–78
Buchanan, James, 232

Bunyan, John, 93
Burdick, Quentin, 60
Bush, George W., 323n

cable television, 59–61, 74–75, 162, 163, 302
camera technology, 32–33, 34, 35, 127
Camp Chaos, 106
CARP (Copyright Arbitration Royalty
    Panel), 324n
cars, MP3 sound systems in, 191
Carson, Rachel, 129
cartoon films, 21–25
Casablanca, 148
cassette recording, 69–70, 314n
    VCRs, 75–76, 77, 158–60, 194, 297, 320n
Causby, Thomas Lee, 2, 3, 7, 11, 12, 256,
    307n
Causby, Tinie, 2, 3, 7, 11, 12, 256, 307n
CBS, 164
CD-ROMs, film clips used in, 100–104
CDs:
    copyright marking of, 291
    foreign piracy of, 63, 64
    mix technology and, 203–4
    preference data on, 189–90
    prices of, 70, 302
    sales levels of, 70–71, 314n
cell phones, music streamed over, 298
chimeras, 178–79
Christensen, Clayton M., 166, 313n, 321n
circumvention technologies, 156, 157–60
civil liberties, 205–7
Clark, Kim B., 321n
CNN, 44
Coase, Ronald, 232
Code (Lessig), xiii, xiv, 121, 318n
CodePink Women for Peace, xiv, 269
Coe, Brian, 33
Comcast, 321n
comics, Japanese, 25–26, 27–28, 29, 309n
commerce, interstate, 219, 236, 326n
Commerce, U.S. Department of, 126
commercials, 36, 45–46, 127, 167–68, 321n
common law, 86, 90, 91, 92
Commons, John R., 318n
Communications Decency Act (1996), 325n
composers, copyright protections of,
    55–59, 74

compulsory license, 57–58
computer games, 37
Conger, 85, 87, 88–89, 90, 91
Congress, U.S.:
  on cable television, 61, 74–75
  challenge of CTEA legislation of,
    228–48
  constitutional powers of, 215–16,
    219–20, 233, 234–35, 238–39, 240
  in constitutional Progress Clause,
    130–31, 236
  on copyright laws, 56–57, 61, 74–75, 76,
    77–78, 133, 134–35, 193, 194, 196,
    197, 294, 324n
  copyright terms extended by, 134–35,
    214–18, 219–21, 228, 236
  on derivative rights, 294
  on digital audio tape, 315n
  lobbying of, 217–18
  on radio, 196, 197
  on recording industry, 56–57, 74, 196
  Supreme Court restraint on, 218–19,
    220, 234
  on VCR technology, 76, 77
Conrad, Paul, 158, 159, 160
Constitution, U.S.:
  Commerce Clause of, 219, 233, 244,
    326n
  copyright purpose established in, 130–31,
    220, 221, 308n, 326n
  on creative property, 119–20, 130
  Fifth Amendment to, 119
  First Amendment to, 10, 128, 142, 168,
    228, 230, 234, 244, 319n
  originalist interpretation of, 243
  Progress Clause of, 130–31, 215, 218,
    232, 236, 243–44
  structural checks and balances of, 131
  Takings Clause of, 119
Consumer Broadband and Digital
    Television Promotion Act, 324n
contracts, 320n
Conyers, John, Jr., 322n
cookies, Internet, 278
"copyleft" licenses, 328n
copyright:
  constitutional purpose of, 130–31, 220,
    221, 308n, 326n

Creative Commons licenses for material
    in, 282–86
  duration of, 24–25, 86, 89–94, 130, 131,
    133–35, 172, 214–18, 220, 221–22,
    292–93, 294–95, 309n, 319n
  four regulatory modalities on, 124–26,
    132
  infringement lawsuits on, see copyright
    infringement lawsuits
  marking of, 137, 288, 290–91
  as narrow monopoly right, 87–94
  of natural authors vs. corporations, 135
  no registration of works, 222–23, 249
  in perpetuity, 89–90, 91, 92–93, 170,
    215, 243, 246, 318n, 325n–26n
  as property, 83–84, 172
  renewability of, 86, 133–34, 135, 289–90,
    293, 309n, 319n
  scope of, 136–39, 140, 169–72, 295, 320n
  usage restrictions attached to, 87–88,
    143–44, 146, 320n
  voluntary reform efforts on, 275, 277–86
  see also copyright law
Copyright Act (1790), 133, 137–38, 319n
Copyright Arbitration Royalty Panel
    (CARP), 324n
copyright infringement lawsuits:
  distribution technology targeted in,
    75–77, 190, 191, 323n
  exaggerated claims of, 51, 180, 185, 187,
    190, 206, 322n
  individual defendants intimidated by,
    51–52, 185, 187, 200, 270
  in recording industry, 50–52, 180, 185,
    190, 200, 270, 322n, 323n
  statutory damages of, 51
  against student file sharing, 50–52, 180,
    322n
  willful infringement findings in, 146
  zero tolerance in, 73–74, 180–81
copyright law:
  authors vs. composers in, 56–57
  on cable television rebroadcasting,
    59–61, 74–75
  circumvention technology banned by,
    156, 157–60
  commercial creativity as primary pur-
    pose of, 8, 204, 308n

copyright law (*cont.*)
    copies as core issue of, 139–40, 141–44, 146, 171, 319*n*, 320*n*
    creativity impeded by, 19, 184–88, 308*n*
    development of, 85–94, 316*n*
    English, 17, 85–94, 316*n*
    European, 137, 250, 327*n*
    as ex post regulation modality, 121–22
    fair use and, 95–99, 107, 141–42, 143, 145, 146, 157, 160, 172, 186–87, 283, 292, 316*n*
    felony punishment for infringement of, 180, 215, 223, 322*n*
    formalities reinstated in, 287–91, 329*n*
    government reforms proposed on, 287–306
    history of American, 132–38, 170–71
    illegal behavior as broad response to, 199–207
    innovation hampered by, 188–99
    innovative freedom balanced with fair compensation in, 75, 77–79, 120, 129–30, 172–73
    international compliance with, 63–64, 313*n*
    Japanese, 26, 27–28
    lawyers as detriment to, 292, 304–6
    malpractice lawsuits against lawyers advising on, 190–91
    on music recordings, 55–58, 74, 181, 195, 291
    privacy interests in, 308*n*
    as protection of creators, 10, 131, 204
    registration requirement of, 137, 170–71, 248–54, 288, 289–90, 291, 327*n*
    on republishing vs. transformation of original work, 19, 136, 138–39, 144–45, 170–72, 294–96, 319*n*
    royalty proposal on derivative reuse in, 106
    statutory licenses in, 56–58, 64, 74, 194, 295–96, 300
    Supreme Court case on term extension of, 218, 228–48
    technology as automatic enforcer of, 147, 148–61, 181, 186, 203, 320*n*, 324*n*
    term extensions in, 134–35, 214–18, 219–21, 228–48
    two central goals of, 75

Copyright Office, 252–53, 289, 291
corporations:
    copyright terms for, 135
    in pharmaceutical industry, 260
"Country of the Blind, The" (Wells), 177–78
Court of Appeals:
    D.C. Circuit, 228–29, 231, 235
    Ninth Circuit, 76, 105, 323*n*
cover songs, 57
Creative Commons, 270, 282–86
creative property:
    of authors vs. composers, 56–57
    common law protections of, 133
    constitutional tradition on, 118–20, 130–31
    "if value, then right" theory of, 18–19, 53
    noncommercial second life of, 112–13, 114–15
    other property rights vs., 117–24, 140
    see also intellectual property rights
creativity:
    labor shift to, 308*n*
    legal restrictions on, 19, 184–88, 308*n*
    by transforming previous works, 22–24, 25–29
    see also innovation
Crichton, Michael, 37
criminal justice system, 167
Crosskey, William W., 318*n*
CTEA, *see* Sonny Bono Copyright Term Extension Act
culture:
    archives of, 108–15, 173, 226–27
    commerical vs. noncommercial, 7–8, 170–72, 225
    see also free culture
Cyber Rights (Godwin), 40

Daguerre, Louis, 31
Daley, Elizabeth, 36–37, 38, 39–40, 46
DAT (digital audio tape), 315*n*, 330*n*
Data General, 279
Day After Trinity, The, 97
D.C. Court of Appeals, 228–29, 231, 235
DDT, 129–30
Dean, Howard, 43

democracy:
  digital sharing within, 184
  media concentration and, 166
  public discourse in, 42, 45
  semiotic, 301–2
  in technologies of expression, 33, 35,
    41–42, 43, 44–45
Democratic Party, 249
derivative works, 329*n*
  fair use vs., 145
  First Amendment and, 319*n*
  historical shift in copyright coverage of,
    136, 170–72
  piracy vs., 22–24, 25–29, 138–39, 141
  reform of copyright term and scope on,
    294–96
  royalty system proposed for, 106
  technological developments and, 144, 171
developing countries, foreign patent costs
    in, 63, 257–61, 313*n*
Diamond Multimedia Systems, 323*n*
digital audio tape (DAT), 315*n*, 330*n*
digital cameras, 35, 127
Digital Copyright (Litman), 194
Digital Millennium Copyright Act
    (DMCA), 156, 157, 159, 160, 181
Diller, Barry, 165–66
DirecTV, 163
Dirty Harry, 101
Disney, Inc., 23–24, 116, 145–46, 218, 231
  Sony Betamax technology opposed by,
    75–76
Disney, Walt, 21–24, 25, 26, 28–29, 33–34,
    78, 115, 139, 213, 220, 309*n*
DMCA (Digital Millennium Copyright
    Act), 156, 157, 159, 160, 181
Doctorow, Cory, 72–73, 284
doctors, malpractice claims against, 185,
    323*n*
documentary film, 95–99
domain names, 289
Donaldson, Alexander, 90–91, 92
Donaldson v. Beckett, 92–94
Douglas, William O., 2–3
doujinshi comics, 25–26, 27–28, 29
Down and Out in the Magic Kingdom
    (Doctorow), 72–73, 284
Drahos, Peter, 267

DreamWorks, 106–7
Dreyfuss, Rochelle, 18
driving speed, constraints on, 123–24, 207
Drucker, Peter, 103
drugs:
  illegal, 166–67, 201, 207, 321*n*
  pharmaceutical, 257–61, 266, 327*n*,
    328*n*
Dryden, John, 316*n*
"Duck and Cover" film, 112
DVDs:
  piracy of, 64
  price of, 70
Dylan, Bob, 270

Eagle Forum, 231, 232
Eastman, George, 31–34
Eastwood, Clint, 100–103, 295
e-books, 144, 148–53
Edison, Thomas, 3, 53–54, 55, 69, 78
education:
  in media literacy, 35–40
  tinkering as means of, 45–47, 50
Eldred, Eric, 213–15, 218, 220, 221, 229,
    249, 325*n*
Eldred Act, 249–54, 255
Eldred v. Ashcroft, 220, 228–48, 292
elections, 41–42, 43
electoral college, 120, 131
Electronic Frontier Foundation, 205
Else, Jon, 95–99, 186
e-mail, 42
EMI, 162, 191
Eminem, 270
eMusic.com, 181–82
encryption systems, 155–56
England, copyright laws developed in,
    85–94
Enlightenment, 89
environmentalism, 129–30
ephemeral films, 112
Errors and Omissions insurance, 98
Erskine, Andrew, 91
ethics, 201
expression, technologies of:
  democratic, 33, 35, 41–42, 43,
    44–45
  media literacy and, 35–40

Fairbank, Robert, 105
fair use, 141–43
    circumvention technology ban and,
        157–58
    Creative Commons license vs., 283
    in documentary film, 95–99, 316*n*
    fuzziness of, 292
    Internet burdens on, 143, 145
    legal intimidation tactics against, 98–99,
        146, 172, 186–87
    in sampling works, 107
    technological restriction of, 160
Fallows, James, 163–64
Fanning, Shawn, 67
Faraday, Michael, 3
farming, 127, 129
FCC:
    on FM radio, 5–6
    on media bias, 321*n*
    media ownership regulated by, xiv–xv,
        162, 269
    on television production studios, 165
Felton, Ed, 47, 155–57, 158, 160
feudal system, 267
Fifth Amendment, 119
film industry:
    consolidation of, 163
    luxury theaters vs. video piracy in, 302
    patent piracy at inception of, 53–55
    rating system of, 117
    trade association of, 116–17, 119, 218,
        253–54, 256
    trailer advertisements of, 145–46
    VCR taping facility opposed by,
        75–76
films:
    animated, 21–24
    archive of, 111, 112
    clips and collages of, 100–107
    digital copies of, 324*n*
    fair use of copyrighted material in,
        95–99
    multiple copyrights associated with, 95,
        101–3, 224
    in public domain, 223–25, 254
    restoration of, 224, 226
    total number of, 114
film sampling, 107

First Amendment, 10, 128, 142, 168, 319*n*
    copyright extension as violation of, 228,
        230, 234, 244
first-sale doctrine, 146
Fisher, William, 197, 301, 324*n*, 330*n*
Florida, Richard, 20, 308*n*
FM radio, 4–6, 128, 196, 256
Forbes, Steve, 249, 253
formalities, 137, 287–91
Fourneaux, Henri, 55
Fox, William, 54
Fox (film company), 96, 97, 98, 163
free culture:
    Creative Commons licenses for
        recreation of, 282–86
    defined, xvi
    derivative works based on, 29–30
    English legal establishment of, 94
    four modalities of constraint on, 121–26,
        317*n*, 318*n*
    permission culture vs., xiv, 8, 173
    restoration efforts on previous aspects of,
        277–82
Free for All (Wayner), 285
free market, technological changes in, 127–28
Free Software Foundation, xv, 231–32, 280
free software/open-source software (FS/
    OSS), 45, 65, 264–66, 279–80, 328*n*
French copyright law, 327*n*
Fried, Charles, 233, 237
Friedman, Milton, 232
Frost, Robert, 214, 216–17, 220
Future of Ideas, The (Lessig), 148, 150, 189,
    292

Garlick, Mia, 284
Gates, Bill, 128, 266
General Film Company, 54
General Public License (GPL), 265, 280
generic drugs, 266
German copyright law, 327*n*
Gershwin, George, 233, 234
Gil, Gilberto, 270
Ginsburg, Ruth Bader, 234, 235, 242
Girl Scouts, 18
Global Positioning System, 263
GNU/Linux operating system, 65, 232,
    264, 280

Godwin, Mike, 40
Goldstein, Paul, 295
Google, 48–49, 50
GPL (General Public License), 265, 280
Gracie Films, 96
Grimm fairy tales, 23, 28, 213–14
Grisham, John, 57, 294–95
Groening, Matt, 96, 97, 98
Grokster, Ltd., 323*n*
guns, 159–60, 219

hacks, 154
Hal Roach Studios, 223, 232
Hand, Learned, 312*n*
handguns, 159–60
Hawthorne, Nathaniel, 213, 214
Henry V, 85
Henry VIII, King of England, 88
Herrera, Rebecca, 96, 97
Heston, Charlton, 60
history, records of, 109
HIV/AIDS therapies, 257–61
Hollings, Fritz, 324*n*
Hollywood film industry, 53–55
  see also film industry
Horovitz, Jed, 187–88
House of Lords, 92–93, 94
Hummer, John, 191
Hummer Winblad, 191
Hyde, Rosel, 60

IBM, 264, 279
"if value, then right" theory, 18–19, 53
images, ownership of, 34, 186
innovation, 67, 313*n*
  copyright profit balanced with, 75, 77–79
  industry establishment opposed to, 75–76,
    188–99
  media conglomeration as disincentive
    for, 164–66
  see also creativity
Innovator's Dilemma, The (Christensen),
  166, 321*n*
insecticide, environmental consequences of,
  129–30
Intel, 194, 232
intellectual property rights, 11–12
  components of, 309*n*

of drug patents, 260–61, 328*n*
international organization on issues of,
  262–64, 265–67, 328*n*
U.S. Patent Office on private control of,
  266–69
international law, 63–64, 258–59, 313*n*
Internet:
  blogs on, 41, 42–45, 310*n*–11*n*
  books on, 72–73, 143–44, 148–53,
    284–85
  copyright applicability altered by
    technology of, 141–44
  copyright enforced through, 149–57,
    161
  copyright regulatory balance lost with,
    125–26
  creative Web sites on, 185
  cultural process transformed by, 7–8
  development of, 7, 262, 276–77
  domain name registration on, 289
  efficient content distribution on, 17–18,
    193–94
  encryption systems designed for, 155–56
  initial free character of, 276–77
  music files downloaded from, 67, 180–82,
    199, 313*n*, 323*n*, 324*n*
  news events on, 40–41, 43
  peer-generated rankings on, 43
  peer-to-peer file sharing on, *see* peer-to-
    peer (p2p) file sharing
  pornography on, 325*n*
  privacy protection on, 278–79
  public discourse conducted on, 41–45
  radio on, 194–99, 324*n*
  search engines used on, 48–50
  speed of access to, 297–98
  user identities released by service
    providers of, 186, 205–6, 322*n*
Internet Archive, 108–10, 112, 114, 222, 232
Internet Explorer, 65
interstate commerce, 219, 236, 326*n*
Iraq war, 44, 310*n*, 317*n*
ISPs (Internet service providers), user identities revealed by, 186, 205–6, 322*n*
Iwerks, Ub, 22

Japanese comics, 25–26, 27–28, 29, 309*n*
Jaszi, Peter, 216, 245

Jefferson, Thomas, 84, 120, 284
Johnson, Lyndon, 116
Johnson, Samuel, 93
Jones, Day, Reavis and Pogue (Jones Day), 229–30, 232, 237
Jonson, Ben, 316n
Jordan, Jesse, 48, 49–52, 185, 200, 206
journalism, 44
jury system, 42
Just Think!, 35–36, 41, 45–46

Kahle, Brewster, 47, 110–15, 222, 226–27, 317n
Kaplan, Benjamin, 294
Kazaa, 67, 71, 179, 180
Keaton, Buster, 22, 23, 28
Kelly, Kevin, 255
Kennedy, Anthony, 234, 239, 244, 248
Kennedy, John F., 116, 195
Kittredge, Alfred, 56
knowledge, freedom of, 89
Kodak cameras, 32–33, 34, 127, 184
Kodak Primer, The (Eastman), 32
Kozinski, Alex, 76
Krim, Jonathan, 265

labor, 308n, 318n
land ownership, air traffic and, 1–3, 294
Laurel and Hardy films, 223
law:
    citizen respect for, 199–207
    common vs. positive, 86, 90
    as constraint modality, 121–22, 123–24, 125, 317n
    on copyrights, see copyright law
    databases of case reports in, 65, 280–81
    federal vs. state, 133
law schools, 201
lawyers:
    copyright cultural balance impeded by, 292, 304–6
    malpractice suits against, 190–91
Leaphart, Walter, 285
Lear, Norman, 164, 165
legal realist movement, 322
legal system, attorney costs in, 51–52, 185, 186–87, 304–6

Lessig, Lawrence, xiii, xiv, 121, 148, 150, 189, 292, 318n
    Eldred case involvement of, 215, 216, 218, 228–48
    in international debate on intellectual property, 263–64, 267–68, 328n
Lessing, Lawrence, 5–6
Lexis and Westlaw, 280–81
libraries:
    archival function of, 109, 111, 113, 114, 173, 227
    journals in, 280, 281
    privacy rights in use of, 278
    of public-domain literature, 213–14
Library of Congress, 110, 111, 198
Licensing Act (1662), 86
Liebowitz, Stan, 313n, 330n
Linux operating system, 65, 232, 264, 280
Litman, Jessica, 194
Lofgren, Zoe, 253
Lott, Trent, 43
Lovett, Lyle, 179, 189
Lucas, George, 98
Lucky Dog, The, 223

McCain, John, 162
Madonna, 59, 121
manga, 25–26, 27–28, 29, 309n
Mansfield, William Murray, Lord, 17, 91
Marijuana Policy Project, 321n
market competition, 128, 147
market constraints, 122, 123, 125, 188, 192, 318n
Marx Brothers, 147–48, 152
media:
    blog pressure on, 43
    commercial imperatives of, 43, 44
    ownership concentration in, xiv–xv, 4–6, 44, 162–68, 269–70
media literacy, 35–40
Mehra, Salil, 27, 309n
Metro-Goldwyn-Mayer Studios, Inc. v. Grokster, Ltd., 323n
MGM, 116
Michigan Technical University, 51
Mickey Mouse, 21–22, 139, 220, 221, 231
Microsoft, 100
    competitive strategies of, 65

340 INDEX

on free software, 264, 265, 328*n*
government case against, 155
international software piracy of, 65
network file system of, 49
Windows operating system of, 65
WIPO meeting opposed by, 265
Middlemarch (Eliot), 148–50, 151
Mill, John Stuart, 318*n*
Millar v. *Taylor*, 91, 92
Milton, John, 89, 93, 316*n*
monopoly, copyright as, 88–94
Monroe, Marilyn, 195
Morrison, Alan, 232
Motion Picture Association of America
    (MPAA), 116–17, 119, 218, 253–54,
    256
Motion Pictures Patents Company
    (MPPC), 53–54, 63
Movie Archive, 112
Moyers, Bill, 165
MP3.com, 189–90
MP3 players, 191
MP3s, 125
    see also peer-to-peer (p2p) file sharing
Mr. Rogers' Neighborhood, 158
MTV, 69–70
Müller, Paul Hermann, 129
Murdoch, Rupert, 163
music publishing, 17, 55–56
music recordings:
    total number of, 114
    see peer-to-peer (p2p) file sharing;
        recording industry
MusicStore, 302
Myers, Mike, 106–7
my.mp3.com, 189–90

Napster, 34, 60, 105
    infringing material blocked by, 73–74
    number of registrations on, 67
    range of content on, 68
    recording industry tracking of users of,
        206
    replacement of, 67
    venture capital for, 191
Nashville Songwriters Association, 221
National Writers Union, 232
NBC, 321*n*

Needleman, Rafe, 191
Nesson, Charlie, 201
NET (No Electronic Theft) Act (1998),
    215
Netanel, Neil Weinstock, 10, 329*n*
Netscape, 65
New Hampshire (Frost), 214
News Corp., 163
news coverage, 40–41, 43, 44, 110–12
newspapers:
    archives of, 109, 110
    ownership consolidation of, 163
Nick and Norm anti-drug campaign, 167,
    321*n*
Nimmer, David, 105
Nimmer, Melville, 304
1984 (Orwell), 108–9
Ninth Circuit Court of Appeals, 76, 105,
    323*n*
Nixon, Richard, 293
No Electronic Theft (NET) Act (1998),
    215
norms, regulatory influence of, 122, 123,
    125

O'Connor, Sandra Day, 234, 238
Olafson, Steve, 310*n*–11*n*
Olson, Theodore B., 240
open-source software, *see* free software/
    open-source software
Oppenheimer, Matt, 51
originalism, 243
Orwell, George, 108–9

parallel importation, 258
Paramount Pictures, 116
Patent and Trademark Office, U.S., 265–69
patents:
    duration of, 54–55, 242, 292
    on film technology, 53–55
    on pharmaceuticals, 258–61, 266, 328*n*
    in public domain, 135, 214
Patterson, Raymond, 90
peer-to-peer (p2p) file sharing:
    benefits of, 71–73, 79
    of books, 72–73
    efficiency of, 17–18
    felony punishments for, 180, 215, 322*n*

peer-to-peer file sharing (*cont.*)
    four types of, 68–69, 296–97
    infringement protections in, 73–74,
        181–82
    participation levels of, 67, 313*n*
    piracy vs., 66–79
    reform proposals of copyright restraints
        on, 296–304
    regulatory balance lost in, 125, 206–7
    shoplifting vs., 179–80
    total legalization of, 180
    zero-tolerance of, 180–82
Peer-to-Peer Piracy Prevention Act,
    324*n*
permission culture:
    free culture vs., xiv, 8, 173
    transaction burdens of, 192–93
permissions:
    coded controls vs., 149–53
    photography exempted from, 33–35
    for use of film clips, 100–107
    see also copyright
pharmaceutical patents, 258–61, 328*n*
phonograph, 55
photocopying machines, 171
photography, 31–35
Picker, Randal C., 324*n*
piracy:
    in Asia, 63, 64, 65, 302
    commercial, 62–66, 313*n*
    derivative work vs., 22–24, 25–29,
        138–39, 141
    in development of content industry,
        53–61, 312*n*
    of intangible property, 64, 71, 179–80
    international, 63–64
    profit reduction as criterion of, 66–71, 73
    p2p file sharing vs., 66–79
    uncritical rejection of, 183–84
player pianos, 55, 56, 75
PLoS (Public Library of Science), 262,
    281–82
Pogue, David, xiii
political discourse, 41, 42–45
Politics (Aristotle), 150
Porgy and Bess, 233
pornography, 233, 325*n*
positive law, 86, 90

power, concentration of, xv, 12
Prelinger, Rick, 112
Princeton University, 51
privacy rights, 205, 277–79
Progress Clause, 130–31, 215, 218, 232,
    236, 243–44
prohibition, citizen rebellion against,
    199–207
Promises to Keep (Fisher), 301
property rights:
    air traffic vs., 1–3, 294
    as balance of public good vs. private
        interests, 172–73, 322*n*
    copyright vs., 83–84, 172–73
    feudal system of, 267
    formalities associated with, 287–88
    intangibility of, 84, 315*n*
    Takings Clause on, 119
    see also copyright; creative property;
        intellectual property rights
proprietary code, 279–80
protectionism, of artists vs. business
    interests, 9
p2p file sharing, *see* peer-to-peer (p2p) file
    sharing
Public Citizen, 232
public domain:
    access fees for material in, 281
    balance of U.S. content in, 133, 170–72,
        318*n*–19*n*
    content industry opposition to, 253–56
    defined, 24
    e-book restrictions on, 148–50, 152–53
    English legal establishment of, 93
    films in, 223–25, 254
    future patents vs. future copyrights in,
        134–35, 214
    legal murkiness on, 185–86
    library of works derived from, 213–14
    license system for rebuilding of, 281–86
    protection of, 220–21
    p2p sharing of work in, 73
    public projects in, 262–63
    traditional term for conversion to,
        24–25
Public Enemy, 285
Public Library of Science (PloS), 262,
    281–82

Quayle, Dan, 110

radio:
  FM spectrum of, 3–6, 128, 196, 256
  on Internet, 194–99
  music recordings played on, 58–59, 74,
    195, 312n
  ownership consolidation in, 162–63
railroad industry, 127
rap music, 107
RCA, 4–5, 6, 7, 128, 184, 256, 275
Reagan, Ronald, 233, 237, 263
Real Networks, 302
recording industry:
  artist remuneration in, 52, 58–59, 74,
    195, 196–97, 199, 301, 329n–30n
  CD sales levels in, 70–71, 314n
  composers' rights vs. producers' rights in,
    56–58, 74
  copyright infringement lawsuits of,
    50–52, 180, 185, 190, 200, 270, 322n,
    323n
  copyright protections in, 55–58, 74, 181,
    195, 291
  international piracy in, 63
  Internet radio hampered by, 196–99,
    324n
  new recording technology opposed by,
    69–70, 314n
  out-of-print music of, 68, 71–72, 314n
  ownership concentration in, 162
  piracy in, 55–58
  radio broadcast and, 58–59, 74, 196, 312n
  statutory license system in, 56–58
Recording Industry Association of America
  (RIAA):
  on CD sales decline, 70, 71
  on circumvention technology, 158, 160
  copyright infringement lawsuits filed by,
    50–52, 180, 185, 190, 200, 270, 322n
  on encryption system critique, 156–57
  on Internet radio fees, 197, 198–99
  intimidation tactics of, 51–52, 200, 206
  ISP user identities sought by, 205–6, 322n
  lobbying power of, 52, 197, 218
*Recording Industry Association of America
  (RIAA) v. Diamond Multimedia
  Systems*, 323n

*Recording Industry Association of America v.
  Verizon Internet Services*, 322n
regulation:
  as establishment protectionism, 126–28,
    188–99
  four modalities of, 121–26, 317n, 318n
  outsize penalties of, 190, 192
  rule of law degraded by excess of,
    199–207
Rehnquist, William H., 219, 234, 239–40
remote channel changers, 127
Rensselaer Polytechnic Institute (RPI), 48
  computer network search engine of,
    49–51
Republican Party, 104, 249
"Rhapsody in Blue" (Gershwin), 221
RIAA, *see* Recording Industry Association
  of America
"Rip, Mix, Burn" technologies, 203
Rise of the Creative Class, The (Florida), 20,
  308n
Roberts, Michael, 189
robotic dog, 153–55, 156, 157, 160
Rogers, Fred, 158, 320n
Romeo and Juliet (Shakespeare), 85–86, 87,
  316n
Rose, Mark, 91
RPI, *see* Rensselaer Polytechnic
  Institute
Rubenfeld, Jed, 319n
Russel, Phil, 55

Saferstein, Harvey, 104–5
Safire, William, xiv–xv, 269
San Francisco Muni, 321n
San Francisco Opera, 95, 97
Sarnoff, David, 5
Saturday Night Live, 106
Scalia, Antonin, 234, 238, 240, 247
Scarlet Letter, The (Hawthorne), 214
Schlafly, Phyllis, 231
schools, gun possession near, 219
Schwartz, John, 79
scientific journals, 280, 281–82
Scottish publishers, 86, 90–91, 93
Screen Actors Guild, 60
search engines, 48–50
"Seasons, The" (Thomson), 91

Secure Digital Music Initiative (SDMI),
    155–56
semiotic democracy, 301–2
Senate, U.S., 120, 131
    FCC media ownership rules reversed by,
        269
    see also Congress, U.S.
Sentelle, David, 228–29, 231, 235, 243
September 11, 2001, terrorist attacks of, 40,
    41, 111–12
Seuss, Dr., 233, 234
Shakespeare, William, 29, 85, 87, 88, 93, 316*n*
sheet music, 17, 56
Silent Spring (Carson), 129
Simpsons, The, 95–98
single nucleotide polymorphisms (SNPs),
    262–63
Sites, Kevin, 310*n*–11*n*
60 Minutes, 105, 111
Slade, Michael, 101
slavery, 120
Smith, David, 309*n*
Snowe, Olympia, xv
software, open-source, *see* free software/
    open-source software
Sonny Bono Copyright Term Extension
    Act (CTEA) (1998), 134, 135, 215,
        218, 221, 223
    Supreme Court challenge of, 228, 230,
        231, 234–48, 252, 304
Sony:
    Aibo robotic dog produced by, 153–55,
        156, 157
    Betamax technology developed by, 75–76
Sony Music Entertainment, 162
Sony Pictures Entertainment, 116
Sousa, John Philip, 56
Souter, David, 234, 235, 242, 244
South Africa, Republic of, pharmaceutical
    imports by, 258–59
speech, freedom of, 318*n*
    constitutional guarantee of, 128
    film-rating system vs., 117
    useful criticism fostered by, 156
speeding, constraints on, 123–24, 207
spider, 108
Spielberg, Steven, 107
Stallman, Richard, xv–xvi, 279–80, 330*n*

Stanford University, 282
Star Wars, 98
Starwave, 100–101
Statute of Anne (1710), 86, 87, 89, 90, 91,
    92, 133
Statute of Monopolies (1656), 88
statutory damages, 51
statutory licenses, 57–58, 64, 74, 194,
    295–96, 300
Steamboat Bill, Jr., 22–23, 26, 34
Steamboat Willie, 21–23, 309*n*
steel industry, 127
Stevens, John Paul, 234, 235, 242
Stevens, Ted, xv
Stewart, Gordon, 229, 230
Story, Joseph, 252
Sullivan, Kathleen, 232–33
Superman comics, 27
Supreme Court, U.S.:
    access to opinions of, 281
    on airspace vs. land rights, 2–3, 307*n*
    annual docket of, 229
    on balance of interests in copyright law,
        77, 78
    on cable television, 61
    congressional actions restrained by,
        218–19, 220, 234
    on copyright term extensions, 218, 228–48
    factions of, 234–35
    House of Lords vs., 92
    on Internet pornography restrictions, 325*n*
    on television advertising bans, 168
    on VCR technology, 76–77
Sutherland, Donald, 102

Takings Clause, 119
Talbot, William, 31
Tatel, David, 229
Tauzin, Billy, 324*n*
tax system, 201
Taylor, Robert, 91
technology:
    archival opportunity afforded through,
        113–14, 115
    of circumvention, 156, 157–60
    of copying, 171
    copyright enforcement controlled by, 147,
        148–61, 181, 186, 203–4, 320*n*, 324*n*

copyright intent altered by, 141–44
cut-and-paste culture enabled by, 105–6,
   203
of digital capturing and sharing, 184–85
established industries threatened by
   changes in, 69–70, 126–28
innovative improvements in, 67, 313n
legal murkiness on, 192
television, 6
advertising on, 36, 127, 167–68, 321n
cable vs. broadcast, 59–61, 74–75, 302
controversy avoided by, 168, 321n
independent production for, 164–66
industry trade association of, 116
ownership consolidation in, 162, 163
VCR taping of, 75–76, 158–60
Television Archive, 110, 111–12
Thomas, Clarence, 234
Thomson, James, 91, 92
Thurmond, Strom, 43
Tocqueville, Alexis de, 42
Tonson, Jacob, 85, 86, 316n
tort reform, 323n
Torvalds, Linus, 280
Trade-Related Aspects of Intellectual Prop-
   erty Rights (TRIPS) agreement, 313n
Turner, Ted, 269
Twentieth Century Fox, 116
twins, as chimera, 178–79

United Kingdom:
copyright requirements in, 327n
history of copyright law in, 85–94
public creative archive in, 270
United States Trade Representative
   (USTR), 258–59
United States v. *Lopez,* 219, 220, 234,
   235–36, 239, 241, 242, 243
United States v. *Morrison,* 219, 234
Universal Music Group, 162, 191
Universal Pictures, 75–76, 116
university computer networks, p2p sharing
   on, 48–51, 180, 206–7, 270, 322n
used record sales, 72, 314n

Vaidhyanathan, Siva, 316n, 322n
Valenti, Jack, 205, 238
background of, 116, 117

on creative property rights, 10, 117–20,
   140
Eldred Act opposed by, 253
perpetual copyright term proposed by,
   326n
on VCR technology, 76
Vanderbilt University, 110
VCRs, 75–76, 77, 158–60, 194, 297,
   320n
venture capitalists, 189, 191
Verizon Internet Services, 205, 322n
veterans' pensions, 293
Video Pipeline, 145–46, 187
Vivendi Universal, 182, 190
von Lohmann, Fred, 205, 207

Wagner, Richard, 95, 97
Warner Brothers, 101, 116, 147–48, 152
Warner Music Group, 162
Way Back Machine, 108, 109, 110
Wayner, Peter, 284
Web-logs (blogs), 41, 42–45, 310n–11n
Web sites, domain name registration of,
   289
Webster, Noah, 8
Wellcome Trust, 262
Wells, H. G., 177–78
White House press releases, 317n
willful infringement, 146
Windows, 65
Winer, Dave, 44–45
Winick, Judd, 26–27
WJOA, 321n
WorldCom, 185
World Intellectual Property Organiza-
   tion (WIPO), 262–64, 265–67,
   328n
World Summit on the Information Society
   (WSIS), 263–64, 266
World Trade Center, 40
World Wide Web, 262
WRC, 321n
Wright brothers, 1, 3, 11–12

Yanofsky, Dave, 36

Zimmerman, Edwin, 60–61
Zittrain, Jonathan, 324n

ABOUT THE AUTHOR

LAWRENCE LESSIG (http://www.lessig.org), professor of law and a John A. Wilson Distinguished Faculty Scholar at Stanford Law School, is founder of the Stanford Center for Internet and Society and is chairman of the Creative Commons (http://creativecommons.org). The author of *The Future of Ideas* (Random House, 2001) and *Code: And Other Laws of Cyberspace* (Basic Books, 1999), Lessig is a member of the boards of the Public Library of Science, the Electronic Frontier Foundation, and Public Knowledge. He was the winner of the Free Software Foundation's Award for the Advancement of Free Software, twice listed in *BusinessWeek*'s "e.biz 25," and named one of *Scientific American*'s "50 visionaries." A graduate of the University of Pennsylvania, Cambridge University, and Yale Law School, Lessig clerked for Judge Richard Posner of the U.S. Seventh Circuit Court of Appeals.